CW01086032

Faithfulness
In The
City

Edited by

John Vincent

Published 2003 by Monad Press,
St Deiniol's Library, Hawarden, Flintshire, CH5 3DF

ISBN 0 907450 334

Acknowledgements

The members of the Urban Theology Collective are all deeply committed to this book, none more so than the books editor, John Vincent. The book would not have seen the light of day without his energy and determination.

The Urban Theology Collective is an annual gathering of urban theologians and practitioners at St Deiniol's Library. It is the forum in which these chapters were first written and discussed. Each year the week's meeting of the Collective is supported by the Library's scholarship funds. Thanks are due to Kate Sury and Andrew Hunt of St Deiniol's Library for preparing the text for publication. Thanks are due to the Trustees of the Library for agreeing to underwrite the publication and for their belief that this is the sort of project that the Library is uniquely placed to support and encourage.

Thanks are also due to the N.C Bellefontaine Trust, the Faith and Justice Committee of the Diocese of Sheffield, for generous financial support of the project and to the Urban Theology Unit, Sheffield, for their invaluable secretarial support.

As we have searched around for funding for this important book, I have been heartened by the generous practical and financial support of the following individuals: the Rt Revd Graham Dow, the Rt Revd James Jones, the Rt Revd Stephen Lowe, the Revd Colin Marchant, the Rt Revd Jack Nicholls, the Rt Revd John Packer, the Rt Revd John Sentamu and Micah Purnell who photographed and designed our striking cover. All of the above have demonstrated their commitment to an important yet unfashionable book – urban theology is in danger of fading from the agenda. These stories indicate time and time again that things have got worse since the publication of *Faith in The City* in 1985.

Peter Francis
St Deiniol's Library
November 2003.

Faithfulness In The City

Introduction   Page

Part Two: Reflections And Discernments

God is with us in our brokeness and powerlessness
yet the Church aligns itself the established and the powerful

God who values everyone
yet the Church picks its leaders by worldly standards

God who offers joy here and now
yet the Church promises other worldly happiness

God who is good news for the poor
yet a Church which isn't

God who is present in a mixed community
yet a Church which presents God as an educated Englishman

God who calls people together to send them out
yet the Church acts like a social club for private members

God who set us free from all that enslaves us
yet the Church shackles us with convention

Tower Hamlets, Theological Reflection Group
Submission to Faith in The City, 1984.

Chapter One

Peter Francis

Setting The Context

William Ewart Gladstone, rural Hawarden and Urban Theology are not as remote from each other as might at first be thought. Gladstone, was Prime Minister four times, a Chancellor of the Exchequer who delivered thirteen budgets. He was in Parliament for sixty-two years. In his final years he founded St Deiniol's Library, and after his death it became the National Memorial to him.

St Deiniol's, the Gladstone Memorial Library, is in the Welsh border village of Hawarden. It's equidistant from the English Cathedral City of Chester and the Welsh market town of Mold. Hawarden is a quiet and picturesque village famous for producing the English footballer, Michael Owen, and for being the home of William Ewart Gladstone. Rural Hawarden seems an unlikely setting for an eight-week consultation on Urban Theology.

It is in Hawarden that Gladstone set up his Library "for the pursuit of divine learning." Gladstone was a voracious reader, his personal Library held over 32,000 volumes. Many of these books were works of theology. Towards the end of his life he began to consider making his books accessible to others. His daughter Mary Drew wrote that he would often ponder *"how to bring together readers who had no books with books who had no readers, gradually the thought evolved in his mind into a plan for the permanent disposal of his library. A country house for the purposes of study and research, for the pursuit of divine learning."*[1]

Gladstone moved 32,000 volumes from his study in Hawarden Castle to a temporary corrugated iron building, the original St Deiniol's

Library. When he died the present building and residence were erected as the national memorial to him. The Library now contains 250,000 volumes.

Gladstone sited this *"home of learning"* in Hawarden, not only because it was his family home but because it was near the new industrial cities of Liverpool and Manchester. He deliberately did not send his Library to Oxford or Cambridge or even London, as many urged him to do. Gladstone wanted to provide a resource for the new society, the new spheres of influence of the rapidly approaching new century.

Gladstone wanted to find a home for his books that was accessible to the new industrial cities. However, a further motivation towards the establishment of St Deiniol's Library was the disestablishment of the Anglican Church and its possible consequences. Gladstone steered the disestablishment of the Church of Ireland through Parliament and had prepared the way for disestablishment in Wales. He believed that inevitably disestablishment in England would follow. However Gladstone worried that with disestablishment theology would be pushed out of increasingly secular universities. This might mean that the church would 'stop thinking,' it would cease to be in dialogue with the intellectual and cultural movements of the age. There would be the danger of the Church becoming a sect remote from woof and warp of society and its institutions. *"The negative movement of the age,"* wrote Gladstone, *"aims at establishing a severance between the Christian system and the general thought of the time; but no enlightened Christian will ever admit that our Christianity was intended to be an isolated thing standing apart from all other conditions of our life."*[2] St Deiniol's Library was set up as a safety net to keep the church thinking, and to ensure that Christianity did not stand apart from other conditions and influences of contemporary life.

This thinking took a new direction and its greatest impetus in 1939 when William Temple charged Alec Vidler, who was then Warden of the Library, to use St Deiniol's as a theological think-tank. At the same time Vidler was appointed editor of the journal *Theology* and this was to be the organ that would disseminate the work done at Hawarden. During World War Two, St Deiniol's provided a home for a number of distinguished theologians, may of them refugees from Nazi Germany. In conversation and reflection with Vidler, Temple and other British theologians they started to forge a prophetic, relevant theology that would not acquiesce in the face of political tyranny.

It could be argued that it was under Vidler that Gladstone's intentions for St Deiniol's came to fruition: a small community of scholars, the discussion and dissemination of ideas about the future of society and the role of the church within that society. In one of the preliminary papers setting the Trust to oversee St Deiniol's, Gladstone wrote what would nowadays be called a mission statement; he envisaged *"a fellowship of scholars committed to solid and serious work for the benefit of mankind in inexpensive lodgings together with congenial society."*[3]

All of this is by way of saying that a consultation on Urban Theology at the cusp of the century is not out of character for St Deiniol's. If St Deiniol's was still concerned with the life of the new cities, if St Deiniol's was still concerned with forging a prophetic contemporary theology, if St Deiniol's was still engaged with issues about the future of society and the church's place within that society then this was the sort of subject with which we should be engaged.

It was clear to me, from my previous involvement with Urban issues in the Episcopal Church of Scotland, that the best Urban Theology is done by practitioners. It was obvious that there was such relentless day to day pressure on urban clergy and practitioners that there was very little time for them to reflect, read or write about their experience. From friends who still worked in urban situations I was aware that since 1985, when *Faith In The City – The report of the Archbishop of Canterbury's Commission on Urban Priority Areas*[4] was published, things had actually got worse despite the huge amount of money from the churches that had supported urban initiatives. Our working title for this volume had been *Faithless City*, emphasising this decline and the need for new reflection, new initiatives. There is a danger that *Faith In The City* and the resulting interest in Urban Theology is seen as belonging to the 1980s, a hallmark of Thatcherism. There was a vain hope that with a new Labour Government there would be a new commitment to the poorest in our society. Those who tell their stories unveil the real situation facing urban priority areas fifteen years after *Faith In The City*.

I persuaded the Trustees of St Deiniol's Library to provide scholarship and bursary funds to enable this process of urban reflection to take place. The Librarian also made sure that the Library contained an up to date collection of Urban Theology – now one of the strengths of the collection.

A little bit of advertising and a number of discussions with John Vincent, who agreed to act as consultant, ensured an encouraging up-take. The eight week period saw 55 residential participants and a further 28 occasional day visitors. These were drawn not only from Britain but also from USA, Canada and South Africa.

Several participants arrived with their own writing projects and were encouraged to bring them to fruition, benefiting at times from sessions with John Vincent and others. So far, in addition to this book we have seen two publications from the St Deiniol's Programme. Joe Hasler has published *Mind, Body and Estates*, on outer estate ministry and working class culture.[5] Dan Rudalevige has published *Urban Mission Training*, concerning the work of ministry courses arranged in the United States by the Urban Theology Unit.[6]

In addition several members contributed to the communal project by developing work which is still to be completed – Geoff Reid on *Urban Rivers and the Character of Cities*, Keith Argyle on *Action Reflection and Community Work*, Tim Stratford on *Anglican Liturgy and Urban Mission*, David Hill on *Theology From Tower Bridge*, Stephen Skinner on *Stories and Scripture on the Raffles Estate*.

11

Of course, this collection of essays mainly tells the stories of Anglican churches. Of the 19 situations or writers represented in this volume, 13 are Anglican, 3 Methodist, 1 Baptist and 2 from other denominations. The complete story of urban mission and ministry in Britain today would have to include the phenomenal presence and distinctive witness of the black-led churches, and the black majority congregations in the white churches; likewise Roman Catholic churches.

We debated whether we should invite other contributors, to ensure that a more complete picture was given. However, we decided against this. The volume as it is records the results of a 2-month conversation with many contributors to the ongoing work. John Vincent's three pieces give a sense of the mutual search, and the emergence of major themes. These were reviewed and critiqued in a further week long meeting, with six of the contributors and six other colleagues, at the Urban Theology Collective at St Deiniol's in December 2000, and the pieces were revisited and updated at the Collective in 2002. The Urban Theology Collective is an ongoing committed enterprise, involving the sharing of new work as it is being developed.

The decision to publish this volume was taken during the centenary of St Deiniol's Library in Autumn 2002. It is entirely fitting that a volume reflecting the sort of work that is undertaken at St Deiniol's should be chosen as one of our centenary books. Gladstone would be horrified to think of his library being a museum, a place concerned only with looking back or concentrating on his own life and works, it was to be a working library. Gladstone was a conviction politician who grappled with the major issues of the day, even when those issues proved unpopular with the electorate: the Balkans, Afghanistan, Ireland, social conditions in the cities, integrity in public office, human rights – all of these consumed his energy (how contemporary these issues remain). His library remains a place that *does not stand apart but engages with all conditions of our life.*

12

Part One

People and Communities

Chapter 2

John Vincent

Urban Realities

Beginning at the Bottom

The stories in this book belong with the few but significant annals of life at the bottom of British society at the turn of the third millennium. Every now and then, the realities of existence as experienced by the least privileged suddenly achieve a voice, and for a brief time, public opinion registers its astonishment, then its disbelief, then its rationalisations and finally the oblivion of its unconscious.

This is not a new phenomenon. Certainly for the last 150 years, there has been an intermittent but regular stream of stories coming from the underprivileged – from Charles Dickens to William Booth to William Beveridge, right up to our own time, with Davies' *Dark Heart*.[7]

In our own time, increasingly, the reports of organisations and charities have supplanted the single volume accounts. The frequent reports could be named over the last ten years by the Rowntree Trust, by Child Poverty Action Group, or by the child care charities like Barnardo's, the Children's Society or NCH Action for Children.[8]

Rarely have the poor told their own stories. There have been recent exceptions – Bob Holman's *Faith in the Poor* and Nick Dansiger's *Danziger's Britain*.[9] Many autobiographical or ghost writer books have appeared alongside them.

However, in the main, the poor do not write books about themselves. The reasons are not hard to find. Precisely because they are poor, they lack access to writing opportunities, to books to read, to supportive friends, to the circles within which writing is recognised as a legitimate means of self-expression, much less a tool for political change. In any case, the poor do not imagine that the non-poor want to know about them. So that the demand that the stories of the poor should come from the poor themselves, understandable as it is, and desirable too, is usually met only in the recollections of the once-poor. Even such recollections are autobiographical and specific, and limited in terms of coverage and significance.

All the stories in this volume come, not from the poor, but from a group of people who, they believe, are a crucial part of the liberation of the poor. They come from people who, for reasons of conviction or vocation, place themselves alongside the poor and live amongst the poor. Often they are "incomers", who do not initially share the situation which they join.

As "incomers", some of them are people who have felt a "call" to take a "journey downwards" to become part of a situation, and be amongst a community, in the hope of helping other locals towards changing the situation "for the good". There is, of course, a great danger in this – as well as a great presumption. But it is arguable that such people can function as significant seeds of change, as facilitators and enablers, as those who by their "incarnations" act as people who awake in others a sense of their own value, and assist others to get themselves together, and help enable the beginnings of the "regeneration" from below, which is both the desire of current Social Exclusion policies, and which is also so elusive to all outside-directed schemes and programmes.

These matters are the subject of ongoing discussion, to which this volume makes its contribution in terms of a variety of stories and some tentative discernments and projections. The question of how regeneration can begin in deprived areas is the question which is provoked by the Christian model of incarnation, which inspires and supports the "incomers"' vocation.[10] And the question as to how far government, national and local, is prepared to see and promote the

15

emergence of a genuine self-run neighbourhood government, neighbourhood economics, and neighbourhood workers, is also very much up for grabs in the contemporary rush for "regeneration" and "capacity building".[11]

However, "Beginning at the Bottom" in this book means beginning with particular groups of people at the bottom. The people who belong to the groups in deprived areas who work with the writers, the "incomers", are themselves people who have made significant choices. Often, they have chosen to be or become significant people within their own areas, by their own capacity for leadership or determination to survive, or by hard-won bloodymindedness in the face of outside officials (church ones included!). Sometimes, they have made decisions to secure education, or employment, or family lifestyles, or habits of self-discipline, quite outside the normal expectations of their neighbours. Sometimes, they have felt called to remain in places of need as servants and saviours, refusing consciously the temptations to "better themselves", and even "improve" the lot of their children, by moving out into better neighbourhoods, where their own lives and futures might be more fulfilled and secured.

These stories, then, come from people who would not normally describe themselves as heroes and heroines, or significant change agents, or social entrepreneurs, or community leaders. But, in fact, they are often some or all of these. Their stories illustrate at least three things. First, that, at the "bottom" there are not monochrome societies, but richly diverse ones. In the midst of the "cycle of deprivation", there are contrary elements, battling to service pockets of meaning, and love, and acceptance, and even pieces of success. Secondly, these stories illustrate the ways that elements of change, or success, or regeneration, or fulfilment, or value, always occur in single, often small, usually insignificant happenings and histories, people and projects. There is no "master plan" from outside. Third, these stories suggest that a new way of looking at the Christian story is also implicit in this practice. To that we will return later, in Chapters 16 and 21.

The Hard Realities
All the experiences come from certain locations. So I will say something about the locations, and the hard realities there, which are the backgrounds for the experiences which our stories here describe.

Faith in the City (1985)[12] was concerned with the Urban Priority Areas (UPAs) of the cities. *The Cities* Report (1997)[13] attempted to speak about cities as a whole. Now in 2003, we have to say that the situations of deprivation, hardship and inequality in certain urban areas are infinitely worse, and seem locked into wider complexes of gross inequality between wealth and poverty, expansion and stagnation, fulfilment and despair, often cheek by jowl in areas next door to each other in our cities. And we must further observe that "pockets" of acute deprivation are to be found now in almost all residential areas, be they inner city, housing estate, market town, villages and growing parts of so-called suburbia. UPA and inner city are now often small-scale phenomena in many parts of our cities and beyond them.

In many places I have been in recent years, of 10,000 people or more, I have asked, "Where is your inner city area?" Without hesitation, people have pointed to a specific neighbourhood, often of council housing, and replied "Well, it's down there" – beside the railway, the other side of the ring road, or near the old works.

Indeed, one recent Report has rather upset the ability of authorities or churches to name "areas of deprivation" about which "something can be done", and directed attention to the smaller pockets of deprivation near to or within larger areas.[14] To deal with such "pockets" of deprivation is possible in terms of one-to-one services. But to concentrate on them alone will not cure the overall deprivation of the larger areas.

17

The situations that are the contexts for these stories are those of present day deprived areas all over Britain. The borderlines between one kind of area and another are sometimes geographical, sometimes historical. They are often related to private or public ownership, and frequently related to long-established "progressive" or "blighted" reputations which neighbourhoods acquire. The "pockets" of acute deprivation in the midst of otherwise thriving areas which recent Reports have observed, are but another manifestation of the growing divide between privileged and deprived.

It is possible to discern at least four major types of area which become visible in these stories from "deprived" places of Britain today.

The outer city council housing estate is the location of many of the classic "slums" of our day. Sometimes these are vast sprawling survivors of housing policies of the 1930's or the 1960's. Frequently, it is a more or less isolated estate, built outside the main areas of residence, peripheral to them, as an out-of-town development, a "township" on the model of a "garden city". Often, today, these are areas of neglect, isolation, poverty and despair, which build up an all-pervading air of depression, inactivity, abandonment, failure and, from time to time, become the scene of anti-social behaviour, gangs, police harassment (both ways!), and violence, with the consequent stigma attached to such "sink" estates, to which people "at the bottom" are sent. There are at present 1,370 run-down estates suffering multiple problems, including 18,000 excluded school children, two-thirds of heads of household in council and housing association homes with no job, and 73% having incomes under £200pw.[15]

The outer city estates featured here are in Wood End, Coventry (Ch.3), Heartsease, Norwich (Ch.6). Milton Keynes (Ch.7) belongs to the same genre, but is mainly a middle-class version of the garden city concept, with only smallish pockets of deprivation. But the story told there also reflects much of the philosophy of the New Town, and the outer Housing Estate, often places of "exile" (Ch.13).

The second type of urban location described in the stories is the large urban sprawl of inner suburbia, in which pockets of deprivation exist alongside more middle class areas, but where the dominant feature overall is of the apparently endless rows of houses, privately built, usually between 1900 and 1950. Interspersed in these areas are sections of more recent housing, sometimes built after the slum clearance schemes of the 1960-1970's. Newton Heath, Manchester (Ch.5), Plymouth (Ch. 10) and Bradford (Chs. 11 and 12) belong to this genre.

The third type of "urban priority area" is that of the classic inner city. Here, the issues of multi-cultural, multi-ethnic and multi-faith Britain are seen in their sometimes violent forms, together with the environment of the visibly "twilight" areas of our cities. For instance, Bradford (Chs. 11 and 12), Newham, London (Ch.8) and East London (Ch.16). It is also the context of the Urban Theology Unit in Sheffield, in which Ian Duffield and I myself work.

The fourth type of "urban priority area" is the former coalfield, steel industry or heavy manufacturing works area, where the works have closed. The villages and towns built around the pit, the woollen mill, or the industrial plant are now depopulated and devoid of finance and purpose. Denaby and Conisbrough (Ch.4) tell something of their stories.

The Darkened Room
One more thing has to be said before we turn to hear the stories. These stories are often deeply moving accounts of heroic pieces of human survival, of courageous endeavour against all the odds, of communities "hanging in there", of Christian discipleship and ministry, of discernment of unexpected and unnoticed "treasures" in the midst of urban tragedies. But before the curious reader smiles, or wonders, or ridicules, and before the Christian reader exalts in the bits of "salvation" here – there is one further thing to say.

Many of those who took part in our Urban Programme at St Deiniol's told stories that they refused to put their name to. They refused for various reasons – because the stories would expose their bishop or other church leader; because the story might prejudice their plans for future policies, or their own future ministries; or because they still lived and worked in the places they described and did not want the truth about them published, out of fear of reprisal against themselves or their families, or of blighting still further the reputations of the areas, often areas to which they were still committed.

Yet some hints of the pain of these testimonies must be recorded, or some elements in the background of the stories which follow will not be understood. So here are a few tiny portraits and scenarios from "the Darkened Room" of contemporary Britain, with names and locations camouflaged.

*   *   *   *

What a wonderful place this once was! Built in the 1930's by the Council, it has 1,500 houses in the west of the City for 5,000 people. 50% of the houses are semi-detached, 50% terraces of four. It was a "Garden Suburb", the pride and joy of the city. It had a nice park and beck running through – great for kids. It had a low crime rate and back doors were left open. Every house was occupied until the last 10 years. There was a very strong and close neighbourly spirit.

In the nineties, things went down hill because of anti-social behaviour. There are weekly, even daily, updates on problems! There are the usual problems – drugs (hard and soft), vandalism (stone throwing to break windows is most popular), intimidation, alcohol abuse (from the off-licence because there are no pubs on the estate). Youth are blamed (6-7 year olds up to 20 year olds, roughly) and people fear their presence, loitering on the streets and speeding around on bikes and motorbikes and joyriding. CCTV cameras are not seen as effective and the police are widely regarded as being too "soft". There are not a lot of burglaries – criminals go elsewhere to commit crime! Problems are often caused now by "outsiders" from the rest of town coming in and causing trouble. Two major incidents have in particular given the estate a bad "stigma" from which it has not recovered: a murder in the park (drugs related) and a small "riot" (stone throwing against the police and their vehicles).

Alongside all this, there is a catalogue of failures by the city council. There is the misuse of millions of pounds of government regeneration money on projects of little benefit to local people – who were barely consulted about what they might want or need. There is a very poor record of consultation – so residents feel that there is no point in expressing their views. This estate is part of a larger ward, and councillors are more interested in votes from the posher part of the ward. Councillors and officials of the city have never admitted their part in the poor use of money ("prettifying" the estate with trees, shrubs and sleeping policemen). The place now feels that it is seen by the civic officers as the "sink" estate of the city, which is being sacrificed to save the rest of the council housing stock. People don't have much confidence in anyone at the Civic Centre, and it will take a long time to regain that trust.

The faint hopes at present are that the recently rejuvenated "Partnership Forum" will give opportunity for agencies and residents to work together on common practical projects for the community. There is also a commitment to a lengthy "Planning for Real" process which will enable local people for the first time to have a real say in the large scale development of the estate, as long as the city council guarantees to take what people say seriously. The other element of hope is that, despite everything, the local people know how to celebrate: Parties, Anniversaries, Births, Parades, Fun Days. So there is a strong underlying spirit.

The general prospects for the medium term future look grim. We are promised the loss of a third of the houses through demolition within three years, leaving large areas of grassland in the central part of the estate. We lost the major shop (Co-op) in October, the Housing Office virtually closed in November and a promised developer pulled out in January. No other developer is yet in sight – not even Housing Associations.

*   *   *   *

There was another stabbing last night. The street opposite is a regular run for the local drug suppliers and drug agents. Every night, groups of them come together in the stair-wells of the block of council flats over the road. Often there are quarrels, and frequently shouting and swearing leads to violence.

This time, the victim was left in a pool of blood. We phoned for the police and ambulance. But the victim would not say who his attackers had been.

* * * *

What is human life here?
1. For some - Day to Day survival (health or money issues, and general hassle). Heroic, against the odds, with help of extended families, neighbours.
2. For some - Steady round of maintenance and daily/weekly settled routines. Looking after their homes, shopping, meeting friends.
3. For some - Gaining of pleasure and a degree of modest prosperity. For those in work, "working" the system well, or illegal activities.
4. For some - Contribution to life of the neighbourhood and its groups/committees, in small-scale and informal ways.
5. For some - Decline and gradual sinking into mounting problems, through increasing ill-health, debts, drugs, alcohol, criminality.

* * * *

Seven types of individual lead to seven types of story:
1. Street-wanderers – Mixing, keeping an eye out. Love a chat!
2. Up-to-no-gooders – Often lads hanging around on bikes or motorbikes.
3. Stay at Homes – Keeping their heads down, their main outing is to the shops.
4. Night Owls – Appear from dusk to dawn, often teenage girls.
5. Working Men – often work shifts, but earn their living! Make little impression on the estate most of the time, stay in when they are home or go to pub or club.
6. Criminals – Travel around in the dead of night in white vans, off to other parts of the county.

22

7. Do Gooders – Helping through formal and informal networks in broadly pastoral ways. This includes the clergy.

* * * *

Winter, it got to be really cold. A few streets away, there was this family of four little girls, living with relations. Fiona, the eldest, had been coming to our club for a few months and we had visited her at home – though never got over the doorstep.

Then, this freezing December morning, she arrived with her youngest sister – aged 4. She was dressed in a thin summer frock. She had no underclothes. And no shoes. Her legs and feet were blue with cold.

I took her into my arms. "Annie, you little darling", I said, as she nestled up to me.
"Are you my Mummy?" she asked.

Ministry at the Bottom
Many of the stories in this book come from those who are often the only "professional" people in these areas – the clergy, ministers and church workers. The following are seven vignettes from some of them.

* * * *

Worshipping in a UPA church, many of us had to exercise patience with respect to car crime. Our own family had all the locks on our minis and metros gradually forced so that they would not lock. We lost three car radios, and a car was entered a fourth time with damage to the dashboard. Finally the whole of one side of a car was rammed.

We said to ourselves: "God has blessed us. Our windscreens have not been smashed, our upholstery was not ripped, our cars (unlike some others) were never torched, and the car that was dented was due for the scrap merchant the next week".

23

Eventually there was so much damage to members' cars that the church employed two guards to keep watch during the evening service at a cost of £20 per week.

* * * *

Still in our mid-twenties, my wife and I with our two children moved to the North to work with a Mission. We were housed in an inner city area. We lived in the church house which was built on to the side of the church. There, our third child was born. The house had an imposing twelve foot wall around and toughened glass windows. The effect was that we were not only imprisoned and isolated from the community, but that we were considered a target by the children in the area. We had a six foot piece of wood stuffed through the letter box, the milk bottles were smashed if we put them out the night before, stones and eggs came over the wall and hit the kitchen window from time to time, and we were unable to leave the baby in the garden as house bricks regularly landed there. The experience convinced us that the idea of this kind of arrangement was a hazardous policy for housing pastors/ministers in an inner city area. The fact that we were isolated made us vulnerable. The couple that followed us only lasted six months, as the situation so affected the wife that she was verging on a nervous breakdown.

When I was appointed to my next ministry, the Mission attempted to resolve this problem, but unfortunately assumed that these areas were too difficult to live in. After eighteen very difficult months, we moved out of the church house provided for us, into a council house. Here our experience was very different. We were only two hundred yards from our new church, but now we were part of the community. While we have sought to minister to this community, they have protected us. Interestingly, those who had the responsibility for our pastoral care placed us in a situation of risk, while those in the community, once we were living among them, took us into their care.

* * * *

When we moved into the vicarage we had one small child of 2, and my wife was pregnant. After a couple of nights, crowds of children and youths climbed onto the roof of the house and started shouting and banging. My wife and I were terrified, and our child was crying.

There are no members of the parish who live anywhere near. And some may have been frightened to come anyway. So we telephoned the police, who took down details. No one came. The next night the same thing happened. We phoned the police again. No one came. We phoned the police yet again. "We can't do anything. It's a church house. Phone the church," they said. So we telephoned the Diocesan office. "We have no-one who can come", they said.

* * * *

My first curacy was in a UPA parish in the middle of a large and very needy overspill estate. Less than six months after I arrived, my rector left – which left me, a deacon, in charge of the church. No specific guidance was given to me or to the PCC or the Church Wardens concerning our working relationship. There was no spontaneous contact from those supposedly responsible for my pastoral care. What contact there was, I initiated. What support I did receive – and was very grateful for – came from other fellow clergy "on the ground", particularly from the neighbouring parish. But even that was limited by distance and the very different nature of the two areas. It was over a year before a new incumbent was found. That time and situation was one I would not wish to endure again, or see anyone else put through.

The social difficulties of the area mean that many of the people are disabled in ways which make it hard for them to find confidence in their own ability and so they need a tremendous amount of encouragement and support. This also made it hard for them to support me in the ways that, given a different social situation, might have been the case. They were wonderful, I could not have wished for better people, but this was as difficult for them as it was for me. For many, the church is where they come when and because they are hurting.

* * * *

Nine months after I came as vicar to this parish in a depressed urban area, the next-door parish became vacant. That this was going to happen was

25

known by the Bishop before I arrived, but he chose not to tell me. He also did not tell me that he had decided to amalgamate it with mine. I was deliberately given selective information about the situation I was considering going into. Perhaps, given the full picture, I might have come anyway, if I'd felt it was the right thing to do. But it would appear that neither I nor God was trusted enough for that risk to be taken. I was being told things – and not being told other things – in order to get me to do what they wanted me to do.

* * * *

I had been told that the previous incumbent had left the parish because of intimidation, but when I accepted the post no one warned me that a gang of people remained opposed to the church. Fires could be lit in our garden so often we kept a bucket of water to hand. We contacted the police but they always turned up too late to do anything. When we found a drug syringe, they didn't even bother to take it away. Our windows were broken so often the Ecclesiastical Insurance office rang up the Diocese to suggest that they board up this empty vicarage! No one from the Diocese appeared to understand or appreciate what was going on. The vicarage was isolated from other housing, and it was impossible to know what was happening on one side, when you were on the other. The final crunch came when a man broke in and threatened me with a gun.

* * * *

In my parish, I was the seventh short-term vicar in 20 years. My predecessors left with stress, illness or physical injury, and two left the priesthood. Since I was "driven out" by local vandalism and threats, the Diocese has had a conference to decide whether or not they dare appoint another vicar to this 9,000-people deprived parish. At the time of writing, the issue has not yet been resolved.

Very little has changed since Faith in the City. There are the same stories of inequality, economic decline, physical decay, social disintegration, and "Two Nations".[16] The situation for churches and clergy is equally dire today as then.[17] The work of the Church Urban Fund has been great; but it has not fundamentally altered either of these harsh realities.

An Urban Renaissance?

Will it all change? I was one of the 1500 delegates at the Government's "Urban Summit" in Birmingham 2002. Amidst considerable razzmatazz, what we basically heard was a progress report on the Government's November 2000 White Paper, *Our Towns and Cities in the Future*, which was sub-titled "Delivering an Urban Renaissance". [18]

The White Paper offers an analysis of the present situation in urban Britain. Issues raised are:

1. There are likely to be up to 3.8 million extra households to be accommodated by 2021.
2. People and jobs have left our major towns and cities for the suburbs, smaller towns and rural areas.
3. In some parts of our towns and cities the quality of life is poor and there is a lack of opportunity.
4. The economic performance of some urban areas has been poor and has adversely affected the wider region; and
5. These and other aspects of the way we live can damage the environment locally and globally. (Para. 2.1)

The needs for more homes (1 above) can only be met by reversing the current exodus from the cities. The answer to the question, Why do people move? is given as:

> The evidence from some surveys is that people move mainly for accommodation and personal reasons but also because of job factors. Those who were looking for better areas appeared to identify with suburban and rural areas. Other surveys and research have identified low crime rates, good health facilities and

low cost of living as key factors. In assessing the importance of local services in decisions on moving, people cited schools most frequently. (Para 2.9)

One of the four main consequences of the exodus is given as:

Previously healthy communities near city centres experience increasing social polarisation, with those who cannot move living in a poor local environment with high levels of crime. In some areas this results in a very low demand for housing and the areas potentially face abandonment. (Para. 2.10)

Urban areas "perform less well than the rest of the country on most key indicators" such as education (2.13), crime (2.14), health (2.15) and general levels of deprivation (2.16).

The key factor is identified as Poor Economic Performance, which has wide implications, notably:

- There is a clear link between poor economic performance and poor performance on key quality of life indicators: growing prosperity is an important driver in tackling deprivation;
- The impact on the wider region: the economic performance of an urban area affects the surrounding area – the main conurbations affect their entire region;
- The under-performance of the economy as a whole. (2.26)

"We cannot allow such poor performance to persist if we are to meet the challenges of the future," the White Paper comments (2.27).

A special problem which receives considerable attention is "the environmental impact of urban living". Urban areas create vast amounts of waste, pollution, noise, traffic congestion, fouling by dogs, litter and rubbish (2.28). Urban areas especially need "A Better Quality of Life" (2.30).

There are differences within urban areas. "The gap between the poorest and the rest of society appears to have widened in the 1980's, and become more concentrated in some areas" (2.17). In addition to longstanding problem areas, like East London, there are striking differences between areas in the same city. Sheffield has "two wards amongst the least deprived in the country just across the city from some deeply deprived areas" (2.19).

However, there are some good signs. Some city centres are re-populating – central Manchester from 300 in 1988 to 6,000 in 2000, with singles and couples without children as the main arrivals. Total employment in the cities has risen. But "these positive developments depend in part on the wider improvements in the economy", and are "not yet shared by all the major cities" (2.35).

The Vision that the White Paper holds out is that we will:
- Build new homes on brownfield land, and adapt older buildings,
- Help people move back into urban areas,
- Tackle the poor quality of life and lack of opportunity "as a matter of justice",
- Strengthen factors which will enhance economic success,
- Make sustainable urban living practical, affordable and attractive (2.36).

We return to this "Vision" at the end of our book, to try to assess, in the light of the stories we must share, how far it is a realistic hope. Immediately, the reader might wonder whether the Report's modest and tepid language is describing the same realities at all, which we have been looking at! A

"Renaissance" can only come if and when the true realities of a "Dark Age" have been faced.

Chapter 3

Nerissa Jones

Justice, Kindness And Humble Walking
Six Weeks In 1999 – Wood End Coventry

Urban Theology

Urban theology is what it's like, and more importantly what *happens,* when a church in an urban place talks about God; when it talks together about what God requires, and about what has to be done in consequence. It's going to vary tremendously from place to place. After all, urban can mean almost anything that's not a village. But obviously, the particular place exerts a great influence on how the people of the church respond to what they hear about God's requirements by way of scripture, tradition and reason. Their experience impinges upon how they hear, and how they, as members of the church, react.

Six weeks in 1999

To show what I mean, I will tell you what some people of St Chad's, Wood End, were doing during six weeks late in 1999. When I say people "of St Chad's", I mean that they all tend to come to the Eucharist on Sundays, and that without exception they talk freely and with interest and speculation about God. I'm also going to add a few notes from the day-book in which I record significant meetings, events and conversations.

I have changed many names to protect people's privacy.

One day I wrote:

> I went to see Roseanne, and her daughter, who has moved onto Wood End. Her brother came to fetch me. She's come from Leicester, her husband's left

31

her. She had another child, who died last year. She's about 25, and her surviving daughter is 3. She sat on a box; I crouched with my back against the wall. We discussed where she might get some furniture. She'll go to the Wood End Advice Centre to make sure she's getting the benefits she should. She needs money for the gas meter. Writing this makes me feel like a *Victorian* parson. It's monstrous. She asked me "Is this a good place to live? Will it be all right for us?" It was hard answering. She's moved into a street where people are leaving, and it's bleak around.

Brian, Henry, Mike and Foster

On Sunday a member of St Chad's, Brian, talked with enthusiasm and clarity on BBC Coventry and Warwick. He'd never broadcast before. He was talking about the organisation *Send a Cow*. Its aims are practical help with livestock breeding for farmers in Uganda and Kenya. The strong and hardy East African cattle, goats, chickens etc. cross very well with European breeds. The increased yield, and handing on of cross-bred stock from one family to another, improves quality of life in many ways; nourishment, clothes, small marketable surpluses which pay for education or medicine etc. *Send a Cow* is the Millennium Project for St Chad's and a local ecumenical group of churches. Brian is our representative on the local Committee, and he is an expert in this subject – not so much on animal husbandry, but the human necessity for a basic quality of life. Employed himself (and training as a Reader in the C of E), he sees many people around him, and even from time to time members of his own grown-up extended family, harassed by unemployment and the sheer difficulties of life in this parish.

Three other employed men who belong to St Chad's, Henry, Mike and Foster, I have only seen on and off for several weeks. Having a job means that you work whenever, and more or less however long, your employer demands. They want to come to Church on Sundays and be more involved, but often they can't. If they ask for time "off", the door is always open and ready leading to unemployment, and that will be more than bluntly pointed out. However, while his working life continues under stress, Foster is doing a distance learning theology course, and hopes one day to have his calling to ordained ministry accepted by the wider Church.

Ed
Another person is Ed. While Ed's job does allow him to come regularly to the Sunday Eucharist, last Sunday he was deeply angry and depressed. He's brought up his family here, and they've all done well, but he's thinking of leaving Wood End after thirty-five years. For the second time, his was one of seven cars trashed in our road on Saturday evening. Groups of children aged about six to fifteen do this sort of thing. Over a quarter of the population is under sixteen.

The Embroiderers
Eight more people of St Chad's who are no longer gainfully employed because they are retired, began last week on the third of four twelve by six foot wall hangings to beautify the church. Knowing what I have come to know from each of these members of St Chad's over the years, I marvel at their creative and loving energy. Everyone has been through suffering, and in various ways some are suffering now. They were Roseanne's first port of call when she came (heaven knows what expecting or fearing) to the Church for help. Anyway, she found *them*. They immediately stopped work, collected blankets, cooking utensils, curtains, toys for the little one, helped her in every way by friendly acceptance, showed her where the Advice Centre is, and told her where she might get furniture.

The Advice Centre is, I would say, the most important and valuable service in the Parish. From voluntary beginnings years ago, it now employs six full-time workers, and houses the Credit Union. St Chad's people are deeply involved with the Advice Centre on the Management Committee and working there. Martha, for instance, the Debt Counsellor, also finished her training as a Reader in 1998.

A typical day-book entry reads:

> Fetched thirty bags of good tins from Wood End Primary after their Harvest Assembly. To be recycled back through the community over the next few months. Very glad, as I've got nothing left. The Advice Centre rang directly afterwards, and sent over John Smith, left with an 8 year old who has special needs. They have no food or money whatsoever until the benefit books (which his wife took with her when she left) are sorted out. Could be well over a week.

Another note the same day:

> Discussed with the Head Teacher offer by the X Charitable Foundation to provide up to £1000 for something good that the school cannot give the children … He's delighted, but it doesn't allay his anxiety. The continual exodus of residents from this estate means the school will have £35,000 clawed back from its budget in January. A teacher may have to be laid off.
> NB. When I mentioned it, he too has heard that primary children are being offered free "come-on" crack down by the bridge.

Brian was writing an essay about Jeremiah for his Reader's Course. He is the Parish Treasurer, and came to deliver something to do with that, but as we began talking about the excitements of the essay, he suddenly remarked, "How strange it is that perhaps you and I wouldn't be here in St Chad's Wood End, if it hadn't been for the Exile, and what Jeremiah was thinking and teaching at the time. Would everything, even Jesus, have been different if it hadn't happened?" This question is a mark, I would say, of the readiness of St Chad's people to think, and be open to new ideas. Brian is upheld by the dramatic way in which Jeremiah bought the field at Anathoth, when affairs in Jerusalem were are their lowest and worst (Jer. 32: 7-8), and he inspires other people here to adopt Jeremiah's confidence, that "in *this* place will be heard the sounds of joy and gladness". (Jer.33: 11, etc).

Margery, Joyce and Christine

In late October, three members of St Chad's, Margery, Joyce and Christine, collected the First Prize Award for the Best Kept Churchyard in Coventry and Nuneaton. The churchyard at St Chad's is truly admirable. Winners from other more rural areas were unstinting in their generous appreciation of what this award, won several times, means to us. It is backbreaking, sometimes heartbreaking, work to keep the area around the Church building beautiful as well as greatly used. It takes sustained effort from a dedicated band, who are, we point out, assisted by every single man, woman or child who bucks the trend outside the garden, and does *not* throw any unwanted item over the fence. They are assisted by every child who does *not* tear off branches, pull up flowers and unravel fences. I would say again that these three women are also life-long experts in all kinds of hard work, suffering and heartbreak. They have lived on Wood End for a very long time. They desire it to be a beautiful environment. They work for it to be so. They will not give in. Not only "the sounds of joy and gladness", but the appearance of them.

Still in October 1999 I wrote:

> Void [empty] properties on Wood End have risen this month from 428 to 465. Not far short of a third of all properties. It has taken 20 months of applied and determined effort to get the City Council Director of Housing and Environmental Services to drive out here, and walk round the estate. Today he came. He told me he's never been off the main road before, or into the small streets. I took him everywhere. His

35

smooth self-confidence and arrogance did not appear to be dented much, but I hope he was unimpressed, both by what he saw, and by his Department's level of activity.

George

George, another member of St Chad's, who hasn't been able to work in the earning sense since an industrial injury to his back when a mower fell on him, chaired the third meeting of our new Resident's Action Association. The residents who came to the Church hall that evening were a mixture of furious, fed-up, excited, amazed to be there, slightly scared, frightened, and very frightened. We had all heard that a certain group of people might turn up who don't want a Resident's group to be formed on our estate at all, because it will eventually interfere with their anti-social activities. Such people didn't come in, but a firework was thrown through the door and Martha's car had a window smashed. Intimidation was also spread next day by rumour, which can be as effective as violence. Mothers were told at the school gate that a group of youths had threatened me that they would torch the Vicarage if the Association goes ahead.

George has spent many years encouraging, nursing, arguing, looking for allies in the Church and the wider community. Everything takes a very long time, but at last there is movement. Everyone who came to this meeting is an expert on injustice, on being threatened, menaced, hurt or bullied in some way, either by criminals, or officials, people with power over their lives. This evening everyone had a lot to say. A new robustness emerged. People expressed total lack of confidence in the City Council at any level. So, in a defiant plea for help, letters were written to Jack Straw and John Prescott, asking central Government to intervene.

A note from a year before:
> George and Jayne, Pat and me; the only residents of the estate that the Housing Office asked to a meeting about conditions here. All the rest were Housing Officers. We

complained. We took as an example the rubbish skips which St Chad's PCC persuaded the Council to put out, but about which a high level decision was made that they were not to be marked or advertised "in case we got too much rubbish".

The Housing people seem to feel that I ought to be on their side. They don't seem to include me as a resident, but until they can take a hard look at their practice and change for the better, how can I be on their side? It's a continual battle in treacle for people that I simply come across (like Paulina this week). What becomes of the people who can't find me or anyone else to fight for justice?

Paulina, Giles and their toddler tried for six unusually cold weeks last autumn (1998) to move *out* of the flat they'd just been moved into. Gas and hot water were not connected. Neither the Housing Office, nor British Gas, or Transco, (responsible for supply) would believe that this was the case. No one would listen, though Pauline phoned and visited the office again and again, with Giles and her mother. It turned out that gas wasn't even connected to the flat from the street; it had been disconnected months ago while the flat was empty. But no one would believe them. The injustice of the situation was made worse because it was not possible to sort the matter out until Paulina took me with her to every office. *Then* she obtained her basic, legal, statutory rights as a tenant to heating and hot water. That the matter could only be sorted out with pressure, fury and influence from the vicar, was an awful aspect of the whole situation. You've really reached rock bottom when only someone *else* is listened to about *your* rights.

St Chad's Parochial Church Council has always backed me in the row about this case, and something useful has emerged. A meeting has been held once a month since then between our three Ward Councillors, the Housing Officers and me, to cross reference cases of bad practice and maladministration, and to demand and secure a more efficient and just way of working. It was and is an uphill struggle. It felt like a major triumph for justice when the City Housing Department and Transco communicated with each other about the properties which they own or service. They found out which properties had no gas or electricity, and avoided putting any more tenants into them.

Martha

I've already mentioned Martha as a Debt Counsellor at the Advice Centre. I was very struck with a comment Martha made in the most recent Information and Advice Centre Annual Report. She wrote:

> I have met two people this year who cannot speak. They hear perfectly well but cannot talk. It really hit hard while working with these two people how society discriminates and dismisses them as incompetent *because they have no voice.*

About this time George came over to the Vicarage and asked me to read through the first chapter of Joel. (I've told him I am putting this in and he doesn't mind anyone knowing that, because no one grasped his need for schooling when he was young, reading is still hard for him.) But he can certainly tear the meaning out of what he does read. "Look at this", he said, "I know it all happened a long time ago, but it all reminds me so much of this estate:

> "What the locust has left, the swarmer devours;
> what the swarmer has left, the hopper devours;
> and what the hopper has left, the grub devours…
> A hoard has invaded my land
> they have teeth like a lion's teeth,
> they have fangs of a lioness…
> they have laid waste my vines and left my fig trees broken…
> they have plucked them bare and stripped them of their bark…"

"Look", he said, "it's even here about their dogs and the trees!" George reads into these words an urgency to get up and do something about it all; the vandalism, the drug dealing, the empty houses boarded up on every side, the desolate streets, low-level policing, municipal ineptitude, needy children and trees torn down, stripped of bark by young men training bull dogs to hold on. Everything. "This can't be what God wants", he said.

Late in October several people went off to Central Methodist Hall in the City Centre, about four miles off, with boxes of crockery to help with the Coventry Christian Aid Fair. Christian Aid is supported by St Chad's by sustained efforts to get to grips with the issues. There are loan sharks here, whose stony-hearted activities make understanding the international scheme of things quite easy. St Chad's people swelled the human chains against debt in Birmingham and London. Collections in Lent and Advent and the annual street collection, do pretty well. By pretty well, I actually mean a not inconsiderable sum for us, about £140 a year.

As usual in any week the church buildings, garden, small hall, slightly larger church, were in constant use by children and young people. These are the buildings which the older generation, as it were, gives over for the use of the children, with much kindness of heart. It is no light thing to accept that a much loved building will be rampaged about in, and not always look as good as everybody would like. It doesn't just happen. There is a sustained theological integrity behind a laissez-faire behaviour. It is in fact quite foreign to many of the older generation, and they have to work very hard to maintain this sweetness of attitude.

Jackie
I meet often with Jackie. She is the recently appointed Youth Work Co-ordinator. The Church decided to raise the money necessary for a five-year post, and was helped to do so by many co-funding Churches, Trusts, Foundations and Funds, which appreciate the need.

We started the appeal on Good Friday 1999, and Jackie was in post for the start of the Summer Holidays this same year.

I know she will not mind my revealing her value as a role model as well as professionally. She was brought up here, and lives in the Parish with her eight-year-old daughter. She left a local Secondary School at sixteen, as she now puts it, barely literate. A great many other young people have left, and still do leave, in the same condition. Jackie always worked, wherever she could find work, but at twenty-six decided to be different. She went to Henley College of Further Education for two years (still working flat out of course to support herself and her daughter), then to Coventry University for another three years to do her BA in Sociology and Psychology. She now has agreed time from her work at St Chad's to pursue her MA studies in Youth Work. Meanwhile, not a few young children have been heard to talk about "going to College" as if is was something normal for them, and not something unheard of except for other people. What is unjust is that Jackie's brain and potential were no less available to be taught when she was sixteen as twenty-six, but schools in neighbourhoods like ours have been the ones allowed by their Local Authority Education Departments to get to the state of failing OFSTED, and of failing generations of young people.

On most days and evenings children pour in for voluntary pleasure of one kind and another, including homework club, dance, drama, art and self-defence sessions, and for pool, games and just hanging about with friends. Children excluded from school meet their home tutors there. Holidays away have been organised every half term since 1993.

St Chad's carried out a parish audit in 1993 and found that over 3,000 of the 8,000 people in the parish are under sixteen. The PCC then made a commitment to activities for these young people. We could only afford to start with a small club for thirteen children, but since then, excluding the wages for the Co-ordinator, the annual outgoings for the children's work have risen to over £20,000 a year. The

Constitution of St Chad's Children's and Young People's Activities has this first simple aim:

> to give the young people of this area fun, interest, stimulation and joy which they may not receive at home or at school, and to enlarge their experience.

This may sound so easy and cute, so here is a quote from August 1998 to redress the balance and demonstrate the narrow line we and the young people often tread between tragedy and comedy.

> Teenage Activities. About 30 children behaved very well, pool, darts, table tennis, games, chat and laughter. However, A, B, C, D, and E, can't hack people enjoying themselves so much, and behaved very badly indeed. C stole a pool cue and hit David (a volunteer) with it on the way out. I took it off him in the Churchyard but he had a brick hidden under his coat. A taxi came for David with a woman driver and the boys took the taxi over and mobbed her until we could get help. Later they pulled condoms over their heads as masks and came in hurling stones. A hard evening. Someone peed in a condom, tied it up and hurled it in.

Some young people have lives which for various reasons are so unhappy, and sadly so far from anything that even St Chad's Children's and Young People's Activities can offer them at the moment, that a year later A, B, C and D are all out of school and dealing crack most of the time down at the bridge. Now sixteen, E is still just short of that, and has been away for an adventure holiday with us. During this he behaved excruciatingly badly, and having tried us to the utmost, day and night, he broke down and cried at three in the morning, pouring the kind of misery a child should never have experienced into Jackie's understanding ear.

And now I suppose you may be thinking that all I have done is to flesh out anecdotally a few of the well-known aspects of life in any outer or inner city parish in Britain.

However, I hope that some of it helps to define the idea of urban theology as people of faith and experience, talking together about what God requires, and accepting the implications and consequences. That is why I have told stories about people and what they do. Everything I have told you is quite small, almost unnoticeable on the global scale. St Chad's only has about fifty members. But I would like to suggest that if urban or any other theology is impractical, or attempted in a vacuum, or cannot be compassed by a story, it is not theology. It may be some other sort of learning, but not God-learning, for people who are applying their own reason and experience to Jewish and Christian scripture and experience.

I have not quite finished telling you what some other people of St Chad's were doing in mid October.

Alan, Rose and Millie
Alan, Rose and Millie were walking with the C.A.P. (Church Action on Poverty) Pilgrimage. Alan walked the whole way, 670 miles, from Iona to London. Rather too frequently on the long walk Alan found himself questioned, or even heckled, by people who declared unfavourably that he was bringing politics into religion. This sort of argument was new to him, as well as foreign to his nature. He has recently retired from a lifetime of work, and considers himself fortunate to have had employment all that time. He knows, however, both at first and second hand more or less everything about poverty, and its effects on people. He walked on the Pilgrimage because he felt mystically called to do so; so he could play a part in bringing poverty to an end. He simply replied to his questioners: "Jesus told us to love our neighbours as ourselves, and what else is there if we don't do what he says? If that makes me a politician, then I am, but I'm a Christian first."

In London, Alan spoke simply and movingly in St Martin's-in-the-Fields at the End of the Pilgrimage Service, while Millie socked it trenchantly to a large number of people in Trafalgar Square. Millie is our young Churchwarden, who joined St Chad's as a Brownie when she was nine.

The next day, together with the Church Action on Poverty, they all met the Chancellor of the Exchequer, to impress upon him the necessity for practical fiscal action to eradicate poverty in the United Kingdom. All three are far more expert on that subject than Gordon Brown. They know poverty, unemployment, and every kind of discrimination and exclusion inside out.

They are some of St Chad's team of experts, people who know from their own experience of living here, and who go out and tell of the situation as it is. Our "urban theology" compels this. For many people it is brave, because first it's hard to expose the fragility of one's own existence, and second because what these experts say is often met with contempt and disbelief, or with hard anger; rarely with attention. Urban theology, I believe, means everything I have written above, and is well summed up by this message on my answer-phone.

> "Hallo. It's Rose here. We're having coffee in the Treasury. We've seen the Chancellor, and we've put our points across."

Of course they did.

> "What does the Lord require of you, but to do justice, and to love kindness, and to walk humbly with your God?" (Micah 6: 8).

Facts on Wood End in 1999

St Chad's Parish consists of three fifties-built council estates on the NE edge of Coventry. They are Wood End, Henley Green and Bell Green.

There are no high rise dwellings. Houses and flats were laid out on farmland, with open spaces and green areas. However, particularly in Wood End and Henley Green, the green areas cut the estates off from the surrounding suburban streets.

The OXLIP score is 45.65. In other words, it is estimated that over 45% of the population is living on low income. (NB. 19% is regarded as high!).

In many city wide reports the Parish is described as an area of particular economic and social deprivation. Drugs and their attendant crime level are a noticeable feature of life.

In all three primary schools the entitlement to free school meals varies between 70 to 88% (although not all parents take them up).

12% of children do not attend school on any one day.

Two secondary schools and one primary school failed Ofsted. One is still in "Special Measures" (1999) but hopes to follow the other two out of these next year.

Needs identified by Health Visitors in Wood End include the highest infection rates in the city, the lowest immunisation uptake, small-for-age babies, highest child abuse figures, highest sex abuse figures, highest accident rates in the city, high perinatal, neonatal, infant and cot deaths. 80% default rate at three-year development assessment.

On average the health of people in the parish is significantly poorer than for the city as a whole. Life expectancy in the parish is ten years less than across the city.

Statistics available show significantly higher rates of teenage pregnancies and cerebrovascular disease within the Wood End and Bell Green areas, (*The Health of Coventry*, 1998).

Of 1,576 council houses on the Wood End estate, 465 were vacant on 18th October 1999. At this time, there is an average exodus of 9 dwellings per week.

60% of the population is under 30 years of age, with 30% below the age of 18.

Unemployment in Wood End is 2 to 3 times higher than in the rest of the city. Very few adult men are in full time work, (1999).

Chapter 4

Ian McCollough

Three Foolish Women
Destined To Confound The Wise
Denaby Main / Conisbrough

This is the story of the searching out of responses to local need through prayer and prophecy by a small ecumenical group of lay Christians in Conisbrough and Denaby Main, near Doncaster. At different stages, that which was interpreted as an action to be done "out there", led to an awareness of the need for a similar transformation in themselves and others, to be faithful in putting the Word in to action, and in the development of their own incarnational ministry and understanding. Most of what is written is based on articles written and presented by those involved, on conversations with them, and on my own reflections.

Denaby Main and Conisbrough
Conisbrough has had a Christian church since about 700AD. Denaby Main is the adjacent village created to house miners and their families about 100 years ago. The pits closed in 1968 and 1986. In 1912 the mine owners turned striking Denaby miners and their families out of tied houses. Miners had asked for payments to remove dirt and muck from the pit face, being paid only for the coal they removed from the pit. After 12 months of living like paupers, the men had to accept a cut in wages before getting their jobs back. Denaby Main closed in 1968.

Fifty years ago, Roman Catholic parents from St Albans Denaby walked the seven miles to Doncaster to protest that the Catholic school be kept open. They won their battle.

The other local pit, Cadeby, also in Denaby Main, had suffered a major explosion on 9 July 1912 that killed 85 men, 45 of whom were rescuers caught in the second explosion. Many bodies were never recovered from seams that were sealed for ever. Cadeby finally closed in 1986 after the Miners' Strike of 1984/5. There are no remaining traces of colliery buildings. Had the pit buildings been made available for community use, they could have provided an opportunity for use as workshops, offices and community centres, and helped drive the regeneration process forward at a faster pace, instead of giving local people ten years of degeneration and very low community morale.

The manner of the closure of Cadeby Pit at Denaby and the instant unemployment it created, together with the knock-on effect on ancillary business, was likened by some local Christians to the fall of Jerusalem and destruction of the Temple columns (Jer. 52: 17-18).

> It was the end of our world. A pall of depression hung over Denaby, Cadeby and Conisbrough. There was no point in anything; getting up, going to school, digging the garden, doing your best – why bother when the future had been cancelled?

The people of Conisbrough and Denaby have been toughened by the hard and exacting life they faced, first in the pits, by paternalism and poverty, and later by the benefit trap, massive unemployment, and the sense of having no future.

Following the closure of Cadeby Pit, the Anglican parish of All Saints, Denaby, created a Miners' Memorial Chapel, built on to the church. The tower, representing a miner's lamp, was built with materials from the pit and power station and included a half pit wheel. It is an important link for Denaby people with their history, the only reminder to future generations as to why Denaby came into being, and a symbol to help the regeneration of its community. It is an educational and tourist resource in the Doncaster area, with some special features. Beneath the tower is the holy table made by pit joiners and encased in glass with a solid, one ton block of coal, with mining memorabilia underneath it. The stained glass windows show the ventilation system in the mines, and a miner and lad working the coal face.

The Miner's Chapel was dedicated in 1989 and the opening service included a hymn written, performed and led by Donald Swann of Flanders and Swann fame. It was a real inspiration to the people of Denaby.

Norah, Jan and Jane – and a Highway[19]

Following the Miners' Strike, life in the South Yorkshire township of Conisbrough and Denaby was bleak and cheerless. Facilities of long standing, that helped to cushion the area socially, started to be withdrawn, or to cost more. At the same time, cheap bus travel became a memory, resulting in many members of the Doncaster Branch of the South Yorkshire Christian Unemployment Group being unable to afford to go into town.

A West Doncaster remnant of three women kept up monthly vigils in the parish church at Conisbrough. Norah, the only one in employment, Jan a young single mother, and Jane, a widow and retired school teacher. They tried to extend the group, and though many people asked them to pray for members of their family, no one wanted to join them. They wrote:

> As we saw the dole queue at the parish hall getting longer by the week, we passionately wanted to do something, but what? One day the answer came. A supply of DIY and garden equipment, held for the convenience of local people lacking the tools necessary to carry out a small repair job, was being withdrawn with the closure of the Red House.[20] We felt it would be a simple and practical thing to replace this store, and canvassed unemployed people for their opinion.

An enthusiastic response soon led to the creation of a comprehensive list of tools deemed necessary. Funding was found, but there was considerable difficulty in finding secure lock-up premises, and people began to ask questions. The pressure to provide the facility became so great that it was decided to keep the tools in Jane's garden shed. If they were stolen, at least the group would have tried, and they could then get on with something else.

Jane Commented:

> "I was explaining this to the Lord in my morning prayer time – I was talking out my excuses as if He couldn't see me coming a mile off – when suddenly I had a reference in the Old Testament impressed upon my mind. Such a thing had never happened to me before and I looked it up somewhat sceptically only to read the words – "See that you finish the work you have begun in the Lord" (cf. 1 Chron: 28. 20). It was like the finger of God coming through my roof. I shared this with the others; we agreed that none of us was aware that we were doing anything "in the Lord" – more of a good idea really. The search re-doubled and with a whole hearted intensity."

A few weeks later at a Justice and Peace Week on Iona, Jane consulted the warden, Kathy Galloway, who suggested we write a letter stating what we hoped to do and give it to as many Christians who might be able to help. The letter was written in complete privacy. Some of the women went that evening to a parish church prayer meeting at which a church member said they had a "word" which they did not understand, but which they must pass on. It was: "Though it seems a small thing to do, do it quickly, and I will fan the flame. The black coal will turn brown, the brown turn red and many will be warmed by the fire." Everyone else was puzzled but they just knew it was for them. The letters were delivered.

49

Almost immediately, it seemed, they suddenly noticed some empty rooms, two floors of them above shops in the vicinity of the parish church, which had been empty for almost two years. The windows and roof had been renewed, so it was decided to investigate. They key was obtained. The heavy door opened on a scene of advanced dilapidation, with walls and ceilings falling in, doors hanging off their hinges and no glass at all in the rear windows. Yet the building was strangely warm! A huge pile of old newspapers and circulars was brushed to one side as the door opened to expose a small sheet of paper. It was an old letter from the branch parish church to the community and in big bold letters they saw the words MAKE WAY FOR JESUS. They realised they had stumbled on a vision given in the parish church some eighteen months previously, of a place where people would come and go, happily employed in creative ways. The premises were about five times bigger than they were looking for. Suddenly the plan had changed. There and then they stood in the hallway, put their hands on the walls and claimed the building for the Lord. Terms were agreed for a lease on the building, although they had no idea where the money might come from.

A week later, sanity set in. But they need not have worried – the Lord had promised to fan the flame. The following week they went to the appointed meeting place for any potential helpers, to find twelve volunteers, one building contractor, two bricklayers, two electricians, two joiners, a plumber, a plasterer, two painters and decorators and a general labourer, all unemployed, mainly through ill-health and all willing to help if they could take it very slowly. Resources were pooled and work began.

It was from this activity that Highway got its name, recalling Isaiah 62. 10:

> People of Jerusalem, go out of the city and build a road for your returning people. Prepare a highway; clear it of stones, and put up a signal.

They cleared plenty of stones, about 20 tons. The building was completed in almost nine months to the day and was opened on 16 October 1989.

One of the group had another vision, that Highway was to be a homestead where everybody who came in would be made welcome. It was not to be just a drop-in centre where people sat down and were waited upon, but a place where people could work. Gradually materials were supplied for batik, quilting, macramé, pottery, silk-painting and candle-making. Talents began to develop. Anyone could buy their products at cost price. It was chaotic but everyone seemed happy.

As the weeks and months went by, the group grew to a family of about 30 people, most of whom used the centre every day. No one in the more respectable agencies seemed to want to have anything to do with them, when out of the blue Highway won a national award for community care in the region. Suddenly goodwill flowed towards the project and it was inundated with requests to take placements, and their opinions were sought after. It would have been easy to go down the road of a training agency at that point and to have been relatively secure financially, but once again God intervened.

The members of the Highway Christian Fellowship that met weekly for prayer and discussion began to report seeing, during their private prayer time, a picture of the face of the crucified Christ, wearing a crown of thorns and weeping. This was disquieting and not understood. At that time quite a few people from different churches in the Dearne Valley met at regular intervals to pray for the whole area. At one meeting a number of people were aware of the weeping Christ. Christ said: "You must become so intimately involved with this suffering until it becomes to you as a garment. Then it will be your crowning glory as this (crown of thorns) is mine." Believing this was specific to Highway, it was agreed not to become a more formal institution, but remain informal, with a less secure structure. A little later in 1991, Norah went on a retreat to Mount St Bernard Abbey, Leicestershire, and one of the Brothers there gave her a package of 100 medallions in a variety of styles, each one depicting the head of Christ with a crown of thorns, as a parting gift for the children of Denaby and for Highway. In the Spring 1995, Jane attended a European conference in Wales of Industrial Missioners and people involved in work with unemployed people. During the farewell service the Welsh preacher, present only for that event, gave the address in which he laid out an erudite, scriptural sermon using the same message and imagery of the Crown of Thorns. The group firmly believed this involvement was the way they should try and go, though it was not understood by others and seemed simplistic.

Within three years furniture recycling was started and old and unwanted furniture was refurbished to be passed on to people in need or recycled to create bowls or candlesticks etc.

It was at this time that the *Highway Halliel* was written, as a reminder of all that God had done. In a strange way those involved felt discouraged and needed to remember their blessings.

When everything was dark and hopeless
God gave us a vision
When we had no understanding, he spoke
When we had no courage, he encouraged us
We had no place... but he provided one
That would unite us as we worked on it together
When we had no talent for the job
He provided skilled workers.
When we had no money... he spoke to the
Heart of many people and released it.
When we had no recognition... he says that
We were praised.
Unfitted, unworthy, unfaithful and weak.
Yet…
He gave us a crown as a mark of his service

As a token that through us
He will accomplish his plan.

Now he beckons us to a new highway,
It seems as impossible and unlikely as ever
So…
We sing this song… and remember…
And follow:

Don't be afraid, stand your ground, and
You will see what the Lord will do
For you today.
You will never see those Egyptians again
The Lord will fight for you.
There is no need for you to do anything.

Many of the people who came to Highway wanted to settle in to a comfort zone although it was there to stretch them. The project group recalled Isaiah 62: 10, about "building up the highway". They felt people themselves were being the stones, blockages in their own lives and in the lives of others, and unable to move on. Gradually the group realised that they should be creating employment, and not activity to fill a space. They could see that some people were ready to move on, but to what? To come off Sickness benefit, take a drop in income to Unemployment Benefit, and leave Highway to look for work that was not there, was to court disaster. Soon they would be back "on the sick" again.

A local resident who worked as a consultant engineer to Monsanto suggested that Highway might be able to undertake some sewing work to make a new type of drain fitting out of a geo-textile. The small amount of work was well paid. The cutting was undertaken in Highway and the sewing done as outwork and given to single parents, both men and women, as a modern equivalent of biblical "widows and orphans". They were able to undertake the work without loss of benefits.

Orders increased in the year, and a community business was established which itself soon combined with another Christian business. Then Monsanto Europe decided to pull out of the Hydraway fittings as part of their internal reorganisation, leaving the group with a beautiful workshop, a grant for four years to set it up, workers, but no work! What was God doing? They investigated products for the disabled, work for nursing homes and other care agencies, before discovering that the geo-textile fittings had been taken over by an English firm, and the work began to trickle back.

In collaboration with Morthyng, the Maltby based Churches Training Agency, Prospect Training, British Conservation Volunteers and others, the wood workshop was developed to take trainees. Since then forty or so trainees have passed through the centre each year, as well as volunteers, two thirds of whom have gone on to more formal training or paid work, even though the majority had not previously persisted with their training course.

A second approach from Monsanto led to the modest expansion of the sewing business to produce designer mats, using their Astro Turf that was very profitable in the USA. This very small venture was a source of hope. Doormats have been made for the Anglican Church in Brussels, the Mansion House in Doncaster, the Earth Centre and English Heritage, as well as designs incorporating the Christian "fish" symbol and the Yorkshire rose.

The increasing business activities led to the formation of the Conisbrough Highway Development Trust, a community business run by a board of management. It reflects the vision of Highway and is the umbrella organisation for the sewing workshop and mat business, a street café for young people, and a community enterprise agency, Co-option 2000. It is now developing a disused and neglected building, strategically placed near Conisbrough Castle, as a community Enterprise Centre, with craft workshops, a retail outlet for locally produced goods and a catering area. Co-option 2000 is

54

crucial to this venture, as they service, support and develop the businesses that are housed there.

Debt and Poverty
In neighbouring ex-mining areas, established high street traders, following the payout of redundancy monies, had moved out as soon as the local finances had dried up. In listening to the users of Highway and others, people became aware of the need to tackle personal debt and loan sharks, so a credit union was started. The first collecting point was at Highway, with church friends and relatives helping to build up membership, and training being undertaken with the National Federation of Credit Unions. For many, savings could only be made out of "spare money". The Credit Union was prepared to take deposits as small as 20p a week. It was important, and still is, to take on board the credibility of such members, for many of whom saving is a whole new way of life. Many had never had a bank account. Patience, tact and understanding are still the order of the day.

Norah Hanley was known locally as the "bag lady", collecting in subscriptions, using her shopping trolley. Norah says:

> "We were humbled by the trust of people who had nothing else to give. Behind the plastic smiles and tidy dress was so much anguish, it was unbelievable. When you provide help to someone to handle the little money in their pockets it is real proof of concern, and the reactions for us have been overwhelming. There is a current jargon of 'local people doing local projects'. I don't know of any other way."

Pay back arrangements are agreed to suit individual needs. No member feels pressurised, knowing that if circumstances change, the timing of the arrangement can also be altered. This has reduced any risk of bad debt and proved to members that the intention is to help and not to be another loan shark, trying to rip them off. An action plan can be set up to counteract loan sharks. £500 from a finance company could cost £278 in interest in one year. With Credit Union, the interest at 1% per month on reducing a balance would be £32.50.

The Credit Union was registered in January 1995. In November 1999 it had 400 members (serving 350 families) with assets of £62,000. In five years 460 loans have been processed, totalling £111,000. With the opening of Credit Union premises in Conisbrough in October 1999, Norah's shopping trolley has been put to its original intended purpose.

There has been tension and stress not only for those in debt and becoming members of the Credit Union, but also for the committee members. Trust has had to be built up by building personal relationships.

Among the stress, has also been much humour and celebration. Norah tells of an elderly member who had stopped her life insurance, found herself in her twilight years with no insurance and her family around her in unemployment. Her stress was that they would be picking up her "final bill". After becoming a member of the Credit Union, she felt more secure and peaceful. She had been promised, "We couldn't leave you on top if anything happened to you". Earlier in 1998 she passed peacefully over to the Lord and they had a joyous mass to celebrate her life. Through the Credit Union she had financed her own departure.

As well as humour and celebration, there have also been some remarkable surprises. Norah again:

> "An elderly lady came along to the collection point in Conisbrough. We knew her by sight from meeting in the shops and an odd "Good morning". She very calmly told us she had been monitoring the progress, particularly in the young mums on her estate, some of whom were her granddaughters. She was pleased

with the responsible way they were now tackling their affairs, and the children were much happier. "I would like to help", she told us and passed an envelope across the desk, "This is only sitting in the bank and might as well be doing something useful." There was £1,000 in the envelope and she became a member. Her weekly visit to us is a joy because her release from the stress is notable in her sprightly step."

Norah continues: "Something else has also happened. We have become a family, and already there are signs of people helping each other through small friendship groups and self-help groups. The old community spirit is being revived, and joy is creeping back into people's lives. They are beginning to smile again and to laugh at, and laugh with, each other."

They have a dream that all schools in the area will become actively involved, and the children be in control of their finances. This is already successful in other parts of the country. Whether the children find jobs or not, the Credit Union will provide some stability and financial hope and help them to be part of a supportive community.

Back in Denaby Main, the story continues. Sometime after the opening of the Miners' Chapel in Denaby Main, Peter Atkinson, a local man, was appointed as the Neighbourhood Worker in Denaby Main with responsibility to a local management committee. About ten years after the closure of Cadeby Pit, the Revd Reg Davies, vicar of All Saints Denaby, called together two MPs, a local councillor, the local doctor and the Neighbourhood Worker to predict what the next ten years would bring. There was a common realisation that if the community was to get itself out of its mess, it should do it by itself and not wait around hoping others would bail it out. It needed to drop the baggage of the past whilst remembering, learning and respecting the lessons.

This led to the formation of Denaby Main Forum, through which professionals and local people shared their problems and addressed issues.

Later, Denaby Forum linked up with the Conisbrough and Denaby Development Trust, and, with the Local Authority, have created other partnerships. Use of £2 million European money improved the environment around the village. Funding from the Dearne Valley Partnership of the three councils of Barnsley, Doncaster and Rotherham has been used to improve a clutch of villages with specific difficulties in the Dearne Valley. Money was used to enable the community and the schools to have hands-on experience in creating public artwork.

Smaller projects can have as much impact on morale as larger ones, and a Community Festival culminated in a parade of war veterans to rededicate the memorial park improvements and the war memorial.

A request from a local soldier to honour the Kings Own Yorkshire Light Infantry and a local Victoria Cross holder, resulted in a peace plaque dedicated to all who serviced peace. Three hundred people attended the unveiling service in All Saints Church, Denaby.

Support
As they reflected on what happened, they were amazed at the 'Begats' that sprang from a gathering of three foolish women from a ChUG meeting at St Peter's, Conisbrough and from small scale activity at All Saints, Denaby Main. They believe in the text Genesis 15: "Look up at the heavens and count the stars... so shall your offspring be."

There has been a feeling amongst some lay people that the established church has never really understood what Highway was about in Conisbrough. Their initial financial support was warmly welcomed, but there is a strong feeling that the attitude from many was what was happening in Highway was worthy outreach to the poor, but not really to do with them. Highway has tried to create a different social structure that would take power from the Local Authority which has abused it in the past, and to use that power responsibly at local level, to benefit and not use people.

Incarnational ministry has been focused on those Christians active in Denaby and Conisbrough who, working with others, have built a community around them but never sought to control it. Like Paul in Athens, they have always sought to understand the context in which they have placed their mission strategies. They have been prophetic, priestly and faithful disciples, developing the vision and action with a frightened community. They have been resourced from their own mutual spirituality and prayer life, together with that from their institutional church, where they have often been seen as the agitators and prophetic voices.

Those involved would tell the reader that it was difficult to start with, and continues to be so. Their outworking of faith is one of risk, prayer, mutual support and reliance on God and each other. Their stories are clear examples of responses to the command "Feed my Sheep". Much is summed up in Norah's father's prayer he regularly shared with his family:

> Christ has no hands, but your hands, to do His work today;
> He has no feet, but your feet, to lead folk on His way;
> He has no voice, but your voice, to tell them how he died;
> He has no help, but your help, to bring them to His side.

In the above story, it is clear that power has been with local people, and followed from their prayer, commitment and responses to prophecies, given within their theological tradition. Without faithful lay Christians in their local churches working with their community, none of it would have happened.

Chapter 5

Derek Purnell

Urban Presence
Newton Heath, Manchester

Urban Presence was set up in 1995 by myself and Paul Keeble as a response to the problems we saw in the inner-city areas of Manchester's - small, under resourced churches and organisations struggling to minister to the city's working class population, and largely unrecognised and unsung within the wider Body of Christ. Our burden has grown from personal involvement in inner-city congregations in areas where we have observed prevailing depravation, an exodus of Christians, and declining numbers in local churches. Our vision is to see this decline turned around, to see growing, indigenous inner-city Christian Communities that are serving and transforming their local areas. To that end we seek to make the inner-city situation more widely known, find and channel further resources into the inner-city, and are actively involved ourselves in inner-city ministry. For me this currently includes the early stages of a church plant on the estate where I live. In this paper I will attempt to give an insight into the situation we face and describe some of the problems with which we grapple.

Urban Context - Manchester

Manchester is the third most deprived City in England, [21] and over one third of its working age population are not in work or training. [22] One third of its households are living below the poverty line, and over half of all births are illegitimate. In some neighbourhoods one fifth of houses lie derelict; there are streets or tower-blocks where up to 83% of properties lie empty and in some streets properties valued at £28,000 in 1990 now have no value.[23] Manchester has the lowest life expectancy in England with men dying 4.2 years earlier than the national average and women 2.8 years earlier. [24] Of course there are many good and exciting things happening in Manchester and for some it is a great place to live. The above statistics predominately relate to the inner areas and housing estates.

My wife Maureen and I see many things on the estate where we have lived for the past twenty-three years. Teenagers racing around on a motor bike they have just stolen, Police arresting a group of young people that have just been in a car chase. Being woken up at 2am by the noise of lads transferring, to another vehicle, goods stolen from an off-license they have just robbed. On yet another occasion three young men threatening another who then ran into someone's house and came out with a knife. This is not a record of things that happened over years - all this happened over a period of a few weeks - this is normal life on the estate. At one point in time recently we were watching a car being 'torched' almost every night, often within 20 - 50 yards from our house. Everyone sees it, no one sees anything. How best can one be 'Salt and Light' in these circumstances? Constantly grappling with this, year in year out, can be very wearing!

Even a small estate such as ours has a very complex social mix, even though it is almost totally white working class. It appears to have all the strata of the working classes including a group that some are defining as the 'underclass'. Charles Murray in the book '*Charles Murray and the Underclass: The Developing Debate*' defines 'underclass' by "...illegitimacy, violent crime, and drop-out from the labour force." [25] Ruth Lister in an introduction to a debate on the underclass in the same book writes:

> The danger is that the more that certain groups in poverty, or the poor generally, are described in the value-laden language of the 'underclass', the easier it becomes for the rest of society to write them off as beyond the bonds of common citizenship. The reaction is more likely to be defensive calls for tougher law and order policies than for an inclusive citizenship-based on an anti-poverty

strategy. [26]

Her concern that this group will be 'written off' by the rest of society if they are identified as such is matched only by the view of some of the various sociologists and the politicians in this debate that they don't exist! Murray suggests that any one who has lived on such an estate knows that they do exist. [27]

The Church at large appears to be generally ignorant of the on-going debate! While we fail to acknowledge the reality of this growing group we are in danger of treating them as non-existent which is painfully close to treating them as what Rosino Gibellini refers to as the 'non-person'.

> But in a continent like Latin America the challenge does not come principally from the non-believer, but from the non-persons, i.e. the person who is not recognised as human by the dominant social order: the poor, the exploited, the one who is systematically and legally despoiled of his human nature, the one who hardly feels human. [28]

Historically, this attitude of failing to recognise a problem or deal with it compassionately is nothing new. William Booth exposed systemic injustice in his day. This is clearly portrayed in Booth's work and is particularly illustrated as he writes about the Casual Wards:

> The result of the deliberate policy of making the night refuge for the unemployed labourer as disagreeable as possible, and of placing as many obstacles as possible in the way of his finding work the following day, is, no doubt, to minimise the number of Casuals, and without question succeeds. [29]

Not only did this reduce the costs of such provision but also in the case of London caused many to sleep rough on the Embankment. These homeless 'rough sleepers' did not statistically exist and so this policy also became a means of 'massaging' the figures and thus reducing the official number of homeless and jobless people. When the option of government provision was considered less desirable than sleeping rough or prison, the State had left itself wide open to the accusation of systemic injustice. One contributor suggests, rather tongue in cheek, that she cannot see how we can turn the clocks back to prevent a developing underclass "...short of a massive religious revival..." or the introduction of draconian laws. [30]

There are people living in the inner-city areas who are on the edge of society who function very differently to the 'in work' members of the working classes. These people are often honest about their struggles. One young man was talking to me in my garden, telling me how he had just got out of prison, very pleased because he only served eight months instead of a number of years for firearms offences and threat to kill. We have seen this lad (about 29 years old) grow up; his sisters both attended Sunday school at nearby Heathfield Church. Unfortunately he got into drugs and petty crime and it has just led on from there. While I am able to communicate with him on a superficial level, I realise I am not even scratching the surface on a deeper level. However the church generally does not appear to be really in touch with this group within the working classes. The absence of the working classes in church is generally an invisible one. I often look around a meeting and wonder where are the black representatives? It is not so easy to do that with white working class people. Perhaps if we were to spray all working class Christians green we might notice how few there are! The Anglican Bishop of Liverpool, James Jones, recently identified a major hindrance to urban ministry as the domination of the power structures of the Church by "middle-class people, like me, most of whom live in the suburbs". Those Christians who live and worship in the inner city feel misunderstood by this majority. According to James Jones: "They're right!" [31]

Urban Community and Culture

Words like insecurity, transience and instability are often used to describe inner-city areas, but this is not uniformly true. Given a chance and support, a community can be stable. In a block of six flats for senior citizens younger unsuitable tenants were introduced and within a couple of years there was a complete exodus. The flats could not be re-let and stood derelict for sometime, and they have now been demolished. In our street there is considerable unease when someone is about to move out or even indicates that they might. The remaining tenants often lobby the local housing officer to put decent tenants in. This is not 'snobby' class attitude but just a desire to be able to get on with their lives without intimidation or continual disruption. The common plea is "You won't put any 'smack heads' in will you?" The term 'smack head' is here a generic one that symbolises violence, theft and disturbance, not just drug users.

As I indicated before, stability is possible where real 'ownership' is exercised and permitted. While NIMBY (not in my back yard) has a negative connotation, the simple fact is that if you don't take responsibility for your backyard, no one else will, and when several residents take this attitude together, formally or informally, a significant difference can be made. It only took four persistent local residents to stop a spate of stealing and burning wheely bins that had been going on for several years. Unfortunately it took so long because of the apparent indifference of the Police and local housing officers. Similarly, further destruction of the senior citizen's flats was also stopped by the same action.

I think it would be fair to say that the church has not penetrated the local culture. Some would argue that the local working class culture is breaking down, but culture does not break down, it only changes. What we witness is a change in beliefs, values, and behaviour, which is a result of their changing worldview. Christian values will continue to decrease in the absence of a Christian presence, as Christian values, (as distinct from middle class values) are not embodied or communicated in a text but in relationships. The often

64

negative experience of inner-city people also influences their worldview.

Broken or temporary relationships, fragmented families producing isolation and hostile attitudes to others in the community could easily represent inner-city culture. Yet that is not the whole story. As our experience demonstrates, there can be mutual help and support, neighbourliness and fellowship that many in the church could learn from.

Professionals who work for Statutory Agencies (who 'visit', 9-5, Mon-Fri) don't always generate a great deal of confidence for themselves in the community. Support from the Housing Office is not always forthcoming and one gets the distinct feeling that these may be 'public servants' but serving the public is not always on their agenda. While I can appreciate that Statutory Agencies regularly have dealt with difficult characters in the community, the vast majority of people in the community have genuine and reasonable concerns. Unfortunately when these reasonable people encounter an inappropriate and terse response from representatives of Statutory Agencies it reinforces a 'them and us' attitude, which perpetuates hostility. Often those with poor communication skills express themselves badly which is sometimes interpreted as aggression. Whenever I contact Statutory Agencies I make a particular point of being courteous; however it hasn't always been reciprocated.

Urban Abandonment
Paul and I continue to live and worship within an inner-city community as a first principle of our ministry as we have both watched the exodus from the inner areas. For Maureen and me this has meant continuing to live on the Troydale Estate, now with the intention of starting a relevant and culturally appropriate congregation. I was the minister of Heathfield Church, which, although it is predominantly working class, functions on a middle class model and many of the congregation have experienced 'lift'. [32]

65

At this point it might be helpful to look at my experience at Heathfield over the seventeen and a half years of my ministry there, as a sort of personal case study which may serve as an example of a renewed commitment to the inner areas and city housing estates.

Heathfield Church is a small independent evangelical church (over 70 members and 80-90 in Sunday attendance during the mid-eighties to mid-nineties). The other churches in the area consisted of two other Evangelical Churches which are now without Ministers and are somewhere between 'holding their own' and 'struggling', and a Methodist and an Anglican Church which also appear to be shrinking in numbers. Of the four couples that shared with us in full time leadership as Pastors or Assistant Pastors working with us for between two to five years, all have left the inner-city, though one lives and works on a housing estate. Two went to the rural areas, the other, though living nearby, never lived in the area and sent their children to a private Christian school.

The church was made up of people who predominantly had grown up in the area who could be described as white working class 'done good' (which reflects some of the community). Some lived a little way out but 95% lived within a mile of the Church building in the local community.

Older members had children who were our contemporaries (slightly younger) all moved out or moved further away when they got married. Out of 20 children of church members who were contemporary to our own only two are still attending church. Four went with their parents to the suburbs, two moved to other countries after University, one moved away through marriage, four stopped attending and moved away, another five have stopped attending but continue to live nearby, one joined the forces, and another moved away to get work as a teacher.

Why do they go? On one level the answer seems obvious; it isn't as nice living in the inner city. The fabric of the inner areas can often be poorer, as an inner-city report states:

> A characteristic of living in the inner areas as far as individuals are concerned is that personal and collective deprivation frequently over-lap and reinforce each other. Thus being poor in the inner areas is worse than being poor elsewhere. [33]

The report explains that personal deprivation is recognised as "things, which impinge directly upon an individual and his family....", such as "low educational attainment, few marketable skills, ill health.... poor housing, unemployment and physical and social immobility....". All of these are seen to affect an individual's life and family. The report also describes collective deprivation as 'poor physical environment.... inadequate local facilities, vandalism, and the stigma attached to some areas.... '. This report was written in 1978 and it is evident from a further report done in 1991[34] that there are still problems in all of these areas.

What an individual might be prepared to come to terms with and adjust to is one thing, whether or not that person is prepared to bring their children up in such an environment is another. We have lived on the same council estate since 1980 where we brought up our three children. Some have suggested they couldn't move into the inner city because of their children's education; all three of our children reached University even though our youngest daughter dropped out and joined the Army! However all three have struggled with conventional church but continue to demonstrate their faith within their particular contexts.

Over the twenty years that I was involved in Heathfield Church there was always a good number of young people in contact with the church. Sunday school would range from 20 to 30 in attendance and occasionally more. The teens generally had a solid core of 10-15 with many more when we ran a football team. However, though faith commitments were confessed, none have continued as far as I am aware.

The question must be considered 'what sort of youth programme was available?' While what was available certainly was not comparable with some suburban churches, it was better than a number of inner-city churches. The Sunday school was always well staffed and well attended, midweek fun evenings, holiday clubs, outings and regular fun events. The teens always had significant input from full-time staff, sometimes a part-time youth leader, adventure holidays, weekend trips out, and their own social youth night each week. One Sunday morning service each month was a dedicated all age event with a strong bias to the younger end.

My personal evaluation is that as a church we failed to penetrate the culture of the community in a significant way to hold the youth of the local community as they entered their adolescence. The children of church members have followed the trend of moving away after college or just moving to 'better' areas, in many ways they seem to have mirrored the values of some church members and full-time leaders.

If the trend of the church to move out and abandon the inner areas and city housing estates continues, then before long the Christian presence will be virtually non-existent and remaining elements of Christian values will dissipate. We will in fact discover that *we have permitted* these communities to become demonstrably godless. I state quite intentionally *we have permitted* because Christians individually have the responsibility to be 'salt and light'. It is too easy to say '*the Church* ought to do something'; the theology that identifies '*the Church*' as an institution is faulty theology. The Church is the collective of the individual believers, and only functions as a body when they act together. However only when every Christian starts to examine him or herself and consider their responsibility to the inner areas can we say we are beginning to take the problem seriously.

68

Unfortunately, often as inner-city churches, in our discipleship we also fail to challenge the 'redemption and *leave*' principle because of the assumption that it is part of the 'redemption and *lift*' principle. The general impact of coming to faith on people's lifestyles can produce '*lift*'.[35] Often this can have positive financial implications making a move to a more affluent area possible. Also personal aspirations for children can also change, making a move more desirable. In certain cases wanting to live closer to the rest of the congregation thus making a move seem normative, a problem that could, in principle, be minimised if all the congregation lived locally. There is nothing wrong with having more money and concern for the kids - but this should not automatically equate a move. Hence I see the "redemption and lift" principle as inevitable in certain circumstances but it should not equate to 'redemption and leave'. Also in our discipleship generally we accept a capitalist and unbiblical ideal that our career is the most important factor and where we live and worship works out from that. We do this rather than recognising that *every believer* has a call on their life and needs to discover how and where God wants us to serve Him in this world. Our career should then serve that principle rather than dictate to it. In turn the church needs to support its members in their work rather than just seeing them as a resource for the church's activities.

What will make the difference are individual believers moving into the inner areas. What the Church as 'an organisation' (of whatever denomination) can do is to help encourage and facilitate that remigration. In many cases it will require Christians to enter another world, an alien culture and learn another language. They will have to face up to their own cultural prejudices to permit them to begin to be able to identify what is good, bad or just different. It will be necessary for them to penetrate that culture and not just to colonise within it as the Church so often has done and continues to do. It is quite possible for almost anyone to relocate in the inner city, however appropriate training and orientation is advisable to make the transition easier. Many are under a false impression that because they share a common language that they also share a common culture. Basic instruction about culture will help to reveal the differences and help avoid the pitfalls. Obviously this is essential when working with ethnic minorities. Attention needs to be given also to discovering acceptable approaches to mission and relevant models of church for the groups with which we wish to engage.

The symbol of 'Yeast' often appears to carry a negative connotation. However we do well to remember that Jesus told the parable of the 'Yeast of the Kingdom'.

> He told them still another parable:
>
> The kingdom of heaven is like yeast that a woman took and mixed into a large amount of flour until it worked all through the dough. (Matthew 13: 33, NIV).

If we are prepared to penetrate these inner areas, then even a small number in comparison to the masses can have a significant effect. To have an effect two things are essential. We must 'mix' into the local culture as the yeast mixes into the dough and we must live out our Christianity in that context just as the yeast dispenses its own life on the surrounding dough. Do we hear echoes of Jesus' prayer in John 17:15: "My prayer is not that you take them out of the world but that you protect them from the evil one"?

By moving into these communities Christians can bring their personal resources of gifts and skills to the local community and church, which can help, bring stability to needy situations. As well as fulfilling the Great Commission, they can be 'salt and light' where it is desperately needed - their presence alone can begin to restore and maintain Christian values. Yet we will not be effective if we think we have only come to teach. Jesus said:

> I tell you the truth, the Son can do nothing by himself; he can do only what he sees his Father doing, because

whatever the Father does the Son also does. (John 5: 19, NIV).

We also need to be able to see what the Father is doing. This requires us to be a prophetic people and believe that God is already at work in the community.

Urban Presence
Urban Presence is a small ministry of two workers, Paul Keeble and myself, and five trustees. Our vision statement "to see growing, indigenous inner-city Christian communities that are serving and transforming their local areas" not only expresses our desire but is also our declaration of faith that it is possible.

Our response to this situation as our mission statement puts it is "to help rebuild and strengthen an effective Christian presence in the inner-city areas of Manchester by providing training, advice, help and education to churches, individuals and organisations."

Paul and I undertake to help inner-city churches and those committed to urban ministry generally. My postgraduate research related to "Rediscovering effective principles for urban church models and mission." I am also involved in developing and teaching urban ministry courses with a local Theological college in Manchester, which will involve placing students in inner-city churches and ministry. So far much of our time has been spent providing management support to urban ministry groups, consultation to inner-city churches, liaison with suburban churches and involvement in our local situations.

Paul and his wife Judith come from a middle class background, Maureen and I from a working class one; Paul and Judith live in their own home, we in a council house; Paul and Judith live in a multi-ethnic community within the Brunswick area of Manchester, ours is a predominantly white working class community in Newton Heath; Paul and Judith attend Brunswick Parish Church, we are now attending Evangel Church (AOG) and attempting a church plant on the estate where we live. Paul and Judith are bringing up their three children in that inner-city setting; ours are now grown up. We have different backgrounds and situations but share the same commitment to urban ministry.

For Maureen and myself, being committed to exercise a ministry within our own inner-city community has meant preparing to plant a culturally relevant expression of church on our estate. Although we have lived in the same house for almost twenty-three years we have spent more time over the last few years just 'hanging out' with neighbours and doing stuff as friends such as working on our fences, cars, gardens and going to the cinema as well as campaigning over issues that affected us all. This has helped us significantly understand how we should proceed.

Our experience on the estate has encouraged us to continue to develop a more open view of ministry, which is not restricted to religious buildings. Apart from a few people there is very little or no attraction to attend religious meetings, read religious books or develop a philosophy that offers the answers to life. So what is so attractive about Christianity that working class people might be drawn to? Two things seem apparent to me from my background, experience and research: *transformation and community* (fellowship [36]). The immediate question that might be asked is 'is there an escape from my circumstances and who will help me?'
Transformation: The possibility of significant change in the individual that will affect their situation either in perception or in actual circumstances.
Community: Love, acceptance and belonging, others standing with them as they face their circumstances. Jesus offered change: supernaturally, in miracle; socially, in standing with the excluded; spiritually, in rebirth and eternal life. Jesus taught about maintaining right relationships and modelled community life with his disciples.

A model of church that does not demonstrate *transformation and community* can only be seen to be offering innocuous religiosity. The New Testament appears to endorse personal devotion and corporate fellowship; today's church appears to practice corporate devotion and very little fellowship. The model of church to some degree is difficult to determine until a group of indigenous believers begin to express their faith collectively. It is impossible for that expression to be totally free from traditional and contemporary characteristics of Christianity but these should be limited to what is transferred through *their* culture and endorsed by scripture.

My experience on the estate, studying urban church planting in Los Angeles and my own research has caused us to consider an integrated model of mission and church based on *oikos* evangelism and the principles from the approach of the Manchester City Mission (MCM) in the nineteenth century. [37] Regarding the Oikos Method Thomas Wolf states:

> "An Oikos was the fundamental and natural unit of society, and consisted of one's sphere of influence - his family, friends, and associates."[38]

He identifies four different kinds of <u>oikos</u> that people have: biological (family), geographical (neighbours), vocational (those we work with), and volitional (recreational). He goes on to say:

> "The early church spread through oikos evangelism - evangelising family members who saw the old sinner become a new saint; sharing with the neighbour who questioned how such a difference had come over his old friend, and reaching guys in the local trade union or the oikos that played tennis together."[39]

The idea is that you start with a new Christian/inquirer and evangelise the four areas of that individual's oikos. While one may come from outside the culture, the new Christian/inquirer takes you inside their culture. I became impressed with the possibilities of this method on placement in Los Angeles studying urban church planting under Dr Wolf and his team. They also run a church planting training programme called 'LASER', which is developed around the oikos method. My opinion is that this approach is easily transferable to the British scene and most appropriate for the urban context.

Concerning principles from the approach of the MCM, it practised intensive wholistic mission and produced informal culturally relevant faith communities, initially as small groups, developing to congregations based in Mission Halls. Four main areas of circumstantial dynamics can be clearly identified. These are cultural identity, social engagement, business-like approach, and spiritual vitality. These dynamics occurred out of the circumstances and context in which the MCM originated. Possibly the most formative was the spiritual environment, as the MCM was significantly influenced by Evangelical Nonconformity. This produced the atmosphere of urgency and the culture of aggressive evangelism within the organisation. These were considered expedient to save the lost among the working classes who were by and large alienated from both Church and Chapel. As a Sodality[40] organisation they were purpose driven to accomplish their Mission:

"The simple object of "city missions" was to carry the gospel amongst the poor, and to their dwellings..." [41]

They met with the working classes in their own environment, where they lived, worked or took their recreation. The small groups (Cottage meetings) and congregations (Mission Halls) were informal and enthusiastic, and participation was encouraged. They employed Missionaries and recruited volunteers from the working classes. In 1899 they had over 80 Missionaries[42] and 1300[43] volunteers!

Making the break in preparation to start something fresh has been helpful. What I have discovered since not attending a regular church is how I resent having been made to jump through middle class hoops just to exercise a ministry. Like many working class people, I

74

am very sensitive to the way people react to me, and have had to discipline myself not to write others off on first impressions. God calls me to be vulnerable to both groups. Also I discovered how much I dislike 'Services'. When I meet with other Christians I long for two things: real engagement with them, and encounter with God - not 'Services'. It is those same two things that I long to bring to my neighbours and friends.

The situation we face may seem impossible but what keeps me going through the disappointments, difficulties, lack of support and general disinterest from the broader Church is primarily a vision of a vibrant, indigenous working class church that is able to express a biblical faith through its own cultural patterns. Also, I have the desire to see the same for urban areas with an ethnic mix, even if this means developing through the process of language churches initially. Whether this occurs through planting new churches or the renewal of established ones is unimportant. I do not believe this vision is an image of a vain hope but a picture of a reality. Whether we achieve it depends on our desire and determination to see it realised.

Chapter Six

Peter Howard

The Story Of Frankie's
Heartsease, Norwich

Doing something for the 8-12's
The story of Frankie's is about how members of a forty year old church on a forty-year-old council estate on the edge of Norwich sought to make contact with a new generation growing up on the estate.

Frankie's came about because we wanted, ('we', means me and my gang at St.Francis'), to work with young people. Or rather we wanted to enter into conversation with young people. We wanted to give them something and we wanted to receive in return something of their life, their energy, vitality, experience and knowledge. Church life somehow, did not seem complete without a work with young people! I think it is good to own up to the unwritten agenda when we seek to set up a piece of 'church outreach'.

There had been contacts with young people already. Holiday clubs, visits to schools by myself as local vicar, and the occasional child that would drop by on a Sunday morning. The problem was, that the obvious plan, a youth club of some kind meeting week by week seemed to demand skills and commitment we did not feel with confidence that we had in our small estate church membership. We looked further afield to our ecumenical grouping to see if there were the resources and interest to begin - but similar doubts about the availability of leadership were expressed and nothing seemed to happen.

Meanwhile two sets of upwardly mobile parents with roots in the community asked if they could rent the hall for a children's disco. They were enterprising people who felt that they could provide a service that would be enjoyed by children, including their own, as well as being a self-supporting endeavour. Indeed, door receipts and income from the sale of hot dogs and bags of chips would guarantee an income that would pay their expenses and provide inward investment into disco equipment and new recordings.

The Church was not involved in this, though we sought to be as supportive as possible and one lay leader attended on a regular basis. There was little opportunity for conversations at the disco, however, and we found it very difficult to be involved. Meanwhile our own explorations into what we might do with young people continued. Links with the Middle School (8-12) and contacts at occasional events led us to believe that the age group that would be best for us to start our work was indeed this age. Again, not because this was necessarily the prime area of need but because we had a tentative instinct that we might be able to do it -if only we could get the leaders. In the end we decided it was for us and that we would need to try to get a group together to do this work.

We were still toying with this one when the Disco leaders announced that they were having too many behaviour problems with the youngsters (5-12) and would need to cut down to meeting once a fortnight. Immediately this struck us as our opportunity. If we provided something for the older end of the disco clientele, fortnightly on the nights when there was to be no disco, we would have a continuity of activity on one night of the week which children could identify with. Could we find leaders even for this restricted provision? We looked amongst ourselves, a congregation in which the majority were middle aged or older, and wondered how we were to do it. Believing however that it was willingness and an interest in young people that were most important, we sought to draw a team together. In order to compensate for our lack of training and to cover for sickness and other calls we knew that we needed a high staff ratio if we were to survive.

When we asked in our local congregation for people interested in being involved, we stressed, 'formal qualifications not required' and, 'age no barrier'. We reckoned that the 'granny figure' might go down quite well. Well, we certainly did get grannies, and a grandad. We also got a teacher/parent, a full time carer/parent, a mature single mum, a person unemployed due to disability, and myself. We were later joined by a suburban Christian who worshipped in a town centre church out of denomination loyalty, but wanted to be involved in Christian service amongst disadvantaged young people.

What kind of club?

We then had to decide what kind of club or project it was to be. None of us were great sports enthusiasts nor did we warm to the kind of club based on organised games. We settled for the traditional youth club model, but we wanted to give it a new twist that invoked a sense of fun and openness to the community. We looked at the kind of thing the church was doing amongst adults, especially the elderly with the Coffee Bar and Luncheon Club. I'd also heard of Cafe projects organised by churches in various parts of the country. We also looked at the older teenage/twenties scene with the new kind of Cafe Pubs and reflected upon the way children like to emulate their elders. We also wanted to make the most of the excellent facilities that we had developed at the church, with a lounge served by a kitchen through a servery.

So was born the idea of "Frankie's Cafe-Bar, 'the cool venue for mids' (i.e. middle schools age youngsters). Everyone warmed to the idea and its potential 'theme' quality. Dealing with children who were in the most imaginative stage, we worked on the idea of selling colourful cocktails, sodas, popcorn and assorted goodies in a venue where there was opportunity to chat and play board games as well as moving into the hall for the more traditional youth club activities of snooker, pool, and table-tennis. From the beginning, however, we decided that there was to be one other component, a five-minute slot when we would talk with them about the Kingdom of God. We wanted to be up front about where we were coming from, and what one of the things we wanted to share with them was. Hopefully they would be as frank in return and we would have the grace to listen.

From the beginning we had involved the church community and now we went back to them to ask for their help. Money to acquire equipment, gifts of equipment in kind, offers of baking for the Cafe. We also appealed to the local community through the parish magazine for offers of equipment that we might use. Everyone came up trumps and we were ready to open. Publicity, in the form of A6 leaflets with fun artwork by one of our team, were sent for distribution to the middle school. The Frankie's Cafe-bar was to meet fortnightly on Wednesdays (alternate with the Disco), admission was free, though a register would be taken for safety reasons, and club income would be raised from the profits of the Cafe.

We had prayed, we had planned who would do what. We had no training, but then how can you train for the unknown? We had our faith and our wish to give the children a good time, and try to get to know them and hopefully show something of Jesus to them. We might not be ready but we were going to start!

We arrived to set up. Fortunately our kind churchwarden had popped in earlier and put up tables and equipment. Children were already gathering 30 minutes before opening time and entertaining themselves around the vicinity etc. There was about 30+ the first night and this grew to nearly fifty. The children loved what we had but we just didn't have enough staff or activities to prevent a breakdown into chaos! The five-minute slot, a sort of epilogue, was a disaster. We couldn't get the youngsters together, nor could we get enough aural space to communicate. We also had to contend with the few who just disrupted things for everyone. And then there was the extra-curricular activity outside, disturbing residents and the environment, not to mention the air pressure in my car tyres.

The response to these problems was more knee-jerk than considered. Early closure on one night when things got out of hand, was disastrous - we couldn't send everyone home, it was irresponsible and impractical, and those excluded remained outside to create havoc. Exclusion of troublemakers, meant those youngsters who would not respect their peers space to enjoy the activities we offered. It was clear that we needed to go away to think on strategy. How could we create a safe environment, in which children could enjoy the company of both their peers and the adults that came?

A revision of the initial 'drop in' concept seemed to be necessary. The notion of club membership was introduced. Membership was to be free, and was open to all that fell in the age band that demonstrated their ability to respect the ground rules of the club (based on respect for other members, the building and the equipment). Anyone who continued to disregard this would be asked to leave. Membership would be marked with an attractive membership card and a full register would be kept. After a discussion it was agreed that 'Frankies five minutes' would remain but be moved to the beginning of the evening after registration. The other thing that we realised was that we needed to restrict numbers if were going to have any chance to offer sufficient activities to all and find the space to build relationships. Core membership was to be offered to those who had been coming and had not been disruptive. They would be admitted first of all, whilst potential members would be admitted on trial according to space. We were not happy about excluding anyone but we knew that we owed the majority of youngsters who came, a place of safety and friendship and we needed to find a way to defend that.

When we came to try to implement our policy we found it was flawed. We never realised how small our regular core was and how large was the circulating membership of children who came one week and never returned for a while. This meant that we always had a large pool of non-members waiting to be admitted. How were we going to choose who got in? In the end, apart from the troublemakers

80

who were excluded for a meeting or two, we ended up letting everyone in and continued with the problem of dealing with too high numbers. Fortunately we still had a reasonable number of adults to cope most weeks, and by being firm on excluding those who would not listen to our appeals for respect we were able to achieve a basic level of order to survive the night. The new time for Frankie's five minutes at least provided us with an opportunity to share with the whole club, though the size of the group made communication difficult. Most popular were the sketches involving the children. Interestingly, it was the youngsters who were the most challenging in their behaviour that always wanted to take part! During this time some of our helpers reluctantly withdrew, having made the decision that Frankies wasn't for them. They are still behind the work and support it in other ways, but the stress levels were such that it wasn't working out for them to be involved at the front line. And front line it seemed still to those who remained, staying on out of their commitment to the children and strengthened by the relief that it was only every other week!

So we continued on this basis until a major change happened when the Children's Disco, meeting the other week, decided to close. The leaders had decided that they were no longer prepared to carry on with some of the disruptive behaviour they were experiencing. This meant that there was no longer a weekly activity to focus children's consciousness. Children now needed to focus their thoughts upon a fortnightly activity. The result of this was that our number dropped significantly, the children came that wanted to come enough to remember to do so. The result was a complete change of atmosphere, children had more to do, staff began to relax and even have fun, and relationships began to be built. Even 'Frankie's five minutes' entered into new life with genuine dialogue developing.

Then came the long school summer holiday. As in previous years we decided to close the club - staff holidays etc. made it impractical to continue.

When we returned, the only publicity was to ask the head at the middle to school to announce it for us in assembly. We found out later that his deputy took assembly and our request was unfortunately overlooked. Twelve children still found their way to our door and everyone was pleased to meet again. No further publicity apart from word of mouth was envisaged and our numbers gradually grew to a manageable 20-30 which is where we are now.

Theological Notes on Frankie's

What do we make of all this? What connections do we make? What sociological analysis is there? What theology can we do with our experience?

1) The Church's call to proclaim the gospel to the poor (Lk. 4: 18 etc). Our children are the poor in comparative terms in our society. Their educational expectations and achievements measured by national criteria are at the bottom end of the scale.[44]

2) Some of our children are abandoned by their parents to the school or street. Parental involvement in the local school is regarded as quite low. The school works hard and is making progress with the youngsters but there are those whose behaviour is constantly challenging in school and out of school, who roam the streets at will. Like the crowds who flocked to Jesus they are like sheep without shepherds (Mk. 6: 34). Frankie's is like a sheep fold, a place where they can come and find good food (Jn. 10: 7ff). (The number one attribute highlighted in a recent 'straw poll' at Frankie's!), warmth (especially attractive in winter!) and friendship. We also hope that, like the crowd attracted to Jesus, there was some good news and signs of God's life-restoring presence as well.

3) Some of our children have burdens placed upon their shoulders, especially the care of younger siblings. In Jesus' name we want to take off that load. ("Come unto me all you who are burdened and heavy laden", Mt. 11: 28). For this reason younger children are not allowed in except under special circumstances. We encourage

children to take sister home and return to the club. This might seem hard on the younger child and maybe we need to address that. But for the time being our concern is to give the older child a reason to say no and have some time with friends unencumbered by child care duties.

4) As we have already seen, food is an important part of Frankie's. Not food for physical hunger. We have not come across any children that are undernourished, but food is a social and soul enriching experience. Many children do not eat together at home though occasional family outings to Macdonald's may feature in their social calendar. Our Café provides an affordable means to eating with friends in a festive way with 'out of the ordinary food'. In a modest way we offer a 'feast'. One cannot therefore escape the connections with the many Biblical uses of the Feast as a metaphor of the Kingdom of God[45] and not least how Jesus uses meagre but generously given resources to feed a multitude as in Mk. 6. 38ff. Metaphor is in fact not the right word for such feasts for they are an actual participation in the Kingdom. That is a mind blowing thought about what is going on at St. Francis' Church Centre every other Tuesday evening!

5) We believe our club provides a Gospel statement not only in what we are doing for the benefit of the children but also what the process itself is saying. The first connection made is with Paul's words in the first chapter of 1 Corinthians. God has called the 'foolish' to shame the wise, (1 Cor.1: 27). Our crew of pensioners, low-income single parents, disabled, unemployed, homemakers, teacher and middle-aged clerics do not appear the obvious staff for a youth club. These are those who have been prepared to come and who have so far stayed the course. They have brought unexpected skills that have been indispensable, including street knowledge, skills in making popcorn, ability to play table tennis and work the old computer game. Above all, they have within them a love for the children and a love for God that they wish to share.

6) Another example of Gospel statement in what we are doing is with regard to the involvement of a wider community in the work. Church members and unexpected supporters from the community were behind us supporting the ministry in prayer interest and in little practical ways that meant so much. The elderly widows not only baked cakes fortnight after fortnight (reminders of Elijah and the widow of Zarephath[46] but also put such thought into the decorating of the same with decorative sweets they thought might appeal to the children. The account of the women who followed Jesus and the other disciples, meeting their needs from their own resources, also comes to mind here, (Mk. 15: 40-41). How would Jesus' mission have moved forward without them? The Café, its theme of fun, food and drinks is a key component to our model and just wouldn't be the success it is without their contribution. The same is also true with regard to the donations of equipment, and the sense of being undergirded by prayer. Important also is the wear and tear on the building and the occasional acts of abuse it suffers.

7) In the lounge at St. Francis', there is a framed copy of an illustrated text, Hebrews 13. 2, itself an allusion to Genesis 18.

> 'Do not forget to entertain strangers, for by so doing some people have entertained angels unawares.' (Heb. 13: 2).

This was placed in the building in memory of a lady who had helped in the Morning Coffee Bar for many years, serving refreshments to any passer by who had responded to the invitation to enter. We see ourselves as continuing in the same tradition. The text, however, demands closer scrutiny. It suggests that amongst those who enter, unbeknown to the host, will be God's angels. Too much apocalyptic symbolism has blinded us to what an angel actually is, namely anyone who communicates God, his word and his blessing upon human beings. So who are the angels at Frankie's? Who is God speaking to us and blessing us through? This requires some retrospective discernment. I believe that we are learning about God from the children and one another, and God is blessing us through those who come. Sometimes it is easy to detect the work of angels in some of the words and acts of the children. What is more difficult is being able to see the word of God in the children with more challenging behaviour. I am still waiting for this discernment, though I have a strong instinct that it is from such a source that we will receive the most profound word God has for us.

Frankie's is still in its early years. There is much potential for development both in terms of the number and age range of the young people we work amongst and the nature of the work undertaken. It may yet prove to be short term in its life span. In itself that would not be a negation of what has been achieved, Jesus' earthly ministry lasted only three years, though its consequences have permeated two millennia. We don't know the answer to this, though whilst the youngsters come and we have sufficient staff we will want to continue and develop.

Chapter 7

Christopher Baker

From The Land Of The Concrete Cow
Milton Keynes

Milton Keynes – The Garden City par excellence

Milton Keynes, as Britain's fastest growing and newest city, occupies a strange place within the national psyche. It could best be described as a love/hate relationship and always, always, people's opinions are framed by a reference to those famous concrete cows. As a contemporary urban symbol their power to evoke strong reactions seems extraordinary, especially given the very humble and innocent subject matter they depict. Their power would appear to derive from their ability to tap into a wider and ongoing national debate (one could almost say obsession) about the nature of urban living and community. The view one holds on this debate will doubtless colour whether one loves or hates the concrete cows and whether one endorses the type of large-scale urban planning Milton Keynes epitomises, or despises it.

One narrative places Milton Keynes in the Utopian tradition of heroic and visionary planning and proudly proclaims it as the future of urban design. ('One day all places will be like Milton Keynes was the ambitious claim of the 80s advertising campaign sponsored by the Milton Keynes Development Corporation to attract thousands of people to come and live in the New City). The other narrative places Milton Keynes as a quasi-suburban Hell devoid of character or individuality, a massive monument to the tyranny of the planner. A magazine article in 1986 characterised it thus:

> Milton Keynes has managed to become a modern myth….Its name has become a shorthand for a whole

herd of bete noires: insensitive public planning, vapid corporate culture, rootless suburbia, hick provincialism, ugly modern architecture, faddish new technology, car-mobile lifestyles, horrid modern housing and so on.[47]

In the meantime, the mainstream Christian denominations have attempted to meet the challenge of Milton Keynes (and the other new towns that preceded it) with their own 'bold' experiments in church design, ecumenical integration and team working, aware that cities like Milton Keynes offer a unique chance to start with a clean sheet of paper, to rewrite what 'church' could be without the weight of past tradition or outdated architecture to hold them back.

However, this has proved a difficult and often demoralising task, and has called into question for some people the whole wisdom of the top-down approach to planning historically adopted by the churches in the New Towns. In the heavily planned and regulated environment of the new city, what is needed from the churches is not more of the same but something more subversive – open, chaotic, small, intimate. That is why in the late 90s, I with some other like-minded people founded The Well: an ecumenical lay Christian community on the north-east fringe of Milton Keynes. What now follows is an attempt to raise some of the important theological and pastoral issues which arise from the urban experience which is Milton Keynes.

Milton Keynes is a Mark 3 New Town designated under the New Towns Act on January 12th in 1967. About 20% of the city has yet to be built, but is rapidly reaching its target figure of 250,000, with around 4,000 people moving in each year. It is the largest and most ambitious in the line of new towns built immediately after the war to provide decent housing and employment for those whose homes in the large conurbations were destroyed by bombs and compulsory demolition. New towns were in turn directly influenced by the ideals of the Garden City Movement which sprung directly from the vision of one man – Ebenezer Howard, who in his small book *Garden Cities of Tomorrow* (published in 1899), first proposed self-contained new towns with sufficient jobs to be self-supporting, spaciously laid out to give light, air and gracious living surrounded by a green belt that would provide farm produce for the population and the opportunity for recreation and relaxation. These towns would also be linked together by a clean and efficient rapid transportation system (electric train) to form regional units of a quarter million or so.

Like so many late Victorian reformers, Howard was also concerned to deal with the moral and social inequities of urban living. Therefore, familiar Victorian concerns such as temperance (the first garden city to be built, Letchworth in Hertfordshire, had as the centre of its social life a teetotal pub) were laced with some radical attempts at economic distribution. For example, he proposed that the betterment of the land value (caused as a result of a new town being built) should be ploughed back into the new community for its development under the terms of an independent trust. The communities were also designed not only to attract the factory worker, but also middle and higher management.

Milton Keynes has therefore a Utopian pedigree which has undoubtedly helped to create some uniquely attractive contexts. What other city of nearly a quarter of a million souls would have beautifully landscaped linear parks and river valley, 180 miles of cycle ways, a young and dynamic population (46% of the population are under 30), an unemployment rate of 1.8%, the latest retail and leisure opportunities (including a brand-new, 1,600 seat state-of-the-art theatre and gallery, the largest indoor snow dome in the UK and a mile-long glass shopping centre), and easy access to 25 million people within a two-hour drive? And you can still get to anywhere in Milton Keynes within 10 minutes - even at peak commuter times (provided you can cope with its 100 roundabouts). In terms of economic success and bustling energy, Milton Keynes may now be having the last laugh against those for whom it still represents a national joke.

'If Tony Blair were a place, he'd be like Milton Keynes'
(The Independent, 4th July 1996)
There is of course a downside to this Utopianism, as quite accurately summed up in this 'insult' levelled at Mr Blair by a newspaper columnist when he was the leader of the opposition. His detractor was attempting to expose (as he saw it) the blandness and inoffensiveness that lay behind the New Labour repacking; a political edifice built around a gleaming modern image, but with no depth or substance. Milton Keynes is like a gleaming new edifice. The city centre for example is a fairly brutal foray into linear and rectangular architecture; huge swathes of glass and concrete which can look beautiful when they reflect the changing light of the sky. And yet that is all they do. They simply reflect back what is going on outside, and in that sense the buildings are extraordinarily passive. You can't see any human intimacy or interaction going on behind the opaque glass. And as a recent visitor pointed out to me, cities built on glass look and feel insubstantial and fragile: there is little sense of the solidity, history and evolving tradition one gets with buildings made of stone and wood.

There is a lack of identifying cultural or architectural landmarks, to the extent that even the older villages are now neutralised in their power to evoke a sense of history by their schizophrenic juxtaposition within vast tracts of suburban, executive housing. You can venture out to the shopping centre (or one of the conveniently provided monster retail parks within the city boundaries) in your car, never seeing a person en route (because all pedestrians and cyclists are separated from the grid system of roads), enjoy the anonymity of mass participation in the ritualised consumption of leisure and retailing, and return to your new home, perhaps nodding to your neighbour as you put the car back in your garage.

Meanwhile behind the immaculately landscaped dual carriageways lie isolated estates, built in the early days of Milton Keynes, almost all social housing, containing within them the usual clusters of factors associated with social exclusion: poor housing, lack of cheap and

89

reliable public transport, low paid work, poor school attendance, higher health risks and high incidence of drug related crime. Within these estates the so-called 'problem families' and those requiring emergency housing are constantly re-cycled. For some citizens of Milton Keynes, access to the glittering cathedrals of life-style and retail therapy is a myth, as is access to the socially balanced environment so dear to Howard's original vision.

Brave New Church

In order to meet the challenge of the 'brave new' world of the physically planned large scale new community, the churches attempted to build a 'brave new' church. Largely under the impetus of the New Town planning programme, there emerged the dual-purpose church building, the multi-purpose church building, the ecumenical town centre church and the pastoral centre. My recently completed research clearly indicates that the success of this programme has been limited.[48] New congregations struggled to resource new buildings which in the early days were far too numerous to be sustained. They were often poorly sited, tight budgets meant that building materials were cheap, and designs were often inadequate, thus producing buildings with a lack of spiritual luminosity inside and external presence and visibility outside. Absence of clear management structures hampered a proper integration of community and church use in the later multi- or dual-purpose buildings. Ecumenical ventures often foundered on different levels of expectation, resourcing and management by the parent denominations. The most damning criticism of church planning the new towns stemmed from an inability to carry out proper analysis of community projections before the churches were built.[49] It was all a classic case of placing the latest theological thinking and theory *before* analysis and reflection.

A reflection on the experience of churches in the new towns would be as follows. First of all there is the lack of belonging experienced by people in new towns. New Town people can expect to feel more vulnerable and lonely because of the anonymity and lack of extended family networks in newly-developed districts. This used to be called 'new town blues', following the classic sociological survey undertaken by Wilmot and Brown in the late 1950s which followed groups of East End Londoners to new settlements in Essex.[50] The extent to which new town blues is still an ongoing phenomenon needs to be researched, but as one delegate to a New Town Ministers Association Conference in the 70s remarked 'the more uprooted and lonely people feel, the less inclined they are to seek social contacts, and the more firmly they withdraw into their own homes and the activities they pursue.'[51]

This has particular implications for activities like church-going and church growth, a situation further compounded by other factors. For example, the traditional loyalties to the church which you find in older communities is absent. In older communities, elements of an original understanding of the church as part of some total organic community still remain and prevent the separation of the church from the wider community. In new towns, the church has not inherited its integration within the life of the wider community – it is therefore not 'basic' to the community and thus not a strong focus for civic identity.

This leads us on to both the opportunities, but also the problems of ecumenism. The planning of the second and third generation (or Marks) of new town building (plus the expansion of some Mark 1 new towns) fortuitously coincided with the high-tide mark of ecumenical adventure in the 60s.[52] In this new consensus, new towns and housing areas were to be designated 'areas of ecumenical experiment.' Many bold projects from that era survive to this day.[53]

However, there is a downside to ecumenical working which can be summarised in numerous ways. In places like Milton Keynes, a few people may well turn to the church as a way of belonging, but in an ecumenical context, one is being asked to belong to something that transcends a denominational affiliation which is both particular and familiar. The danger that people will turn away to find and travel to something they find more reassuring is further compounded by the pressure from the parent denominations for ecumenical churches to deliver the goods. The unmistakable message from their hierarchies is that they are there to form a community that is better than the existing model; that rises above the tribal and local to form something new which is based on deeper roots. They remind the local ecumenical projects (LEPs) of the high investment in terms of new buildings and person power that has been invested in the ecumenical enterprise. But they rarely offer the ongoing support and understanding that pioneering work requires. Rather, the parent denominations insist on maintaining their existing administrative and management structures instead of allowing an ecumenical area to have a unitary system of management. This causes confusion and resentment, and means that most ecumenical ministers and congregations end up having to resource two overlapping structures instead of one. It feels a very top-down form of church planning, where the ideal of ecumenism is attempted without real conviction or commitment.

Then there is the impact of physical planning we have briefly alluded to already, which can affect a new community in many ways. The compression of time and the vastness of the planning scale reduces the normal haphazard and incremental growth of communities to a single planned process, when it is apparent from people's experiences that more than physical design is involved in developing community spirit. A sense of shared history can only come when people eventually share together key communal experiences of adversity and celebration. Then there is the upheaval impact on existing residents, typically in market towns or villages whose rural or semi-rural community history and sense of identity is swamped by thousands of people who have come from an urban or suburban background, and whose values and class identity are very different. The church can have a key role in managing the transition from the old to the new, but is often too overwhelmed by the presence and needs of the newcomers to properly address the needs of the existing congregation.

Finally there is the modern church design in New Towns. Particularly in the 60s and 70s, churches sought to reflect the new incarnational, 'humankind coming of age' and secularist theology of that era in buildings that were non-contentious on the outside and multi-purpose on the inside. The clear missiological message was that the church was coming alongside the community as a servant, not dominating it as a beacon of conversion and spiritual power. While commendable in its theology at the time, the reality is that these churches were often shunned for their uninspiring and utilitarian interiors and ignored because of their lack of identity and visibility on the outside. In a landscape crying out for some kind of physical landmark or identity, many new town churches fell woefully short on impact.

From Willen Priory to The Well
At this point in our narrative, I want to stop talking about the church, and talk about communities. As far as Christian communities are concerned, there have been two significant responses to Milton Keynes, and their experiences I think offer a glimpse into how a new church might evolve within a new city.

The first of these is Willen Priory, established by an Anglican missionary order founded in the nineteenth century by Fr Herbert Kelly, the Society of the Sacred Mission (SSM). Like many other Victorian missionary orders inspired by the Oxford Movement, the Society was an attempt to bring the sacramental mystery of the church into the midst of the urban working class and to nurture and train men from those communities for the priesthood. With proceeds from the sale of their theological college at Kelham in Nottinghamshire, they decided in 1972 to establish a new Priory for the new, and as yet largely unbuilt, city of Milton Keynes. Their mission statement was to be 'a still centre of the city's busy life' and to provide people with the opportunity 'to share in the experience of living in community.' People were indeed attracted to the Priory, especially in the early days, by its peacefulness and quietness, plus the many training events which took place there, often run by local community groups. Yet, over a period of time, the numbers of monks living in the Priory declined and within a dwindling community a safety-first principle appeared to operate. The monastic model asserted itself over the more radical ideas that were around in the early days – including the profession of women and the development of lay associates. The Priory was used and loved by a core group of people, but these people were by and large a self-selecting group drawn from a wide area (sometimes beyond Milton Keynes itself). Its impact amongst the rapidly growing areas appeared to be negligible. Some 25 years after its foundation, in stark contrast to a booming and bustling Milton Keynes, the Priory appeared to be diminishing, both in terms of its internal membership and external impact.

In a radical move, SSM took the decision to lease the site to a new community. An ecumenical lay community called The Well was eventually formed in 1997, comprising seven adults and five children. If the Priory was a monastic model of community, we are a more family model. For one thing, we have yet to define a concrete vision for ourselves (despite our best efforts to do so). Nor can we look back to a founding father. However, each supports the initiative of another person within the group. The Well is thus an entity made up of contrasting activities, which nevertheless appear to coalesce into a holistic package – a commitment to hospitality, a commitment to issues of peace and justice (in particular our work with asylum seekers in Milton Keynes), a commitment to partnership working with other agencies in the city, and a commitment to exploring spirituality and faith through art and creativity rather than merely the spoken word. This package is often held together at great cost in terms of learning to trust each other, forgive each other, learning to love and work within the limitations of each other rather than our own idealised projections. More often than not, the space at The Well is chaotic, unstructured, spontaneous and small-scale. It is extremely open to the wider world, often through an inability to keep proper boundaries – but the number of people coming in and out and using our facilities suggests that they at least do find The Well a place of refreshment, hospitality and encounter (to use some of its biblical norms). Often we are tired and tetchy. Sometimes we are exhilarated and amazed at what is achieved through the interaction of human commitment and openness, and the Spirit of God. Above all however, it feels important in an urban context planned 'from above' to a supposed blueprint of what a city and church should be, to have a small, hospitable but creative space where a few things can run wild, a few risks can be taken, and the outcome be often anything but certain.

Five Marks of Mission for a New City
I would like to end this article by summarising what I consider to be 5 marks of mission for a church, or more accurately, a church community (since you would not need a specially dedicated or large building for any of these things). They will hopefully speak to a way of being church in the many new towns and settlements that will emerge in the next 30 years.[54] As such they belong to that part of the urban experience that speaks of newness and displacement, of a search for an identity and experience of belonging which can be elusive in an increasingly post-modern and post-industrial urban landscape.

The first mark a church community might offer is a sense of rootedness which comes from the experience of community. Within new towns and expanded areas there is still a pronounced lack of kinship and feeling of community. In cities like Milton Keynes there are no extended families to visit or look after, people work late and go away for the weekend and they have probably been sent to Milton Keynes to work for a few years in one of the many multinational and service sector head offices based here. There is also evidence to show that aspirational motives mean high levels of mobility *within* Milton Keynes itself, as families move in order to secure (supposed) better education or housing opportunities for their families. Meanwhile for those excluded from accessing the more suburban elements of life there is an equally high transient population due to local authority housing policies which tend to move the 'problem' families from one poor estate to another.

If Milton Keynes is a city always on the move, then it seems to me that the churches need to accept that core, committed, stable membership levels will be low. This core membership needs to be committed to providing a sense of belonging and community to people within their locality for as long as those people are with them. This to my mind requires an approach to hospitality which is fairly unconditional and open – requirements of attendance and participation need to be kept at a low threshold. It is hard work, and without the right mental and theological approach we have found at The Well (and I have heard the same from other ministers working in the new areas of Milton Keynes) that it is easy to get resentful and angry; to feel that people are taking you for a ride. However, there will always be a few for whom the more committed form of community membership will be their salvation, as they join the existing core group.

A second mark a church community might offer in a new town is a sense of spirituality and an offering of symbolism. The endless low density 'prairie planning' of the new towns produces a landscape generally devoid of cultural or spiritual signpost. If Lewis Mumford is right when he proclaims that the main function of a city is to act as a cultural container for its citizens[55], through the community narratives set in the stone of older buildings and districts, and through a wide range of cultural and visual stimulation, then the new towns are at a distinct disadvantage. The church in the new town, along with other religious communities, is one of the few existing organisations that understand the importance of cultural depth and spirituality; symbols like bread and wine, icons, crosses, candles and darkness, the peace, the confession, exodus and creation, Advent and Lent, living for the sake of the neighbour. 'Church' is the one place in a new town where one can experience the richness and nourishment of religious and cultural symbolism by which to develop a spirituality that can help cope with the arid materialism of a Milton

Keynes. It must be said that deep symbolism is difficult to communicate in a landscape of ubiquitous MacDonalds and Marks and Spencer megastores on the one hand, and on the other the privatised 'suburban' layout of a new town where each person has a house and a garden – 'an Englishman's home is his castle'.

A third mark of mission for the new town is that of ecumenical witness – a strand of experience that has evolved as the new towns themselves have evolved. It seems to me that ecumenism presents a challenge, and yet needs to be realistically attuned to people's needs. As we have seen, some people settling in new towns perhaps have a greater need of familiarity and a strong liturgical identity. For others new towns still offer the potential for bold experiments in radical co-operation. However my research suggests (and our experience as an ecumenical community bears witness) that the uniformity model of ecumenism feels like a parallel to the top-down model of the new town planners and Development Corporations. You can try and impose a model on people; you can try and impose orderliness and structure that intellectually makes sense, but emotionally feels conforming and restricting. It is better to allow ecumenism to happen in a natural and spontaneous way: a more grassroots based model that allows self-expression and individuality, but which is nevertheless committed to partnership working: a flexible approach which is happy with difference and spectrum, but is also alert to the possibilities of mutual creativity.

Which leads us on to the fourth element of a church community model – a commitment to partnership working with others for the social development of the local community. In the early days of the New Towns programme, the church was seen as having a pivotal role in the development and integration of new communities. Lord Reith, whose committee paved the way for the New Towns legislation in the 1940s saw the churches having a pivotal role in the social cohesion required for community growth, because they could be regarded as 'societies having a strong common bond and disposed to service.'[56]

However, by the 60s and 70s, most development corporations of new towns saw the church as just one of the many voluntary associations whose main role was to provide for its members. Perhaps the course for church communities in the new millennium is to avoid on the one hand the paternalism of the 1940s and on the other the timid fatalism of the 1920s, and instead to recognise that while they don't have the resources single-handedly to 'build the Kingdom', and while the overwhelming majority of the population will not require their services, they can nevertheless be a key player in the social and economic generation of their locality. It would appear that the Priory/monastic model finally withered because the partnerships with the wider community were not strong. The Well/family model, with its members committed to partnership working beyond the structures of the community and an active marketing policy to bring outside users to share our resources appears to be bearing fruit in the range and quality of initiatives and relationships that have been developed with others in the wider community.

But partnership does not always have to rely on consensus and agreement. Authentic partnership also requires from time to time the counter-cultural critique – the fifth mark – the more prophetic stance which is not afraid to point out injustice or imbalance. At The Well, when our way of being lurches (as it often does) towards the chaotic, passionate and unplanned, it is, on reflection a useful counterbalance to the Utopianism of the planned environment, be it secular or ecumenical, which is tempted to 'play God' with other's lives. It reminds the church and the urban planners that authentic community is far from perfect, but constantly in flux and evolving, growing (one hopes) to greater maturity. It critiques the modernist belief in the science of planning to resolve fundamental human complexities, and dare I say it, sinfulness.

The sharing of community, the working for and with others also offers a counter-critique to the post-modern notion of the individual which is expressed in terms of the right and freedom to consume whatever is required for your own personal happiness and self-constructed lifestyle, regardless of the cost to others' human rights and the environment. Milton Keynes, as we have seen, is being developed on the premise that choice and individual freedom is all.

Meanwhile in The Well's work with asylum seekers, in our opening of doors as far as we can to the stranger who has no material goods to offer, but brings instead their cultural perspectives and richness, we are hopefully valuing those individuals caught up in the globalisation of poverty and inequality.

Conclusion
The purpose of this article has been an attempt to locate within the emerging theological spectrum of urban theology some reflection on what it means to belong to a very new community among urban communities at the cusp of a new Millennium. A theology of New Towns offers us a fascinating glimpse into the whole history of Utopian planning in Britain, and explores how the churches attempted to change themselves in order to meet their challenges. In Milton Keynes in particular however, we also have a glimpse of the city of the future – quintessentially suburban, post-industrial and dominated by the retailing and leisure sectors. The traditional narrative of community appears to be under threat from a new narrative built on techno-information based on ways of living, which stress the power of the individual to work, consume and communicate without necessary human interaction. As such, this feels a world away from the inner-city and the peripheral housing estate, and yet the challenges it poses to church communities of the future may in the end be common strands in the continuing building of God's Kingdom.

Chapter 8

Greg Smith

The Christ of the Barking Road
Newham, London

Out of the mouth of babes

- Is Jesus stronger than Allah?
- I want to be a Hindu so I can put Mehndi paint on my hands.
- Are we Christians or are we English?
- Will Parmesh go to heaven?
- Aleisha's a Hindu, so do we have to get her a Christmas present?
- It's not fair… God should have made Jesus a girl.
- If Ahmed can't eat pork and Saffron's a vegetarian why do I have to eat my vege- troubles?
- That man doesn't need to be homeless… Can't he share our house?
- Is it really true that Auntie Myrtle's grandmother was a slave in Jamaica?

Such questions are day to day reality for many of the children and young people of East London. Children have a habit of going straight for the heart of the difficult theological questions. Perhaps our theology should be far more childlike and thus closer to the kingdom of God.

My kids as part of our committed Christian family regularly worship in a majority black church, and attend a primary school in which over 80% of children are Asian and about 60% are Muslim. I experience daily hopes and fears for their development. Will they, as I hope, come out of it all as strong but open minded Christians, secure in a personal faith and clear in their values, knowing what they believe, but respectful in their friendship with others? Or will they drift into a fog of unknowing rootlessness, picking and choosing the bits they like in a desire not to offend anyone, or worse still turn into narrow racist bigots willing to fight for the flag of St. George and the dominance of the English "Christian" supremacy. Whatever happens in future the present reality is that they at age six and eight are far more sophisticated in identity work, and appreciation of different religions, than many of us were at eighteen.

Personal Journey
I want to structure this chapter as a journey... a short journey no more than 4 kilometres from West to East (literally and metaphorically) along the Barking Road in Newham. Indeed this was a journey a group of us made on foot one summer evening a year ago during which we counted 44 places where religious activity evidently took place. In fact in the whole borough of Newham in our recently published directory of religious groups we document 294 organisations of which 181 are Christian congregations and around 20 are mosques* (see table at end). The Barking Road certainly has plenty to offer for the multi-faith tourist or pilgrim.

When I came to Newham to live and work in 1975 there was a real sense of it being a missionary journey. Arriving on the Barking road from a rural Methodist upbringing, via a university where I had found evangelical faith, and a year as a volunteer teacher in India where I encountered non-western cultures and religions for the first time, I felt a definite sense of calling to work for the church, the gospel and the community of the (in)famous East End for a year or two at least. Through various jobs over two decades in church, community work and academic research, I found fellow travellers on the journey, the closest companions being a peer group of like-minded Christian incomers. On a shared journey, for many years in one new church fellowship, we have stayed together through stages of evangelical outreach, community work and political activism for and against the Labour Party. Twenty five years on, our paths have diverged though we are still together. One of our members has become an MP and government minister, another is completing training for Anglican ordination having moved from Brethren roots through depression to High Anglicanism, a third is training for the URC ministry while her husband is teaching English to refugees and Religious studies at a secondary school on the Barking Road. We have all made decisions to stay and bring up families in the area, with all the dilemmas in education that poses to middle class families, and to white Christians living as a minority among diverse ethnic and faith communities.

We have walked the Barking Road together and that journey has shaped our lives. It has shaped also our religious understandings, as for most of us the exclusive certainties of 1970's evangelicalism have broadened to include more Catholic, Celtic Christian and Orthodox understandings, and we have come to see Muslim, Sikhs and Hindus as neighbours, friends and community allies rather than just "benighted heathen ripe for conversion". The church too has changed over the last three decades, from a tiny dispirited remnant of white old ladies to a lively growing and noisy multitude. Our fellow travellers in both mainline and independent churches are the peoples of the Two-thirds world; it is now African, Asian, Latin American, Pentecostal and Catholic, prosperous professional and poverty stricken, global and local and all mixed up.

Religion on The Barking Road
We begin our journey down the Barking Road on the millennium line of 0 degrees with a fine view of Canary Wharf and the Dome. If the first represents a temple of Mammon the second celebrates a memory of Christendom culture with a Faith zone covering something from each major faith community in Britain today. We risk our lives navigating on foot the Canning Town flyover and roundabout where the A13 shoots off to sever the two halves of the local neighbourhood, and the huge new transport interchange heralds economic

regeneration for the most deprived ward of the most deprived borough in England. The first religious buildings we encounter are two hostels for the homeless, a temporary one linked to Newham's ecumenical night-shelter project the second a Catholic hostel for seafarers, now used for otherwise homeless men. There is a Catholic parish church and the sites of a Methodist chapel (now a garage) and an Anglican church (now a Macdonalds). But there are also the signs on the shops, His Grace Photos, Amazing Grace Groceries, Signs and Wonders Hair Salon, Mount Zion General Store, Faith Electronics and just round the corner Saraswati Newsagents, and the Old English Pawnbroking Company.

Next in the religious landscape is the Islamic Centre, formerly the local synagogue. On one side it is flanked by bookies, on the other by the worship centre of Calvary Charismatic Baptist Church. Across the road is Mansfield Settlement, a multi-agency centre that used to specialise in the muscular Christianity of boxing clubs but is now known for its work on HIV/Aids and its links with the Gay Christian Movement. Back on the other side is Glory Bible Church and Green Pastures Christian ministry, occupying a huge complex which was once a Baptist chapel, then a draper's shop and warehouse until five years back it became a church again. The congregation is large, lively and mainly African, with the flags of fourteen nations flying in the auditorium. They are engaged in partnership with the Council in a multi-million pound project to establish a day nursery and training centre.

At the Abbey Arms, (a not very religious pub), there is a cluster of mainline church activity. The House of the Brown Brothers or Society of Saint Francis, the Anglican Parish Church, the huge barn of Memorial Baptist Church and the associated West Ham Central Mission. Together these groups form a network of Christian care and support for poor and vulnerable people, for refugees and asylum seekers, for people with mental health needs and learning difficulties. With volunteers from other churches they run Newham Organisation for Stopping Hunger (NOSH), a Sunday lunch club where people from all these groups dine cheaply in good company. The sign on the church wall proclaims that the building offers a base for at least four new Pentecostal congregations, though they come and go so quickly that you can never be sure if the information is up to date. A bit further on there is St. Andrews, a former parish church now housing a new independent evangelical congregation and its various ministries, and a former snooker hall housing the Foursquare Gospel Church.

The next section of the Barking Road contains the URC church, thriving and evangelical with a daughter congregation, English classes for refugees and fellowship groups in Spanish for Latin American refugees. Across the road is a Pentecostal storefront church, and along it a shop front mosque operating in an unmarked building. At the traffic lights we stand within a hundred metres of a Catholic Parish Church, and a newly renovated St Martins Church of England, which shares its premises with a large secular youth work agency. The shop front of Sree Narayan Guru Mission, (next door to Emmanuel Enterprises) is dwarfed by the obviously prosperous West Ham United Club Shop, and the nearby football stadium.

The last kilometre of the Barking Road takes us past two mosques, a Church Army Youth Centre which also hosts three Pentecostal congregations, and another Parish Church and Community Centre (home to two or three more congregations), a "Mecca" Bingo Hall and the book-shop of Holy Tabernacle Ministries. We then arrive at the Town Hall, where if it is Sunday a banner proclaims that the Redeemed Church of Christ, Royal Connection Parish meets here to worship. During the week of course this is where Newham Council meets in secular state, although with seven Councillors and the local MP as signed up members of the Christian Socialist Movement, with half a dozen Muslim councillors including the Mayor and Deputy Leader, three Sikhs and a couple of Hindus the undercurrents of faith are never absent.

How then should we read the story of the Barking Road? Clearly it is about globalisation, the numerous international public phone call shops speak clearly about and to the connections back home, in Pakistan, Nigeria, Colombia, Croatia, and Mozambique. Clearly too it is about global and local politics and economics, of economic migrants and asylum seekers, fleeing poverty and oppression at home, ending up in a part of London that is paved not with gold but with litter and racism, overcrowded housing and low paid casual work. In all of this religion offers some hope of building identity and community, practical mutual help and spiritual resources. The churches and mosques in one sense operate in a religious supermarket, or rather a set of niche markets purveying hope and friendship, meaning and faith. But for disciples of a Jesus who drives out with a whip the traders from the house of prayer for all nations, the prosperity of this religious environment can only raise difficult questions.

People and Ministry on the Barking Road

A road is a place for people journeying and the Barking Road is no exception. As people move up and down the road, crossing from one side to the other the short journey links with each life journey, each pilgrim's progress. Some of the journeys are very local, some are stages in transcontinental travel, some have clearly set their sights upon their vision of the Celestial city, others are struggling with Giant Despair or foundering in the Slough of Despond, or simply going round in ever decreasing circles. It would not be fair to spell out the stories of individuals in their struggles and their dealings with God. So instead we will present the stories of a few of the ministries and try to discern the theologies that lie behind them.

The Night-Shelter was recently renamed Turnaround as it has taken on a wider remit including day centre and resettlement work and is concerned for turning round the situations of homelessness and despair for people in the street. It is ecumenical, seven churches providing shelter on a weekly rota basis, and volunteers from other churches and faith communities helping out as they are able. With so many people involved it includes a range of theologies from the evangelistic through the compassionate to the empowering and the prophetic. There may be a shared gospel understanding around Matthew 25: 35, "I was a stranger and you invited me in" and an obedience to the fast of Isaiah 58: 7 "Is it not to share your food with the hungry and to provide the poor wanderer with shelter". However there are multiple readings within a common commitment, where some of the churches want to present Christ and his love to the homeless and others discern Christ in the persons of the guests.

NOSH, the Sunday Lunch club also operates ecumenically, out of compassionate concern. The sharing of food among pensioners, single parents, people with learning difficulties and African refugees can be seen as a foretaste of the Messianic banquet. One feels that the diners are just the sort of folk that Jesus walked and talked among. It's a shoestring operation, struggling against setbacks as every few months someone more desperate than the diners breaks into the deep freeze and steals the food for next Sunday. People get involved as they are able, some find meaning in helping set the tables, making the tea or washing up. There is pastoral care from each other and from the Christians who hold it all together. There are attempts to address wider issues, like health promotion and plugging in to the Credit Union which operates from the Catholic Church down the road. His name is not often mentioned but somehow Jesus is there.

Just up the Road the URC does its work with refugees. There are English Classes and prayer meetings, bible studies and worship in Spanish as well as English. There are links with the local Churches Immigration Support Group. Over the years this organisation has helped those struggling with Home office rules or threatened with deportation. There is personal and prayer support, legal advice, letter writing campaigns and in some cases sanctuary in church buildings. Some cases are won, some are lost, some people just disappear. There's an understanding that Jesus was a refugee in Egypt, that the immigration rules are racist and unjust and that God cares about justice. For some at least Christ is known as a personal friend and

Saviour. I often support them in their campaigns, and think Jesus would too.

My friend is an American evangelist. He was a drug addict when he was converted, he's a man of great faith and prayer. He and his family served many years as a missionary in Pakistan. He has a calling and a burden to share the gospel with Pakistanis. He is at home in their culture and language and far from naïve about what it would mean for a Muslim to accept Christ. He dare not represent the church, he doesn't talk about being a Christian, for that is a mere "caste" identity, he talks of being a follower of Jesus. And as he and his five-year-old son meet people in the streets and shops they lose no opportunity to talk to people about their faith in a forgiving and saving God. I sometimes wish I could be as up front as them.

I recently got to know a local church leader, a medical doctor originally from Nigeria. He gave up medicine for the cure of souls and is one of the ministers at the Glory Bible Church. It is a large Pentecostal worship Centre, to which hundreds travel from all parts of London. It's mainly African but the flags of a dozen nations hang in their sanctuary. There is a distinct emphasis on faith and on a living Jesus who can bring you health and prosperity in this life as well as the next. The ministry is entrepreneurial, growing, and beginning to reach out into the community to meet local needs. They work with the Health Authority to put on Health Information Days, with Social Services, to develop their day nursery and with the local regeneration partnership to develop employment training courses. I sometimes wonder if the Jesus they worship is the same one I serve, and whether their Christ is not perhaps more North American than African.

The Muslims who worship on the Barking Road are also aware of Jesus. For them he is a prophet, but not the final prophet. They reject the idea that he might be divine, for Allah cannot be associated with anything created, God cannot have a son. There is huge distrust... a Muslim student who approached the mosques to gather information

107

for our religious directory had many layers to unpeel. First he had to assure them he was not from the Council, then he had to explain why he was doing some work for and with Christians. Next although he dressed as a Muslim and prayed alongside them in the mosque he had to explain his own allegiances and beliefs, which strand of Islam did he come from, what were his Islamic agendas? In some cases he had a language barrier to overcome, as an English speaker with some fluency in Punjabi he couldn't get far with Bangladeshis. Finally he discovered he was the wrong age, a twenty-year-old should have more respect when talking to his elders who ran the mosque. Not only are there many Jesuses in the market place, there are a bewildering range of Islams, and unforeseen complexities in the inter faith encounter.

One of the features of our so called post-modern times is that a plethora of fragmented cultures and identities coexist with an evident increase in connectivity. Through international travel and electronic communications a global network entangles the world. At the local level we can also talk of the network society. Traditional dense and closely bounded local communities have tended, especially in cities, to give way to looser associations built up of overlapping personal networks.

In this context an important question is whether the diverse local ministries on the Barking Road are in touch with each other. The answer in short is both Yes and No. Among Christians, denominations provide linkages for some but there are few if any formal ecumenical structures. There are however umbrella bodies bringing together certain groups such as the Newham Christian Fellowships mainly for the white led charismatic and evangelical churches, and the Newham Community Renewal Programme which brings together churches for social action programmes such as the Turnaround Nightshelter, and the Immigration Support Group. There are also informal ecumenical collaborations on specific local projects such as the NOSH lunch club. On the other hand there are cleavages and wide gulfs between Christian Groups. Most of the black majority Pentecostal Churches on the Barking Road are fiercely independent if not sectarian, and not even well networked with similar groups, let alone with mainline Christianity. Traditional party divides such as Catholic / Protestant, Evangelical / Anglo-Catholic are less significant than they once were but new schisms have appeared for example over the gay issue. Inter faith activity is not well developed, one exception being a relationship between a mosque and a Catholic parish in the context of broad based community organising. But the charismatic Baptist church next door to the mosque would want to have nothing to do with Islam. Indeed the very mention of the possibility of interfaith relationships is contentious enough to make some Christian churches break fellowship with others.

One of the few ways in which networking and collaboration between religious groups can move forward is through the proactive networking ministry of a small number of Christian workers, of whom I am one. Together with friends and colleagues, using a variety of action research and community development techniques, we have over twenty years sought to extend and strengthen the networks for urban mission and ministry understood in its broadest and pluralist sense. Such efforts have not always met with success but there are at least some possible channels of communication available between the different faith communities, religious groups and secular agencies that are found along the Barking Road.

Messiahs on the Barking Road
In our church we sometimes sing

> I looked up and I saw my Lord a coming
> I looked up and I saw my Lord a coming down the Road.
> Hallelujah He is coming
> Hallelujah he is here

It often moves me to tears and it leaves me with many questions and few responses. When I was a young Christian in India I read E. Stanley Jones *The Christ of the Indian Road* and understood for the first time that Jesus could come in many guises, and be at home in many cultures. Today as I walk the Barking Road Jesus walks alongside, but in many packages, if not incarnations. It's a bit like the Number 15 bus which travels along the Barking Road. You wait for a Messiah for ages then three come along at once!

However all this pluralist language is highly unsatisfactory. Is Christ divided? Is there one God or many in all this? Even if there are diverse interpretations and its hard to be as certain in our faith as some Christians and Muslims appear to be surely there is a core of truth a basic gospel story, a rock which doesn't roll. Can we not go back to the simple faith of the old Boys Brigade Hymn?

> We have an anchor that keeps the soul
> Steadfast and sure while the billows role
> Fastened to the rock which cannot move
> Grounded firm and deep in the Saviour's love.

The usual route to firm foundations is to return to the original sources, to look at what the Scriptures say. There are many books, and many sermons that try to present easy and unique answers to these questions, using proof texts. They want to be a guide book or street map offering power and control over the urban environment. As urban theologians we have learned to be much more modest, and just to put our stories alongside Bible stories and get people to talk about it. So here we'll only talk about signposts; and all of us who walk or cycle in the city know that signposts are unreliable, for bored youngsters love the game of turning them round to point in the opposite direction.

Gospel Signposts for the Barking Road
The five New Testament Roads that come to mind are all in Luke / Acts.

110

1. The Jericho Road (Luke 10: 25-37)

This is a downhill road, ultimately a road to one of the oldest cities in the world. It is a dangerous road for bandits are waiting in ambush. It's a road where muggings are too frequent and the police, if there are any don't bother to do much about it. The church is there too, but the religious people are not much use because they have a habit of not noticing, of just passing by, or not wanting to get involved in the blood and the muck, of not wanting to risk their necks. But just as you give up hope and you think you are bleeding to death along comes help from an unlikely source. It's the outsider, the foreigner, the one who wouldn't be welcome in church even if he decided to come, that has some oil and wine, and a donkey and a voucher for bed and breakfast at the next travel lodge. In the end it's quite simple, about being neighbours and going and doing likewise. It's a road which leads us to caring in the city. In consequence, as a family we get involved in neighbourly and pastoral concern for people in our street and church, and we give money and time in projects like NOSH and Turnaround. But in doing so we find we often receive as much as we give and often from those whom the world regards as merely a burden on society.

2. The Jerusalem Road (Luke 19 - 23)

This road after passing through the hostile territory of Samaria begins in Jericho and is therefore an uphill trek. It's a road where money and power keep coming into the picture. There is the rich and crooked Zaccheus who repents and starts to do something useful with his resources. There's the challenge to invest our talents and take responsibility for up to ten cities, as a reward! There is the pomp of a powerful king yet riding into the city on a donkey and weeping over it. It's a story of confronting the capitalists who pretend to be interested in religion. It is a road for debating the claims of God and Caesar and coming to realise that they are simply two sides of the same coin. It's a road where the poor widow's contribution is worth more than the credit card of the rich. It's a journey of discerning the signs of the times, where there is apocalyptic meaning. But its a road that leads to betrayal, denial and eventually to unjust punishment for sedition and blasphemy, even death on a cross. In short it's the road of prophetic protest and political involvement in the powers of the city. So we walk this road in campaigns as varied as Evangelical Christians for Racial Justice, Church Action on Poverty and the London Cycling Campaign. And we join Community Forums and Regeneration Partnerships, we stayed involved in the Labour Party until we could bear the Newness no longer, and remain in discussion and prayer support groups with Christians who are local Councillors and MPs.

3. The Emmaus Road (Luke 24: 13-35)

The third road is a more quiet road, a road of retreat from the city. It's a sabbath road, a time to talk over and reflect on dramatic events that have taken place in the city. It's a road where if we are fortunate we may sense someone coming alongside us and restoring our disappointed hopes. It's a journey where he will help us understand the meaning of the Bible story, where we can make the links between our story and his. It's a journey with a living companion, a companion being defined as one who shares bread. And in the breaking of the bread, and perhaps the drinking of wine, we see symbols and memories of what it's all about. Ultimately it is about worship and expounding the Word, the every week ritual of the church for two millennia now. And it is this reflection and resourcing that renews our tired feet and sends us back with Cleopas and his friend into the City to share the Good News of a risen Jesus.

112

Recognising this need we stay in the local church even when despairing that it will ever reflect the Kingdom, we worship with nostalgic old hymns and some trivial new ditties, and retell the old, old story to children in the Sunday school.

4. The Road to Africa (Acts 8: 26-39)

The fourth road leads to the south through the wilderness and is an odd story. Philip goes out of his way and meets the Ethiopian Eunuch on his way back to Her Majesty's Treasury. He's already got most of the story in the book he's reading, and the missionary just gives him the clue that it is something to do with Jesus. There is a quick baptism and Philip leaves him to get on with it. He goes on his way rejoicing. The first African Christian, the first black theologian, the founder of the African church. When you get back on the Barking Road you realise that Africans have just been getting on with it and rejoicing in the faith ever since. It's a road where if we are white and in the mainline church we can do no more than come alongside, to give space for them to do their own worship and theology and perhaps to listen and learn the rhythms from another culture and context. If it's a road out of slavery for them and us so much the better. As white people in a mainly black church we encounter sensitive issues, seek cleansing for our racism, and try not to patronise. On balance it's a privilege to be in a multicultural church, share an image of Christ who is not an English gentleman, and sway to the beat of the gospel songs. The bring and share dinners are a delight, but it's sometimes a pain to let others do it their way, and in their time!

5. The Damascus Road (Acts 9 and 26: 12-24)

The Damascus road marks a radical change of direction, a Turnaround experience as persecution and hate turns to solidarity and love. It's an experience of blazing lights and voices from heaven in which the Jesus Paul never knew in the flesh breaks into the bolted dungeons of his heart. It is a moment when he is commissioned for his life's work and from then on he is not disobedient to the heavenly vision. Though we all have our problems with Paul and people like him, and we may well agree with Festus that "your great learning is driving you insane", there must be a bit of Paul's experience within us if we are to play a role for Jesus and the rule of God in the urban world. Like Paul we need converting to Christ and a radical reversal in our lives (often three or more times every day). And though the Barking Road may not have the spiritual significance of the Damascus Road as Christians committed to urban mission we need the experience of "conversion to the city" while walking such streets. Paul went on to take the Gospel to all the nations. On the Barking Road we should be thankful that God has saved us some long journeys by bringing all the nations to us. The end result in our family life is to obey our vision, to stay with our calling and continue to live close to the Barking Road. At times we've been tempted to move to the country, or at least to a smaller city, closer to the hills and dales of the North which we love. It would be all to easy to say "we'll go for the sake of the children". Yet in the end ours is not a very radical conversion, there are so many advantages and joys of living and serving in the inner city it seems we can do what we want and stay within the purpose of God.

In the end...

In the end I have to admit I cannot answer all my children's questions. The longer I live in the diversity and ferment of the city the more hazy the answers seem to become. But the issues of justice and of cultural diversity, and the need for faith, hope and love will not go away. By setting the story of gospel journeys alongside the story of our own journeys one thing becomes clearer than ever. We walk not alone but with Jesus,

114

and I want my kids and everyone else to walk with him too. For if there is a meaning and purpose of life in the city it must all come together in the Christ, or perhaps we have to say Christ(s), of the Barking Road.

Shall we then give up the quest for a single Christ? Is the conclusion that we are now in the territory of post-modern post-evangelicalism and have left the idea of a single grand narrative behind? After all Jesus walked and walks many different roads, told many different stories, and had many different disciples who got on with their mission in many diverse places in various ways. Perhaps we should see the risen Christ as a divine networker who through the various gifts and ministries and manifestations of the Holy Spirit stays in touch with, but in a relaxed self emptying way, out of control of all this kaleidoscopic mess. We in our human limitations will not be able to understand the totality until Kingdom come. If that is the case we may not after all have to give up on traditional, credal, orthodox and Biblical Christian faith. For on this road we are not far from the teaching of Colossians 1: 15-20, or from the supreme and pre-existent creator Christ in whom all things hold together, and through whom at the last all things will be reconciled.

PS

Early in 2002 our family after much thought and some prayer and for a variety of personal reasons took the road north and settled in exile in Lancashire. We are now established and surrounded by new friends, trying to share our learning from the years in London in very different situations in church and community. Re-reading this piece released floods of tears of homesickness, nostalgia and many questions about the wisdom and guidance for moving on. As we left Newham I wrote this piece.

Newham Exodus

After 26 and a half years I am about to leave Newham.

Throughout that time I have lived
within 500 metres of my present home.
My kids were born here
know nowhere else.

I have lived and breathed
(it's polluted air)
and had my being in this place.
I know the paving stones,
the potholes I've cycled over
in all the local car cramped streets and hidden cycle routes.

I've measured and mapped its space,
calculated and crunched its demography
campaigned and counselled its councillors
even counted its garden birds, (all six of them)
for the RSPB
blown bubbles with West Ham.
I've crossed cultures and tried to culture the cross
Documented doctrines and Docklands
Been fascinated by its faiths
Produced and promoted projects
Evaluated events
And knitted knotted networks.

I've seen it change
Decline, deprived, diversify
White flight
Renew, regenerate,
reject the refugees
and welcome wealth.

This month I leave
Will God divide the traffic on the Barking Road?
Will Pharoah's armies follow?
Will Preston prove the promised land?

Magical memories
Peculiar people
Convoluted communities
Fantastic friends
This Newham nostalgia
Makes warm tears flow.

Greg Smith

Table:

The Contribution of Faith Communities in one Borough

Recent data from a comprehensive survey of religious life in the London Borough of Newham shows *

- There were in 1998 at least 294 faith based organisations of which

- 181 were Christian congregations of which the largest groups were:

BY Denomination	
Pentecostal	72
Church of England	26
Independent Evangelical	15
Baptist	13
Roman Catholic	12
Methodist	7

- 20 were mosques
- 5 were Hindu Temples or Mandirs
- 4 were Sikh gurudwaras
- 1 was a Jewish Synagogue

- The average membership reported (by 166 of the groups) was 134 people.
- A majority of all Christian congregations are majority black and the majority of Pentecostal ones are black-led and almost totally black in membership.
- 82 (40%) of these have started since 1980.
- Between them these groups owned at least 104 buildings, employed at the equivalent of at least 350 full time staff.

- These groups put on at least 437 different religious activities, (conducted in at least 25 different languages).
- They ran at least 183 "secular" community activities ranging from children's and pensioners clubs, a night shelter for homeless people to employment training and advice and support for refugees.

* From Smith G. (1999), *Religious Organisations in Newham in 1998-99,* paper accompanying the 3rd Edition of Directory of Religious Groups in Newham, published by Aston Charities, Durning Hall, London E7 9AB.

Chapter 9

Geoffrey Curtiss

Ministry In The Gentrifying Cosmopolis
Hoboken, New Jersey

From De-Industrialisation to a New Edge City

Hoboken, New Jersey, located on the West Side of the Hudson River directly across from midtown Manhattan is once again a thriving urban village and part of the New York Cosmopolis.

For the last twenty-five years, Hoboken has been retooling itself from an old gritty industrial city into becoming a new upscale residential community for the upwardly mobile in this region. Hoboken is a part of a new "Edge City" on the west side of the Hudson that includes Secaucus and Weehawken and the Jersey City waterfront.

Colonel John Stevens received the lands of Hoboken following the Revolutionary War. Hoboken was an island under the cliffs of the Palisades. At first Hoboken was a place to retreat to on Sunday afternoons. People would ferry over from New York City for a day of leisure and relaxation in the cool, refreshing breezes along the cliffs of the Palisades. New Yorkers would promenade along the Hudson River and picnic in Elysian Fields. It is in Elysian Fields where the first organized baseball game is recorded to have occurred.

The quiet community of Hoboken grew rapidly following the Civil War with the industrial revolution because new shipping and rail transportation industries located themselves along the Hudson River. Hoboken became known as one the new gritty cities of the industrialization of America, which occurred first along the major rivers and then along new transportation networks with the arrival of the railroads. The Stevens family, founders of Stevens Institute of Technology, were engineers who used the power of steam to create

120

engines for transportation and the industrialization of the nation. Hoboken part of the burgeoning port of New York became a point of termination for major railroad lines between New York and Chicago. The city was now prospering and rich in opportunity for the new immigrants to America.

The first immigrants to arrive in Hoboken were of Dutch and German extraction, by the beginning of the 20th century the Irish were followed by the Italians and Eastern Europeans. These immigrants came to work the waterfront industries and the many factories that were part of the city along with the vast opportunities the railroads provided. During World War I, Hoboken was put under marshal law because it was the point of embarkation for the European Theatre. The German Shipping Industry at the centre of Hoboken's waterfront was confiscated.

Hoboken's waterfront and industrial base remained active until 1952 when the newly created Port Authority of New York and New Jersey moved their entire container shipping business on the west side of the Hudson River to a new location in Port Newark. Also in the 50s the Puerto Rican community came to the city as the old industrial base sought to hold on by bringing in a cheap labour pool. This was their last grasp to keep the costs of doing their business in the expensive New York market in line with their costs. However they quickly left the New York metropolitan area because it was much less expensive to create goods elsewhere and ship them to New York. For example Maxwell House Coffee Plant long a staple of the Hoboken waterfront found that it was far cheaper to make their coffee in Jacksonville, Florida and ship it to New York. The old industrial base found it more convenient, more economical and more advantageous to move the industries away from Hoboken and Northern New Jersey. Cheaper labour costs, cheaper operating costs, cheaper transportation costs and the opportunity to build more modern plants all took industry out of the city during the 60s, 70s and 80s.
The 1950s had marked the beginning of this significant change, now by the 1980s many of Hoboken's old factories were vacant. People

who had come to the city in the earlier part of the century for work were left without the kind of work for which they were employable. But a new immigration to the city was beginning to change the city. These new immigrants were looking for inexpensive housing and an easy commute to New York City.

In 1979 I had undertaken the IAF ten-day training which gave me a new understanding of the church as a change or transforming agent within the local community. Broad based organising helped me to understand the dynamics around the issues of power and how to have a broader vision for the role of the church as a mediating institution in the city. This training raised new understandings about my leadership and my role in building institutions that could exercise power in community. These learnings would be very important in the next phase of my ministry, moving from the City of Newark to the City of Hoboken.

My ministry in Hoboken began in the fall of 1979. By this time Hoboken was in the midst of a massive transition from its old industrial base into a new residential community. Hoboken's mixture of Italians, Germans, Irish and Puerto Rican communities was being invaded by a new immigrant group of upwardly mobile professionals. They were now drawn to the city by the forces of real estate interests and the city's proximity to Manhatten. Lipton Tea, Maxwell House Coffee, Bethlehem Steelyards, and Levelor were among the many factories that were abandoning the city. The new financial interests sought to have Hoboken claim a relationship to Manhattan as a residential village. Live in Hoboken and work in Manhattan. Gentrification was underway.

Hoboken's old housing stock was the focus of this new opportunity. The Model Cities Programme provided the opportunity for Hoboken to create its own plan and methodology for implementing change. The major catalyst for this effort was a partnership between the city planners, who secured a developer for section 8 housing and financial institutions, which provided the low interest construction loans to entice people to Hoboken. The old brownstones built by the Dutch and German immigrants with their character and quality were seen as an asset. While these brownstones were in disrepair and did not have the adequate amenities for modern urban living, they represented opportunity for the new urban pioneer.

The first task was to create some new housing to relocate people who would be displaced from the old brownstones. Rather than clearing land for new apartment buildings, the city fathers decided to experiment with the concept of keeping the character of Hoboken by redeveloping existing buildings. In this way the external village atmosphere would be maintained, as the existing housing stock of previously ten family walk-ups would be reconfigured and refurbished. Local residents who were living in what was substandard housing in the old brownstones could be moved into this new housing.

This made it possible for bankers and real estate entrepreneurs to sell brownstones along with a low interest construction loan to urban pioneers. The new Hoboken immigrant would be completely able to renovate the interior of the brownstone and bring it up to modern standards. This planned way of redeveloping the city brought on the forces of gentrification. Young professionals now had the opportunity to buy old brownstones for a very low price, and invest their sweat and financial resources into rehabbing these old buildings into fine urban homes. Along with these urban pioneers came large developers with financial resources who saw the city as a gold mine for housing speculation.

Hoboken was a city in transition. But new contexts provided new ways to discover Jesus and new opportunities to form communities in Jesus' name to practice discipleship. Bishop Spong of the Episcopal Diocese of Newark asked me to explore what could be done with the three existing Episcopal churches in Hoboken. I was sent by the Diocese of Newark in January 1980 to be the Episcopal Missionary for Hoboken because none of the three Episcopal Churches would risk calling this young clergyman. As missioner to the city of Hoboken, I was given some freedom to experiment and explore new models and methodologies for being church. I was learning about these ideas from several creative people that will be referred to later in this work. As missioner, I could gather new people within Hoboken community and not be confined to simply serving the old guard of the three churches. I had permission to not simply serve a local congregation but to serve people within a neighbourhood and the larger city. What was to be the new Episcopal Congregation for the new Hoboken community was my mantra? I could gather a group of people together who would be the new expression of Church within the city. I would look for new people and new groups who had interests and needs that I might either join with or respond to. My ministry began with a mixed role of being partly missioner, partly evangelist, partly repairer of breached walls. But mostly I was given the opportunity to explore new ways of being the Church.

In February 1980, I was called to become the Rector of the Church of the Holy Innocents. Soon some of the young pioneers started showing up at Church and we began talking about the possibilities for a new way of being the Church in Hoboken. We explored what we liked about the Church and what we did not like, what we feared in our lives and what we hoped for. Out of these discussions the level of commitment and expectation grew and I could hear the voices of a new experience with God. They hoped that they could overcome its problems and become a place they would like to live for the long haul. As Missioner, I rolled up my sleeves and side-by-side, we began this great work.

Around this time I was introduced to the work of the Urban Theology Unit. John Vincent and Ed Kessler had been hired by the Diocese of Philadelphia to do a course on Urban Ministry. The design of their course was for experienced urban clergy and lay leaders to meet for three four-day periods (Thursday-Friday/Monday-Tuesday) over the course of twenty-four months to explore their own ministry situations. This introduction and continued relationship with UTU

Sheffield and the Sheffield Inner City Ecumenical Mission has been seminal in my mentoring for urban mission.

The "Hopes and Fears" and "Marks of the Gospel" exercises in the UTU Diploma in Community Ministry course seek[57] to help participants identify gospel stories in their own lives and to provoke lay and clergy into new Jesus actions. There are several key Gospel elements that describe our ministry in Hoboken. I will illustrate seven of them.

Seven Elements from Jesus' Practice
1. You give them something to eat (Mk 6: 30ff).
This is a gospel story that came up early in my ministry in Hoboken. Many of the new pioneers moving into Hoboken were looking for different kinds of food products than were typically offered in the local stores. Of particular interest for them were fresh produce, alternative grain products and assorted cheeses. Given the need to find these food items to enhance the quality of life, a new group at the Church of the Holy Innocents along with other members of the larger community began a small food co-operative. The intention of this Food Co-Op was to serve a variety of needs for both the Hoboken newcomer and the old timer. People from both communities worked together in the Food Co-op, forming new relationships and seeing how together we could respond to our perceived needs. The Church rented a storefront directly across the street and shared it with the Food Co-op. This brought the Church out into the street and forever changed our relationship with the community. Imagine walking by a storefront window and seeing the work of the Church going on, in a modern paradigm people could watch from the street and have a safe way to enter into the common storefront rather than having to enter through traditional church doors. Within three years the Food Co-op was put out of business as new merchants opened stores in many of the city's neighbourhoods that now offered the kinds of foods we were offering.

We also started a choir on Sunday mornings. Robert Putnam has helped us understand the value of choral groups and bowling leagues for the enhancement of community and the exchange of goods and resources. This new group within the new church became connected to another group of young musicians who had also moved into the community. Gary Schneider, a very gifted and talented conductor, brought the enthusiasm and energy of these people together to create the Hoboken Chamber Orchestra. They now approached us asking if they could use the sanctuary of old St. Paul's Episcopal Church for a series of performances. This became a huge success and eventually the Orchestra had to move to the local public school for performance space. The opportunity to provide quality classical concerts was another way of feeding the spirit of Hoboken.

2. "When did I see you hungry, or when did I see you naked" (Mt 25: 31ff).
With the loss of its old industries people were now feeling the effects of poverty and oppression, as a significant job base was lost by the early 1980s. These men who had worked the docks and railroads were residing in dilapidated SROs (Single Room Occupancy Housing) and several SRO Hotels. Landlords now saw the new value of their buildings as a result of the burgeoning residential community. They had to change the zoning laws in order to disband SROs in the community and provide them with the opportunity to rehab their buildings. They could now sell these former SROs by throwing out the residents. The Hoboken housing market was now in crisis for those who had lived in Hoboken through the 50s, 60s and 70s. This crisis had people being pushed out so that buildings could be upgraded to get higher rents. Often the pushing was done through a series of arson fires. Also, ten family railroad apartments that had housed many of the Puerto Rican families were being converted into new rental housing. How could we respond to these forces of displacement that were putting people out onto the street?

The former dockyard workers and railroad workers living with limited means were knocking on the doors of the several Churches seeking help and assistance because the SROs were now being emptied under speculation of development. Fires were becoming too frequent in buildings that were now prized as available for the new rental market. For both the Puerto Rican community and the men of the SRO's, Hoboken was no longer a place that they were welcomed to live in.

The Hoboken Clergy Coalition gathered to share about these common concerns. We decided to act by first going to every building that suffered a fire and offer prayer for the families as well as the building that made up the fabric of this city. We resolved to meet within twenty-four hours of each fire and do a liturgy of witness and lamentation. All of us shared the struggle we were having responding to the needs of the number of people who needed help. A second action we undertook was to mobilise and open a Shelter for the Homeless in the parish hall of the local Lutheran Church. That first winter for about eight weeks, seven clergy took turns sleeping on the concrete floor so that sanctuary could be provided. The Hoboken Clergy Coalition Shelter began out of our commitment to respond to the housing crisis that was impacting the larger community. For more than twenty years now a group of local churches with the local synagogue have spear headed this shelter which feeds up to 100 people a night and shelters 40 people a night and provides additional support systems and services for about 50 guests a week. The guests of the Shelter have changed over the years but the ability to respond to the needs of a changing disenfranchised community continues.

3. "Do not prevent the little children from coming to me." (Mk 10: 13ff).
As a new young father, I knew that one of the key issues for me to stay in the city would be to build a congregation that would support me in raising my son. How will we nurture and raise children in an urban environment? What is the role of the congregation in living out our baptismal commitment to support families in fulfilling their baptismal promises? How could the Church get involved in a

ministry among children? Can the local church be a blessing for children and their families? This became an opportunity for mission. We were leasing out our space to a city owned child care centre and we were involved with two alternative private schools, Stevens Co-operative School and Mustard Seed School who were leasing our buildings. John McKnight from the University of Chicago changed my thinking about all this in a presentation he made to the annual Church and City Conference. He challenged urban clergy to stop leasing out space to others and to set about doing these ministries ourselves. He challenged us to move from being gracious landlords out of convience to active centres of discipleship and ministry where the members of the congregation took ownership and leadership for the way their buildings would be used.

In 1984 we decided to add a second worship service on Sunday mornings. We began a children's Eucharist on Sunday mornings that served as a place for children with their parents to worship and break bread together. Out of this new congregation came a commitment to start a nursery school so that we could undertake this work of ministry ourselves. In the fall of 1986 we opened our own nursery school. Now All Saints Episcopal Day School is celebrating its sixteenth year and goes up to Grade 6. The Sunday family service is now the largest of our three Sunday services. We also teach the values of community in something called "Community Time" in the Day School which focuses on the spiritual life and growth for the children of the school community.

4. "Who are my brothers and sisters, are they not the ones who do the will of my Father?" (Mk 3: 31.ff).
The gay and lesbian community was not very visible in 1989. Even though the parish had been involved with this community for some time, gays and lesbians were yet to be recognised as a significant part of the fabric of the city. In 1982, the parish had been attacked in the city press for being hospitable to a group of lesbians who were invited to use the parish's fellowship hall for social gatherings. They called themselves, "The Dykes of Hoboken" and they met regularly

for fellowship and community service projects. The new local Hoboken Reporter in an editorial, criticised me for allowing the church to be affiliated with such a group of people.

In the 80s, the Diocese of Newark explored the issues of Human Sexuality and issued a report that first affirmed the gay and lesbian lifestyle as a God-given one, and second, by encouraging gay and lesbian people to live in monogamous relationships. This report led leaders in the Diocese to the form of a new ministry, the OASIS mission, which would be led by a gay clergy person and would find ways for the church to do ministry with and among the gay and lesbian community, their families and their friends.

However in time All Saints would be the only parish in the Diocese willing to volunteer as host for this new ministry. This decision made by the new leadership of the parish affirmed who we were becoming as a congregation since several members of our lay leadership team were gay. The OASIS was going to hire a gay man living in a committed relationship as their first executive director and ordain him to the Priesthood. All Saints became the host congregation of The OASIS—standing with the gay and lesbian community we gave generously to support the growth of this work.

5. "Is a lamp brought in to be put under the bushel basket..." (Mk 4: 21ff).
One of the celebrated marks of the new parish community became its hospitality. People remarked how welcome they felt when they visited All Saints. Duncan Wilson in his article, "Gospel Values in Inner City Churches" in *Gospel from the City*[58] notes the alienation we face in urban life and how the church has a wonderful opportunity to provide places of hospitality to express genuine care and love. Many people felt that All Saints' commitment to the larger community made it a place where one could learn about Jesus and God's activities in Hoboken. For the newcomer, as well as for those who had resided in Hoboken for a long time, there was a desire to find places of community in the anonymity of the city. All Saints became a

new light of hope. Instead of keeping it a secret, the parish kept trying to open its doors wider and wider.

6. "We found a treasure of great worth in a field, so we went and sold what we had to purchase the field" (Matthew 13: 44).
As Hoboken changed, the need to bridge across the economic divides became more and more important to the health and vitality of our mission and ministry. We could not simply ride on the benefits of the newcomers to the city but had to reach out to work among the poor, the lost and the downtrodden. One dynamic of Hoboken's changing population was that the number of children in Hoboken decreased dramatically over 15 years. In 1980 there were 15, 000 children in the public school system, but by 1995 there were fewer than 4,000. Of these remaining children, a significant number were living in poverty, living on the West Side of town. Our efforts were focused on the needs of youth. In partnership with the local Baptist Church, the Latino Pentecostal and Afro-American Churches and others, we sought to develop a partnership that would reach out to these children and their parents. The Homework Club, sponsored by our CDC, is operated and run by several local parents who seek to provide a space and an opportunity for children to learn and play after school. As a result of the ministry of our Parish Missioner, we have just completed the building of the Jubilee Centre a 9000 square foot building that will open this May to serve a wide variety of activity for youth and others.

7. "Truly I tell you, there is no one who has left house or brothers or sisters or mother or father or children or fields, for my sake or the sake of the gospel, who will not receive a hundred fold now in this age" (Mk 10: 29ff).
Broad-based Community Organising has led All Saints into new relationships and partnerships. It has required us to let go of old ways of being Church in order that we might be open to work with others and especially to take up the mantle of responding to the needs of middle class families and empowering the poor. The Rich Man was asked by Jesus to sell all he had and come and follow and in

many ways this is what broad-based organising asks us to risk. But the wonderful good news of this work is the new brothers and sisters you discover who share in the hundredfold blessings of this work.

One of the issues we confronted was chromium contamination in our soil. In particular, for neighbourhoods of the city the issue is striking. We heard of neighbourhoods where the rate of cancer was significantly higher than those on another local block. One family had been raising tomatoes in the backyard for years. When they found out their soil was contaminated, it explained why so many members of their family had died of cancer. The concern for justice is more than individual. It must be communal, social. Social Justice means that we seek to build a society where our neighbourhoods are treated fairly and equitably. In our new work in Broad Based Community organising we are creating a regional coalition of faith based communities that are addressing the concerns of worker justice, the ability of immigrant children to get in state tuition rates for higher education and the need for metro equity to be addressed in public education, tax base and the sharing of resources.

The Kingdom Practice of Jesus
William R. Herzog III in *Jesus, Justice and the Reign of God*[59] has discerned that the focus to understand Jesus should be on his actions rather than on his sayings or teachings. In order to understand the true mission of the historical Jesus where he claims to be a prophet for the justice of God and the Reign of God, we must look at his actions. Similarly I realise that our actions in the name of Jesus serve to describe our historical context and similarly speak much louder than what we may be teaching or saying. These seven actions illustrate our work in a way that words cannot. Herzog's work leads to a deeper appreciation for the UTU model of biblical praxis and to know the historical Jesus in our own time.

During these twenty years of ministry within the cities of Hoboken and Jersey City, these Gospel actions have led me to discern God's presence and hear the needs of God's people, in the neighbourhoods and communities where I have walked and listened. The hospitality that the God of Israel, Jesus and the Church offer for the people is unquestionable. Therefore the more I become willing to listen to the cry of those who suffer under the domination of others, the more I am willing to reach out and find allies and collaborators who share in a vocation of responding to their needs. I have found pathways to God and new ways to practice the Reign of God here and now. In practising the actions of Jesus, in searching for the actions of God's inbreaking reign (reign breaking in), and in acting within the movement of the Spirit, I have been driven to new contexts for ministry within my community. From the early prayer services for families whose buildings had been torched by an arsonist to the current vigils at the Elizabeth Detention Centre protesting the ways we detain and incarcerate asylum seekers, there is an abiding concern for God's justice and reign that speaks of a new possibility for the right relationships we have with one another.

These stories are similar to the ones told by Moby Ferrands in *Gospel from the City*,[60] where she describes events of transformation when the Gospel becomes evident. These few examples of joining community needs and issues with Jesus' actions and stories have shaped our ministry and mission in Hoboken. I came to Hoboken in 1980 to three congregations with at best 25 elderly people who worshipped in three dilapidated buildings. The new congregation is now 250 members strong with an assortment of activities that serve another 150 families within the city through our Day School and our Jubilee Centre. People often remark, "I do not go to church, but if I had to choose one to go to, it would be All Saints."

In this community of change and transition, we try to keep our focus on what is happening outside our glass church doors to discern how God is challenging us. By working on issues of community empowerment and community organising, we find ways to partner and collaborate, to enlarge both the scope of our work as well as our capabilities to respond to needs, in effect, we find God already there. As a Christian community we must address the political, economic and social needs for these are the spiritual concerns of our city. We must seek the welfare of the city because the systems of the city have a deep and long-lasting impact on the health and vitality of its people. Whether it is displacement or homelessness, education or health care, the delivery of social services for the needs of children, being a neighbour means finding partners who share a vision for the city of Hoboken. The struggle to make our city a place that can be fair and equitable to all concerned and to accept our responsibility toward the people who are the diversity of our city, is a very unique challenge for the Church.

Many people lost out in Hoboken's transition and were displaced. Many others have been brought to this city without acknowledging the systems that continue to build and shape it. If we are to be neighbours, one to another, then we must understand the complexities that shape the fabric of our city and work for justice, to seek a fair and equitable distribution of the city's wealth and opportunity for all its citizens and residents. The Church is not simply called to care for its own, but to seek both the welfare of the whole community and to recover the lost.

The Biblical Call to Justice
Within the biblical narrative is the demand for justice.

> God has taken his place on the divine council;
> In the midst of the gods he holds judgement:
> "How long will you judge unjustly and show partiality to the wicked?"
> Give justice to the weak and the orphan;
> Maintain the right of the lowly and the destitute.
> Rescue the weak and the needy;
> Deliver them from the hand of the wicked."
>
> Psalm 82: 1-4

Just as justice describes the character of God so it describes the vocation for God's people (Micah 6. 6-8). We who are made in the image of god are to practice the justice, the righteousness of God. Justice describes the right relationships between neighbours (Deut. 10: 18-19). Justice creates the social framework within God's community; justice describes the social practices of the community (Jer. 21: 11-12). Justice vindicates and restores Israel's political, economic and social projects that are to practice the Reign of God. Righteousness and justice create, redeem and preserve God's people (Is. 59: 15-16).

The Torah Law is concerned with social justice to create the moral community. The individual is urged to be generous to those who are less fortunate. The Torah community like the Jesus community is required to practice a law of equity and love that maintains structures or finds alternative ways to meet the needs of the disenfranchised. Israel is designing a social system within the framework of God's Law where the concern for one's neighbour is primary, Jesus is steeped in this vision.

God initiates after listening to the cries or laments of those who are under oppression. The Exodus narrative invites Moses to hear the cry of his people and respond rather than murder the soldiers out of anger for the way they treat the oppressed. God invites Moses to organise and to create an alternative society, one that does not treat people as slaves but as people of God. The concern for Social Justice within the Church has the Exodus narrative at its root. The Church is for the people who practised an alternative social project where love of a neighbour is practised, (Lk 7: 29-30). We are not simply to be chaplains of ease for the maintenance of the security of the status quo in the Church. Like Israel, the Church is also called to respond to laments and cries of the people who are suffering affliction. God hears the cries of the afflicted. God seeks out leaders to create alternative community. God's alternative community is to reflect God's character, which seeks to practice justice.

In the Torah, particularly the books of Deuteronomy and Leviticus, we hear of how the people of God are to care for the alien, the stranger, the practice the Torah Law in a way that demonstrates their relationship with God and God's relationship with them. God calls the people of Israel into a new social contract, a covenant as the prophets understand it, based upon the practice of doing justice, loving kindness (mercy) and walking humbly with our God as described by the prophet Micah (Micah 6: 8). God is seeking right and just relationships within the covenanted community.

God has called Israel, and by extension his Church, into the vocation of building a just society (Ezekiel 45: 9). This is the primary characteristic of God's work. The Torah for Israel becomes revelation, that is, the Torah reveals God's call to a people to a vocation of loving God and loving one's neighbour(s). Justice is the loving way of practising the Torah Law (Nehemiah 9: 13). Justice is doing well to others and showing an active concern for the well-being of the weak and downtrodden. The individual and the society are called to demonstrate an active concern to meet the needs of the powerless and to defend the oppressed.

Justice is an interpersonal concept throughout the Hebrew Scriptures. Doing justice is about how we treat one another in and through our social, political, economic and religious systems, "when God rose up to establish judgement, to save all the oppressed of the earth." (Ps. 76: 9). Justice practised in a social context defies how we treat one another. In our highly pluralistic communities that make up the new Global Community, the concern for Social Justice is a very significant vocation for the Church. Hebrew Scriptures presents Social Justice as the character of their God who is seeking to create, then sustain and finally redeem a moral and ethical community. Within this new community, the individual is related to the community, the individual is expected to be generous to those less fortunate, the individual is called to design and maintain social systems in which the concern for one's neighbour can be practised.
(Is 58: 2-10).

135

At the heart of the call for Justice is the biblical image of the Year of the Jubilee. The Jubilee is about setting us free from the debts and burdens we have laid upon one another (Lev 25: 36). The call for the year of Jubilee is fulfilled in the ministry of Jesus (Lk 4: 16-20) according to John Yoder in his classic, *The Politics of Jesus*.[61]

Christian Scriptures continue this understanding of the character of God. The Reign of God is the coming of justice and righteousness for the poor and the downtrodden, those who are oppressed, the forgotten. Within the Reign of God those who hunger and thirst for justice will be satisfied, those who are persecuted for justice' sake will be redeemed. One will know the living God when one is engaged with the naked, the poor, the downtrodden, those in prison, etc. God's reign is to fulfil the promise of right relationships, justice to those who are far off and to those who are near. There is no disparity among those who know they have been excluded and seek equity. In Luke, the oppressed are to be raised up and the oppressors are to be judged. Luke depicts God as the Just One.

Paul goes one *step* further and sees that in God's Justice now even the community of Gentiles who previously had no rights within the commonwealth of Israel is now being brought into a new relationship with the God of Justice (2 Cor 8: 10-15). This is why the Church must work on new social constructs in order to provide the space and place for this to happen. Justice demands that we open up our ways of practice and find new ways of being in right relationships with one another as neighbours and together with our God.

Social Justice is the cutting edge of the new Cosmopolis. As Leonie Sandercock in *Towards Cosmopolis*[62] has said, difference must be incorporated into the quest for social justice in the multi-racial, multi-ethnic city. The Apostle Paul similarly struggles with this issue in his own time and the Church; the new Israel becomes multi-racial and multi-ethnic. Our times might be similar to the Apostle Paul's in that we also are living in a New World order. It is exciting to hear from someone who seeks to understand and explain the situation, and is not a person of faith, that Justice will be one of the major components along with Citizenship, Community and Public Interest of the new Cosmopolis. Social Justice is more than simply rearranging the distribution of wealth within a capitalistic market economy. The author is talking about decision-making procedures, the division of labour, culture where the dominant cultural groups' experience no longer is universalised to dominate the variety of groups and peoples who will inhabit the new Cosmopolis.

David Harvey similarly in his work, *Justice, Nature and the Geography of Difference*[63], points to how social justice will be a significant force in defining how we will accept one another's differences. Justice hides power relationships and will have to leave its universalistic concepts and become more comfortable with its heterogeneous set of concepts. This good news for Justice is the heart of the biblical narrative. It is a community that seeks right relationships, which sees both God and Israel modelling community to each other, community that is heterogeneous to one another. It is perhaps why the prophetic tradition always lamented that Israel chose a King to model and describe God, instead of remaining in their struggle for equity that God depicted more fully in the Tribal Confederation of Equals. How do we create, sustain and redeem small communities of faith that practice social justice modelled after the biblical vision?

Can God's Justice Reign in Today's City?
All urban communities are undergoing the effects of a significant demographic transition. Vast majorities of the people of the world are moving to cities. The new urban context is a world being urbanised. The new global market economy is changing urban neighbourhoods and communities and will continue to do so.

Within the changing nature of transitional communities, I think the Church has to look out of its doors and engage the communities, the neighbourhoods that it is called to serve. The Church must explore the questions of Justice, which are by nature themselves subjective and relational to the community itself. The issue of Justice within one

137

community or neighbourhood will not necessarily be the same for another. However, the concern for Justice is common among the various faith traditions that will make up our changing neighbourhoods.

Like Amos, Isaiah, Micah and Jesus the concern for Social Justice is a concern for the way God intends us to be. Behold I have come to bring Good News, the poor are fed, the lame walk, the blind see. For too long the Church has critiqued the world and its injustices and yet we remain the voice crying in the wilderness. Social justice must become the lens through which the Good News of God is breaking forth into the world and creates a society that seeks to live out commitment to one's neighbour and to one's God. The language of Social Justice has turned anger into response and invited me to be the one sent. Here I am Lord, send me.

Social Justice has led me to find a new set of colleagues who are also concerned about Social Justice and we are willing to partner together to work on how to respond to the human need. It is a way for Lutheran, Roman Catholic, Presbyterian, Reformed, Latino Pentecostal, Baptist as well as Rabbis and Imams to converse and act upon a common vision we have of God and God's work for Justice in the world.

On behalf of God, we have fed the homeless together and slept on the floor together to resist the forces that sought to close the shelter. On behalf of God's Justice, we collect food together and operate a Food Pantry together that responds to the critical need of mothers and their children. On behalf of God's Justice we support the development of Community-based Police so that people might be safe and secure within their neighbourhoods instead of being a whim of drug dealers and crime. On behalf of God's Justice we can come together to build a Broad-based Community Organisation where Black, Latino, White and other people can share their hopes and fears and together find solidarity and sustenance for their struggle.

God's Justice has formed the way I do my ministry. One of the most liberating images for me is for the local church to affirm all people by supporting their ministries and their commitments to raise Christ up. My role as pastor is to support ministry and mission. The concern for God's Justice is not simply to be an external part of the congregation delegated to the outreach committee but to become the internal dynamic of congregational life centred in our worship. How does our worship help us to practice God's Justice? Our ministry is a shared ministry from the centrality of our Table Fellowship to the ways in which we govern ourselves and share our resources.

This work of Justice has become our work as a community of faith. This pattern of seeking the welfare of the city has made us more open and less defensive, more inclusive and less protective of our traditions. We are willing to be a community of faith that understands that one of our primary roles is to seek the welfare of the places "where we live and move and have our being". As we share with others in the work of social justice, we are able to recognise a need for partners, we are willing to collaborate, which means letting go of some of our vulnerability about our own identity and risk others joining with others. The ministry of social justice demands of us a willingness to weigh the needs and concerns of our neighbour. We took a significant piece of our endowment to create the Jubilee Centre because we believe we have found a pearl of great worth on the west side of our city. We chose to invest our resources that God has given us in the work of social justice and creating more equity among the components of our community. By being willing to do this we have also found new partners and allies who want to collaborate with us and expand this work.

Justice can be one model of formation for Christian Community. The practice of Social Justice, that is to seek to make the city of Hoboken a place of right relationships both with ones neighbour and with one's God, have guided our mission and ministry in this place and time. The practice of justice occurs within our social, political, economic and religious institutions. In order for justice to be practised, we must

139

understand the systems of power that oppress the weak and dominate the less fortunate. Justice can be an operating principle around which we can organise the community of faith. This is learning as well as a practice for congregational building and formation.

Many of the issues that we confront as a Church are very complex because of the new culture we are living into. The Church is about community, the building of community to conform to God's Reign. Justice is a way for the Church to join with others as members of the community. Justice is the way to respond to need and raise up Hope. Mrs Juliet Kilpin, the project co-ordinator of Urban Expression in London says well what we have been trying to do in Hoboken:

> To recruit, equip, deploy and support self-examining teams which will pioneer innovation and relevant expressions of the Christian Church in under-churched areas of the inner city.[64]

Within my situation, I have found that working to bring God's justice and building networks and coalitions that will fight for the oppressed and respond to the weak has brought strength to the local congregation. Social Justice is a way to organise because the language of Social Justice does not have a lot of religious baggage with it but rather turns spirituality into action. We can talk about our vision for Social Justice. This vision brings us to a concern for the welfare of our neighbour, the welfare of the world and calls us to identify those values for which we stand. In the Judaeo-Christian framework, justice creates community. The power to do the work of Social Justice comes from our understanding of the character of God. Community organising concerns the redistribution of power so that there can be right relationships that are a more equitable sharing of power and wealth. The Church that sees Social Justice as a vocation will find itself drawn into the larger community. It will become vulnerable to its neighbours and willing to join in networks and collaborations that cut across many lines and boundaries. It will have a vision for itself of part of a much larger city. Social Justice Churches are ones that become fully incorporated into God's vision.

Chapter 10

John Summers

A New Way Of Being Church For Britain: Can We Learn From The Basic Ecclesial Communities Of Latin America?

St Barnabas, Plymouth

Our Context

We are an inner-urban parish in Plymouth about ten minute's walk from the city centre. The Ministry of Defence used to be the major employer in the city, but following the defence cuts and the advent of privatisation, the workforce has been drastically reduced. Twenty years ago 20,000 were employed in the dockyard, now the figure is nearer 3500. Alternative jobs have often been hard to find, and have been slow to come to the Westcountry. A number of projects, have come and gone having failed to get off the ground. There is an air of passive resignation about the city.

I came to the parish of St Barnbabas in 1981 after a long 'inter-regnum' and found a rather dispirited, middle-of-the-road Anglican Church, with a small, mainly elderly congregation.

Over the next few years, the church was led in an evangelical and gently charismatic direction, with emphases on personal faith, the church as being the visible 'Body of Christ', and with particular importance being attached to the bible, prayer, fellowship and worship. St Barnabas developed into a lively local community church, with a good representation of young people, families and of men and women. The church has a strong sense of being a family, and its worship is characterised by flexibility and informality. The local culture is mixed, but mainly working class, and most of those who participate in the life of the church live locally.

Since 1984, we have tried to replace our large Victorian building with something more suitable both for the church and the community, but without success. Some describe the church as looking 'lived in' which is probably a euphemism for 'untidy', but it aims to look user-friendly. The long delay has drained the enthusiasm and sapped the energy of some people. A great deal has depended upon one key member of the church, Joy Burrett, who has taken responsibility for the redevelopment group since 1992. Significantly she urged us to use the resources we already had, especially the present building, and to work with the local community as much as possible. We realised that the church was the only large building in the area where local people could come together, so we decided to open it up for use by the local community for public gatherings of all kinds.

In 1985 the report *Faith in the City* had been produced by the Church of England, yet it seemed to me at the parish level, eight years later, that few of its recommendations had been heeded and implemented. The Church of England remained basically a middle class phenomenon, in its ethos, its structures, and its liturgy. It was struggling to maintain itself, with the prospect of a reduced number of clergy ever more thinly spread. The institutional church continued to fail to attract a rising generation and even so-called 'successful' churches in the middle-class suburbs attract a relatively tiny percentage of the local population. I found a widespread dissatisfaction among the clergy with an institution which is slowly collapsing. All kinds of solutions have been proposed, but most of them are attempts to improve the present model and its agenda, rather than dealing with fundamental issues.

It seemed to me that in the 'evangelical' wing of the church from which I come, there is an inadequate and narrow understanding of 'the good news of Jesus'. My conviction has grown, that something vital is missing from this version of the 'good news'. In the city, to be

143

honest, eternal life, forgiveness for sins etc. are not the immediate concerns of the ordinary people I meet. Most see little or no connection between our 'gospel' agenda and their everyday experience. It is not surprising that the church which 'preaches the gospel' in these terms, makes little progress in the inner city. We evangelicals carry around the baggage of a theoretical 'good news' which on the whole, fails to engage with people.

For most ordinary people, God, Jesus etc. don't even come into their scheme of things and so we fail to connect. Their first priorities are about the conditions in which they struggle to cope with everyday life in the city. Do we have any good news about any of these things? In his day, Jesus was immediate 'good news' to those he met. He spent much of his time with the poor, the oppressed, the sick, unloved, the lonely, those in trouble with the religious authorities etc. His 'gospel' in word and action, was first and foremost for 'now'. I do not deny the other parts of the 'good news', but they may come later. We tend to miss the impact of Jesus' opening manifesto in Luke 4: I8-19, when we spiritualise his announcement of 'good news for the poor and liberation for the oppressed'. His message was of the beginning of a new way for human society in which the hungry are filled and the rich are sent empty away. Heady, dangerous, and revolutionary stuff. But it is a gospel for today and not just for tomorrow! Jesus actually embodied his message. The church is called to do the same.

The José Marins' workshops
It was during 1993 that I became aware of the theology of Latin America. I began to read Liberation theologians such as Leonardo Boff, Jon Sobrino Gustavo Gutierrez and others. I came to it with the common perception that this new theology was a dangerous form of Marxism which threatened to subvert Christianity.

But what I was actually reading was about the radical application of the gospel to everyday life. It was good news for today, especially for the poor, the oppressed, and those who were on the margins of

144

society. The bible was central, but it was used in a way that was new and disconcerting. Yet this approach seemed right, and it made the Word of God accessible and relevant to ordinary theologically untrained people. I devoured this 'new' material. I was intrigued and excited by it. The approach was very different from anything I had met before, though at first, it was hard to get used to a new way of thinking. My conviction grew that here was something important and relevant for us in Britain.

It all began to come together in 1994 when I took part in a *New Way of being Church* workshop led by a Brazilian Roman Catholic priest, José Marins. For over thirty years, he has been a facilitator to the *Basic Ecclesial Communities (B.E.C.s)* throughout Latin America. He is a member of the theological reflection team to *CELAM (The Latin and Caribbean Catholic Bishops Conference*) and took part in the 'Vatican 2 of Latin America', at Medellin in 1968, and was at Puebla in 1979, where the development of *BECs* and *Liberation theology* was acknowledged and affirmed as the way forward.

The workshop was very different from any in which I had ever taken part before, and it proved to be the most significant and radical turning point in my own ministry since ordination. It was an introduction to a way of 'learning-by-doing'. There was no easy 'DIY kit ' or 'course notes pack' to take back to the parish. It was an introduction, not a model to be copied, but a process in which to be engaged.

Over the following year, my own understanding of the process was consolidated through a series of weekend workshops, facilitated by the U.K. *New Way of Being Church* team.

I was very impatient to share my discovery with others, so I invited the Marins team (with the blessing of the Anglican and Roman Catholic bishops) to run a 4-day workshop in Plymouth during the summer of 1994. Around seventy people took part, mainly from the Plymouth area, but including folk from across the Southwest.

The Basic Ecclesial Communities

Although *Basic Ecclesial Communities* began in the Roman Catholic Church of Latin America, they exist in many different forms as small Christian communities across the world. Here we will confine discussion to Latin America. So what are *BECs*?

Basic: A *BEC* is *basic* in that it is the smallest unit of being church and that it exists at the grassroots level of the ordinary people, who are usually the poorest and most marginalised. It contains all the essential elements of being church. The parish is geographically subdivided into a number of *BECs,* so that a parish becomes a 'community of smaller communities' - the point at which the church as salt, leaven and light, engages in the world.

Ecclesial: It is 'Ecclesial' in that it embodies the essential elements that make it truly an expression of the church. It is an autonomous cell of the church, yet it is interdependent with the other *BECs* which make up the parish, and is linked with the diocese and the universal church, through its ordained ministers. In this structure the members participate together in the various ministries which enable the *BEC* to function. Unlike a traditional group, there is no one 'leader' upon whom everyone else depends. A shared ministry of co-ordination is undertaken on behalf of the *BECs* by its members in turn, not as 'leaders' but as the ministry of one who links together the various ministries within the *BEC*.

The parish priest co-ordinates the mission of the church at the parish level, and is a link between the BECs at the grassroots level, and the Bishop and the universal church.

Community: It is a Community of people whose lives are bound up with one another in practical love and service. It has the minimum of structure and co-ordination to enable the community to function. It encourages the contribution and participation of all the community members, and a sense of mutual responsibility for the community. It values the unique gifts and talents of every member. It seeks to be involved in the issues in the wider community in which its members live or work. It does not depend upon gifted 'leaders' or clergy in order to function, yet it values the ordained ministers and lay workers as animators and facilitators and as co-ordinators at the parish and diocesan level.

There are two particular characteristics of the *BECs* which seem to be on the whole markedly different from the church in Britain.

1. Church as Community

A *BEC* is made up of a household-sized local group of people who know, relate to and support one another. They meet regularly as a small church community, in a home, a local hall or hut, maybe weekly or perhaps fortnightly. They come together with other *BECs* from time to time for parish events such as a Eucharist. (Weekly, monthly or depending upon the availability of the parish priest). They work together on common projects to improve the quality of life for the whole community and to challenge injustice and oppression. Their practice of theology begins with their experience of life. Biblical reflection with a view to action is central to their common life as 'church'.

I met with *BECs* in different parts of Brazil and Bolivia and I was immediately struck by the quality of their community life and their generous hospitality. I felt that I had experienced something of the ethos of the early church. Despite the fact that they are among the poorest people in Latin America, they have a joy and spontaneous generosity which puts those of us from 'the rich church' to shame. Fiesta (celebration) and meals together play an important part in sustaining their common life.

Perhaps the most striking difference between these church communities and our own in Britain is the link between their faith and life. Life is not compartmentalised into 'sacred' and 'secular'. Consequently political, social, economic and 'religious' issues are all part of the *BEC* agenda. There is a robust realism about the worship which I experienced in Bolivia and Brazil. It was certainly not a case of 'Marxism to music'. The hymns and prayers are Christ centred, bible related, and rooted in their often harsh everyday experience. In Britain church groups so often fail to make the connection, and tend to be introspective and escapist. Even if they are outward looking it is usually in terms of evangelism rather than the wider agenda of 'mission' (which also includes evangelism).

2. Church with the agenda of 'Mission'

The fundamental orientation of the *BECs* is mission. They exist to be agents of transformation of the world towards the reign of God.

The primary concern of Jesus in the synoptic gospels is the Reign of God. The agenda announced by him in the synagogue in Nazareth *(Luke 4: 18-19)* was good news for the poor, liberation for the oppressed etc. It was a highly political agenda, and seems to encompass what Jesus meant by the reign of God. In his three-year public ministry he put this agenda into practice, as evidenced by the reception he received from those on the margins of society. He embodied good news to these people. He brought them new life and hope for this life as well as for eternity.

At the end of his ministry, Jesus passed on his mission to the embryo church- 'as the Father has sent me I am sending you' (John 20: 21). Fundamental to the very existence of the church is an orientation to mission. To quote Jose Marins 'The church is by no means the only instrument for bringing in the kingdom, but it is a privileged means through which the reign of God may be mediated'.

BECs in Britain?

I am often asked by those who are well aware of the failings of the current model of church. "It is all very well hearing about what has been happening in the *BECs* of South America, but can you simply transplant a model from their situation to ours?" The answer is, of course, no. But there are a number of characteristics which are fundamental to the very nature and mission of the church in any context, and it is these which are of particular relevance to us.

In the *BECs* of Brazil and Bolivia, I felt that here was the real working base of the church as community, a church of the people who materially had very little, but had a commitment to 'change the world'. I felt a sense of continuity between the ethos of the early church and the *BECs*, and this has encouraged me to explore the possibilities for the church here. After all, they have had over thirty years of practical experience, they have shown us that an alternative model for the church is possible. Thousands of small Christian ecclesial communities across Latin America are the living proof.

My experience in the two churches of which I was vicar, proves that to communicate the vision for a *New Way* to a parish is not easy. I have learned the painful truth that there can be a huge gap between what I may say or print, and what people hear, see and understand. If this different model is to grow from the grassroots, then the people have to 'own' the process. There is a fine line between animating the people with a vision and imposing new ways upon a resentful church. That this is a long term process I have no doubt, and it may well take ten years in order to become second nature to the people here.

Early in the autumn of 1995, following the 'Marins' summer workshops, we started a weekly evening course on *New Way of Being Church,* in which about 25 members of St Barnabas were able to take part. At the end of November, the course ended and we then decided as a church to take the process forward.

The plan agreed was that from the start of 1996, the parish would be divided into three or four geographical 'Mission Areas'.

In each of these a *'Neighbourhood group'* would be formed, made up of church members who lived there (including the children). The primary purpose of each group was to develop as the basic local unit

149

of the church, orientated to mission. There had to be some flexibility, but participation in the group by those who lived in other Mission Areas of the parish was discouraged.

We now had a practical structure for mission and pastoral care which covered the whole parish, with a better chance for the group to know those who lived in their locality, and a structure for the follow-up of contacts.

The Plymouth "Neighbourhood Groups"

The Neighbourhood Group is the basic unit of the church, and its primary purpose is mission. Its members come together to share and reflect upon what is going on in their neighbourhood from the 'Jesus' perspective, with a view to action and transformation.

The members meet to share 'stories' of the people and situations which they have met. They then engage in prayerful reflection on what they have seen, using the bible in order to try to discover the 'word of God for now', and to decide upon any action to be taken. For example, if someone in the vicinity has been bereaved, it is not a matter for a bereavement counsellor, but perhaps a very simple action by a member of the group, such as a word of condolence and nothing more. These actions may seem unspectacular, but I think this is what Jesus meant when he spoke about being *salt, light, and leaven*, in the world. It is mission at the simplest level and a way of mobilising the church at the grassroots. Mission requires the involvement of church members in 'secular' local community life wherever they engage with other people. They do this, not as a way to 'get them into church', but because it is worthwhile in itself and is where the salt, light and leaven are meant to be.

In common with other evangelicals, I used to think of mission primarily in terms of personal evangelism. But the mission of Jesus and the church is much wider than this. Jesus' agenda is the reign of God in the world he loves so much. If it is, then the transformation of all aspects of it towards the reign of God has to be our concern. For

150

many of us, this has meant a radical re-focusing from the church and a 'church programme agenda', to the world and a 'reign of God agenda'.

I am indebted to the insights and the experience of Latin American Liberation Theology for my shift of perspective. I do believe that we need to discover this theology and to develop its praxis in ways appropriate to the British context.

The bible occupies an important place in the life of the *BECs*, but it is used in a different way. Instead of being the object of study it becomes the subject through which the group discerns God's word with a view to action. Various methods of prayerful reflection have been found useful as tools to enable this to happen. Of course, bible study and knowledge of the bible provide a Christian with an essential basic resource, but the purpose in coming together when we use the bible in this way, it is to try to listen to hear what God may be saying. In our parishes those both able and willing to conduct a bible exposition and teaching session are few on the ground, and most church members claim not to have the bible knowledge and background to do it. Using the bible in this new reflective way, the Neighbourhood Groups are not dependent upon 'leaders' and 'teachers', nor is preparation necessary other than that necessary in the ministry of co-ordinator of the group.

We have found that it is very easy for groups used to housegroup bible study to revert to a general discussion, rather than to exercise the perseverance and discipline necessary for silence and reflective listening, and the ministry of co-ordination needs sensitive handling.

Many of us brought up within the evangelical wing of the church may have difficulties at first with this way of using the bible. For me the bible had always been the essential first step, before applying its principles to the issues of contemporary life. As I began to explore Liberation Theology, I was perplexed by the notion of theological reflection as a 'second step'. But now it seems obvious to me that it is

151

'life' which provides the point of contact and the agenda for biblical reflection, which may then lead to action. This approach is illustrated in Luke's gospel. On the road to Emmaus, Jesus engages the two disciples in their conversation *'what is this that you are talking about?'* He listens to their story until they have finished before he introduces a different perspective (and incidentally only then, the scriptures).

Perhaps the most difficult and necessary change is in our mindset, from thinking about *going* to church to *being* the church.

Many parishes have housegroups meeting mid-week for bible study, prayer and fellowship. Each group usually has a leader, appointed and approved by the vicar. In my experience, bible teaching and study together have a special and important place in these groups. Fellowship, prayer, and faith are deepened, and mutual support in good times and bad is a real benefit for those who take part. With neighbourhood groups, as with the *BECs*, while all of these benefits are valuable, the fundamental purpose for which the groups have been set up needs to be grasped by those who participate. They are not primarily for fellowship, but for prayerful, biblical reflection upon their engagement in the world with a view to action towards the reign of God, i.e. looking outward for 'mission', to the wider community.

Ministries within the Group
The first and most obvious difference is the way in which the groups operate. Different ministries or 'ways to serve the group' are necessary to enable it to function smoothly. The following ministries are usually to be found in our groups. The list is neither exhaustive, nor is it prescriptive. Other ministries may be found to be useful to the group. We need a far more disciplined approach to the working of our groups but there is a danger in being either too rigid and seeing this *New Way* as a method rather than the development of a fundamentally different process, or of being so informal that we fail to learn from the experience of the *BECs*, and not make the best use of the time we have together as a group.

Co-ordination

Responsibility for the group does not rest with a 'leader'. Ideally co-ordination of the group is shared by two co-ordinators who share responsibility *to the group*, for linking together the activities of the group for a limited period of time. (This may vary from weekly, monthly, termly but never permanently!). This better models a participative *New Way* of being church. If there is only one co-ordinator our experience has shown the ease with which a group can revert to the old style of the leader-dependency model.

Hospitality

In the *BECs*, hospitality, informality and the welcome into someone's home play a significant part in the development of their ethos. From the New Testament it is evident that meals together had an important place in the life of the early church, indeed the agape and Eucharist stem from such natural expressions of sharing the common life. We are only just realising that this aspect needs a far higher profile if our own British experience of church is to become more communitarian.

Fiesta

Food together is linked inextricably with 'fun' together. Of course the Latin American temperament is much more exuberant than our own, but the ability to 'let their hair down' together in their 'fiestas' is a marked characteristic of their life together as is their music and dancing. We might actually make more progress than we would imagine, in the development of the church, if we gave more time in our programmes to this social aspect of being church and less to the cerebral.

Memory

Each time the group meets, someone records a 'memory' of the evening. This is not the same as the minutes of a meeting. Rather it consists of one member's impression of what happened and what actions were decided upon when the group met. The next time the group meets, the 'memory' is read out. This brings up to date those who were absent, and gives time for the group to evaluate those actions which have been taken.

News
It is always important to keep in touch with what is happening in the world, and items of local, national and international news from radio press and television are discussed. This may provide the starting point for the group's biblical reflection.

Prayer/Worship
This is always an important aspect of the life of both *BECs* and our own Neighbourhood Groups. They are not just groups for social action but are aware of the reality of God and the presence of the Holy Spirit when we meet as 'church'. Thus the spiritual perspective is central to the very existence of the group which seeks to discern the word of God and what he is saying 'now'. As a practical visual aid for our prayers and reflection, our groups sometimes place a candle in the middle of a small table, symbolising the light and presence of Christ among us. Radiating outwards from the candle are strips of cardboard with the names of all the streets in the particular neighbourhood.

Timekeeping
The group needs to decide how in general it wishes to use the time spent together and to agree the proportion of time to be allocated for memory, reflection, prayer news, etc. One person, acting on behalf of the group (acting with some sensitivity and acceptable flexibility), then keeps the group to time in order to achieve its aims in the time allocated for meeting together.

Local Community Involvement
Since about 1992, there had been a natural and almost imperceptible re-direction of our focus towards the local community. Many in the church would say that we had always been involved with the people in the surrounding area. Much of the care and involvement with neighbours takes place on an individual spontaneous basis and by its nature cannot be quantified or monitored. But what was different

154

now was our conscious re-focusing outwards to the local community as a result of a 'Kingdom' rather than a 'church' perspective.

We recognised that the Parent and Toddler's group, which was set up originally by the parish, no longer exists with the ulterior motive of 'getting bums on pews'. Rather we encouraged and participated in it because it was worthwhile in itself and meets a need. It was a place where isolated and lonely parents make new friends and discuss issues of parenting etc. As part of improving the quality of life for the local largely non-church community, it was Kingdom business for us to share with others in this self-help group. Space does not permit to tell the story of growing involvement in the local Community Forum; with local councillors; the local non-church primary school (as members of the PTA school, governors, school and community events together either in the church or in the school); a weekly senior citizens 'Tuesday Teabreak'; a local park amenity group; local residents association.

At the time of writing, we had our first Christmas Candlelight Carol service followed by a community shared tea and a community family quiz in the church chaired by an avowedly atheist local councillor as a joint church/ community effort in which I as vicar had absolutely no part in its planning or execution. Hitherto, we had invited people to come to 'our carol service'. It was a great success and sets a precedent for more such joint community action and celebration in the future. All of this community involvement meant that church and non-church people were constantly rubbing shoulders so that friendships and relationships were made on a far wider basis than ever before.

The church was taken seriously as non-church people see us taking the community seriously. I do believe that we have been getting somewhere when the local councillor, who happens to be an atheist, says that the Church is making a significant contribution to the quality of life in our local area. To extend the Reign of God in every aspect of life is the church's mission. We believe that this community involvement is a vital part of that mission.

The introduction of a *New Way of being Church* and Neighbourhood Groups is not primarily a matter of ecclesiastical re-structuring. At heart it involves a different mind-set for the clergy and people alike. It is a way of thinking about *being* church rather than *going* to church. It means leaving behind the stereotypes of the past which are so deeply rooted.

If there is to be any real change, there has to be a movement of the people of God from the grassroots. We are all too familiar with the top down approach. There is always the temptation to take a short-cut and to imagine we can 'get it done' quickly and efficiently and dispense with the organic process of development. I do believe that God is moving by his Holy Spirit to bring about change, and this may be through the financial and other crises hitting the institutional church.

Finally I share the conviction of the Roman Catholic Archbishop of Adelaide Leonard Faulkner who said in a pastoral letter to his people in 1994:-

> 'I believe that the world-wide emergence of *Basic Ecclesial Communities* is the work of the Holy Spirit in our time, a gift of God to the Church. For this reason they have a central place in our diocesan vision and I encourage parishes to move towards them as a long-term orientation and "preferred way" for our local church.'

AMEN!

Chapter 11

Elaine Appelbee

Shaping A Changing Society
Bradford

A Personal Introduction
This chapter is concerned with specific strategic action and reflection undertaken in the metropolitan district of Bradford over almost a decade. It draws on personal experience and perspective, as well as a collaboration with ecumenical colleagues questioning the role of the churches at a time of great societal change.

The personal perspective is that of a community development worker whose adult working life has coincided with the major economic, technological and social change, tantamount to a third industrial revolution. I have observed from very close quarters the effects of these changes on traditional working class communities within Bradford, both on an outer estate and in the inner city - communities which have borne and continue to bear the brunt of that change.

The collaboration with ecumenical colleagues began in 1991 when I took up the more strategic post of Bishop's Officer for Church in Society. It was then a newly created post, with the freedom to explore the relationship between church and society across a city. This coincided with the decision of the Methodist Church in Bradford to explore a new sort of presence in Bradford city centre, a presence without a congregation, and for a while without even a name, but with staff members freed to pay attention to the city and its needs. This became a presence which has grown from strength to strength, and is now named Touchstone. Together, with colleagues from the other major denominations in the city, we re-formed the Bradford and Keighley Faith in the City Forum. The determination of the group was to be proactive, taking action as well as talking, reflecting and praying.

Having deliberately moved from parish-based project work into a more strategic role, I saw that the insistent questions before us were: What is the strategic role of the church in the regeneration of a metropolitan district like Bradford? Was there any task that was distinctively ours to undertake? Was it possible to work with change, to shape it rather than be shaped by it?

The impact of Isaiah 58
Throughout the previous period as a church community worker, I had been struggling to understand what it meant to be church in a place where significant sections of the population were enduring increasing hardship and where some communities were fracturing before our eyes.

Eventually, whilst on retreat, I stumbled on the text of Isaiah 58: 1-12, and felt the excitement of revelation. It provides a succinct summary of what the Gospel of Jesus is all about. In this passage are to be found some of the major themes of scripture: the right relationship between God and humanity, right relationship between people, sin and repentance, healing/salvation and the true worship of God. These verses prefigure, yet help expound Jesus' teaching in the Gospel of Matthew 25: 31-46, and in James, Chapter 2. If the churches need a short mission statement combined with action plan, then here it is. As my reading and interpretation of this text has helped to develop much of the work that will be described later, I want to share some of my exploration of it.

Whilst it is not desirable to make a direct sociological comparison between church communities today and the ancient nation of Israel, it is possible to discern and identify those aspects of people's relationship with God and with one another, which hold good for all time and for all societies.

158

In the opening verse, the prophet receives the command to speak to the people about why their prayers have not been answered. The prophet is told by God to speak to 'my people' (Is. 58: 1)[65] i.e. those people who have accepted a covenant relationship with God and agreed to be His people. A people who 'worship me every day, claiming they are eager to know my ways'. (Is. 58: 2).

The exhortation to the prophet to speak to God's people, also reveals that they were to be addressed as a community and nation, not just as individuals. This poses a challenge for the churches today because many churches appear to have lost sight of themselves and of their faith, as a *community* of people held together under obedience to God. Faith has become increasingly individualised and privatised, with community only symbolically represented by collective worship on Sunday. The symbol is in danger of being an empty one because too often it does not represent lived out experience. The problem emerging from this state of affairs is that congregations rarely appear to seek the will of God corporately, in order that they might respond in obedience, as a community, to those in pain around them.

The emptiness of symbolic religious activity which is devoid of lived out experience, is a major theme of this passage.

> The people ask, "why should we fast if the Lord never notices? Why should we go without food if he pays no attention'. (Is. 58: 3)

As far as the people of Israel are concerned, they are fulfilling God's Law by religious observance and bitterly complain that this brings them no answers to their prayers. The prophet's reply, on behalf of God, points out that their religious observance appears to have no good effect on the way in which they lead their lives. Their daily behaviour invalidates the ritual of worship as worthy of God.

The Lord says to them, "The truth is that at the same time as you fast, you pursue your own interests and oppress your workers. Your fasting makes you violent and you quarrel and fight. Do you think that this kind of fasting will make me listen to your prayers?" (Is. 58: 3-4).

The vehemence with which the people of Israel protest suggests that they are genuinely convinced that obedience to religious ritual and law is all that is needed in order to offer true worship to God. They seem to have forgotten that the ritual serves only to act as a symbol for a way of living out life in obedience to God, which happens day by day. The symbol becomes a nonsense without the action which it represents.

This question of symbolic ritual and lived out response is pertinent to churches today. There appears to be a similar separation and dissonance between the gospel proclaimed through the symbols of word and sacrament, and the living example of both the churches (as institutions and congregations) and the individual members of whom they comprise. The words of the prophet seems to have a particularly strong resonance through history to the present day.

Although the context in which the prophet speaks is one of community and nation, it also includes the actions of individuals within the nation whose behaviour is the focus of the prophet's criticism.

They are violating the Sabbath which was a token of homage to God the Creator. Secondly, they commit acts of injustice to their fellows the consequence of this unacceptable behaviour by individuals is that the whole nation suffers.[66] When the prophet goes on to describe what constitutes true fasting, he says:

'Remove the chains of oppression' (Is. 58: 6).

Kissane explains that these bonds are not the bonds of slavery which they impose upon the poor by unjust means, but the burden of sin which the whole nation bears.[67]   Bob Lambourne points out that in the Old Testament 'there is a steady insistence that families, villages, cities and nation are under a kind of group contract with God. The action of the individual, especially if he is a leader or a representative, carries with it possibilities of blessing or punishment for the whole group'.[68]

This picture of the relationship between the individual and the community or society in which they live, and their personal responsibility, is very useful for the current context in which Christians live in Britain. The past twenty years has seen particularly strong messages from the political arena, disseminated successfully by a largely uncritical media, suggesting that individualism and individual choice are all that matter; that the family replaces community or society; and that personal responsibility relates only to the individual's behaviour in their own sphere of influence. Far-reaching policies, reflecting these ideas, have been introduced in all areas for which the government has responsibility. The change in government in 1997 has not substantially altered that. Notions of interdependence have been all but lost in the public arena. Indeed this emphasis on individualism and privatisation has infiltrated the churches. Faith has become something personal and individual, an internal relationship between God and the individual; 'a private cultivation of religious life' rather than 'publicly revealed truth'.[69] This has made possible, in many church people's minds, the separation of the 'spiritual' from the rest of their lives and behaviour. It has increased the likelihood that congregations will make the same mistake made by the people of Israel, of believing that ritual, symbolic worship is the true worship of God. It has also meant the loss of understanding that God created unique individual human beings to live in the context of community.

A particularly important aspect of this section of the Isaiah passage is the message that individuals' destructive or unjust behaviour, where

161

it continues as acceptable or unchecked by the community, hurts that community. In this present time that idea would appear to be borne out. For example at the same time as the divide between rich and poor grows ever wider, and as communities become increasingly fractured, there is an growing increase in crime. The effect of this increase is to cause people to fortify their homes, and for women and elderly people to impose voluntary curfews on themselves to avoid attack. The response by the people in power is to focus on the crime and condemn bad behaviour, and only belatedly, to examine other forms of unjust behaviour which have created wealth and poverty, or caused communities to be undermined or destroyed, allowing crime into the vacuum.

Fasting is the specific example of worship under scrutiny in Isaiah Chapter 58. Fasting was the external token by which the people of God expressed their penitence. Once again, though, the external token is mistaken for the actual experience of repentance. The so-called repentance was not borne out by subsequent behaviour.

> Our English word, repentance, does not come close to conveying the actual meaning of what [Jesus] said. In New Testament Greek the word is metanoia, which means a change of word or heart. (Meta= Change, Noia= the whole mind, intellect, feeling, desire and will.)
>
> Behind that word is the Hebrew, Teshuvah, which means returning to God, or more profoundly, a return to the living God who is turning us back to himself and to responsibility for one another.[70]

From this definition can be seen the emptiness of the token response alone. Repentance means changing, change which affects the way in which people behave. Actions speak truthfully about the state of people's relationship with God. The prophet gives examples of the marks of true repentance:

Remove the chains of oppression and the yoke of injustice, and let the oppressed go free. Share your food with the hungry and open your homes to the homeless poor. Give clothes to those who have nothing to wear, and do not refuse to help your own relatives. (Is. 58: 6-7).

The measure of right relationship between God and His people is demonstrated and judged by the way in which the people of God treat one another and those 'who are your own relatives' i.e. other human beings, especially those in pain or poverty. The fruits of true repentance for God's people are described:

"Then my favour will shine on you, and your wounds will be quickly healed....... When you pray, I will answer you.......If you put an end to oppression, to every gesture of contempt, and to every evil word; if you give food to the hungry and satisfy those in need, then the darkness around you will turn to the brightness of noon. And I will always guide you and satisfy you with good things...... You will be like a garden that has plenty of water, like a spring of water that never runs dry. Your people will rebuild what has long been in ruins, building again on the old foundations". (Is. 58: 8-12).

The idea that healing for the people of God, both individual and communal, is tied up with being involved in the healing of others i.e. the avoidance of injustice and meeting the needs of the poor, is a powerful one. It explains why Jesus made the same connection in Matthew 25: 31-46. However when Jesus spoke he did not speak of 'healing' but 'salvation'. In Hebrew, the same word is used for both. A willingness to encounter those in pain or poverty, in obedience to God, signals a right relationship with Him. The consequence is healing or salvation for the people of God, individually and communally. This point is crucial. It challenges both the assertion that there is no connection between private behaviour and public worship and the tendency within churches to see the social responsibility element of the churches' mission as an optional extra.

Translating Isaiah into strategic action

The theological ideas in this particular Isaiah text are clearly helpful to a congregation wanting to make connections and to understand the importance of responding to the community in which they are set. The text not only engages the intellect but suggests practical ways of responding. It invites reflection on the relationship between the congregation and God, the relationships between congregational members as the people of God and the obedient response of the people of God to others. I believe the words of Isaiah are also helpful to the people of God trying to engage in a strategic manner with a rapidly changing society. Our proclaimed relationship with God should enable us to be helpful in creating and sustaining right relationships between people in our diverse metropolitan district, at a time when change seems to be fracturing those relationships.

The ecumenical Faith in the City Forum began to reflect on the contribution it could make from the starting point of focusing on those in the most pain across the metropolitan district. Was there anything different about people's lives and experiences in the 1990s as opposed to the 1980s? On the surface, it seemed that issues such as unemployment and growing poverty, which had begun in the late 1970s, merely continued. However, there were significant differences. Poverty on this scale, with about half the population living on incomes at or below income support level, had never before been experienced over such a long period of time. The politics had changed radically, affecting the key services upon which those living with poverty most relied.

In 1993 the Faith in the City Forum undertook a project called 'Powerful Whispers'.[71] This project brought together the key decision makers within the Bradford Metropolitan District and some of the people living in four of the most disadvantaged areas. The aim was to hear directly from the people concerned, including local

164

professionals, about how life is experienced by them; to demonstrate that even in hard-pressed communities there were people with ideas who would be fitting partners for the work of regenerating the District; and to help to create a public debate about the future of Bradford. Four urban 'hearings' were held and out of these came a common agenda of concerns - poverty; crime; young people; race, culture and religion; consultation and decision making; housing.

The Hearings had a profound effect on the decision-makers who had sat for eight hours listening silently. One of the most powerful effects was to remind everyone concerned that we do share a common humanity and inhabit the same world. The encounters established a direct relationship between those with the power of decision-making and those whose lives are intimately affected by those decisions. It raised the key issue in Isaiah of right (or wrong) relationship. After the first hearing held on a small outer estate experiencing great social distress, one of the 'Hearers' asked with some pain, why was he there, what could he possibly do to change things, it was just not possible. After the second hearing he came back and said 'Now I know'. Another said: 'I never realised that people want the same kinds of things as me'. A third remarked that it was true that resources are scarce but he was left wondering whether the right people were being listened to when decisions were made about how those resources should be allocated.

Through these encounters, the decision-makers were able to move from 'head' knowledge about the impact of poverty, unemployment, and ill-health, to a 'heart' knowledge which came from personal encounter. The seeds of healing were revealed. The people speaking, whilst describing the harsh reality that they face, also revealed the grace, courage and sheer inventiveness with which they often tackle that reality. The people who listened were taken aback by the range of community activity revealed. At the subsequent conference that brought together all the participants in the hearings with a wider cross-section of communities and institutions, two of the key leaders within the district declared publicly their sense of helplessness and

165

powerlessness in the face of the many challenges. The conference participants were less than impressed by this, but it was an important theological moment. The public confession of helplessness signalled that there might be an opportunity to forge new kinds of relationships.

Following the Hearings, the Forum then went to listen to the decision-makers talk in more detail about their responsibility for trying to solve the problems. The Forum then considered how the project might be built upon.

Powerful Reflections
Out of the six common issues, consultation and decision-making was the surprise. It challenged the official view that the regeneration projects which had been undertaken in the District were, bar one exception, 'bottom up'. Furthermore the damage done to the communal solidarity of the District by the competitive nature of the bidding system was palpable, particularly as the decision- making process appeared not to be transparent. Consequently areas of the District that were not involved in these large 'bids' were left feeling even more marginal. It also revealed the desire of people to take an active role in the shaping of their communities.

The Powerful Whispers process also demonstrated that despite diversity there was a clear common agenda around which the increasingly separated and diverse communities of the District could be reconnected.

As we reflected on all the information generated by the process, a picture emerged of a plethora of strategies from the 'top', and at the 'bottom' a great deal of ad hoc activity responding directly to needs. For those at the top, there was a frustration that nothing appeared to move the District forward in the way that had been hoped, and at the bottom a frustration that nobody was listening. There appeared to be a gap in the middle where the top and the bottom were failing to connect. It seemed to the Forum that here was the task for church, to take a lead in attempting to plug that gap, so that people could be drawn together across the divide and draw on each other's strengths to address the challenges and turn them into opportunities. The Forum felt sure that the gap would not be closed without a self-conscious attempt to make that happen. None of the discussions with the decision makers led us to believe that they knew how to set about this work. Nor, to be fair, was there any reason why they should.

Minding the Gap
In the summer of 1996, the Faith in the City Forum came up with an idea for how a piece of work could be constructed to deal with the gap. It was to become known as 'The Centenary - Millennium Project' (C2M) and ran from 1997 -2001. It is not the purpose of this article to detail the whole process of building this project, but it is important to note that this work has involved risk-taking, risk-bearing and persistence in the face of understandable doubt and fear. It has relied on the *faith* and *belief* of people who would not all subscribe to those concepts, but have been willing to share in our obedience to God.

The central idea was a simple one - in partnership with existing networks and agencies, to encourage communities in the District to use the time between the City's Centenary (1997) and the other side of the Millennium (2001) to build local agendas and plans for their communities. This aimed to take community initiatives into a further stage of development, moving from ad hoc response to needs, to a taking stock of all the strengths and weaknesses of the community leading to a more planned response.

Underpinning this concept was theological reflection on the Magnificat of Luke 2. Implicit in the text is the idea of a complete revolution. The only problem with such a revolution is that those who had previously been at the bottom, tend to copy the behaviour of the previously powerful, and the unhelpful cycle repeats itself. The Powerful Whispers project stood revealed as a process of raising up the lowly and bringing down the mighty to the point where they encountered one another, allowing the possibility for new

167

relationships. The essence of C2M was to build on what had been revealed through Powerful Whispers by enabling communities (however they define themselves) to have the opportunity to participate and create a forward momentum.

A model of neighbourhood planning was modelled that happened at an appropriate pace, not driven by funding deadlines. It demonstrated that this could put communities in a strong position to bid for funds, from all sorts of sources.

In order to encourage this type of 'bottom up' audit/planning/action work the Churches brought together a wide ranging, independent, charitable partnership, backed by the major institutions within the district, to set up C2M. As well as inviting and resourcing communities to participate in the programme it enabled three other crucial things to happen.

The first was to link across the district groups and communities who had common emerging agendas, plans or actions. The purpose of these links was to share ideas and learning. C2M received a half million pound grant from the Millennium Commission to make grants to 150 individuals working on the C2M programme. These grants carried a requirement to participate in Action Learning groups with other recipients. In this way people from very different communities become connected through common concerns and actions and from this people across Bradford District came to understand that within diversity we share a common humanity.

In Bradford, along with the rest of British society, we struggle to celebrate our God-given diversity. Perhaps it is because diversity, detached from any understanding that we share common values and concerns, frightens us. This highlights our differences and allows us to view each other only as aliens. Perhaps when we are confident that we hold some key values and concerns in common, then we will be able safely to celebrate and enjoy the riches of diversity.

The second crucial task was to work with institutions to increase their capacity to partner more effectively with communities. If new relationships are to be forged between those who hold the power and those who do not, then those at the 'top' have to be given the opportunity to change and learn. The challenge of the Gospel is to allow everyone, particularly those who are part of the problem, 'to remove the chains of oppression' by offering the chance to change i.e. repent. This work was developed through a process known as Powerful Partnerships. It reflected the steady building of relationships between the churches, C2M and the institutions and agencies.

In February 1999, 160 people took part in a two day 'whole systems' event - 'Powerful Partnerships....Making a Difference'. They were drawn from a broad cross-section of public services senior staff from across Bradford District, together with a number of community and voluntary representatives. The task was to explore how the agencies could be better partners with each other in order to become better partners with local communities. The development of the event was led by the top executive group of the agencies concerned, in partnership with C2M.

The two days were highly interactive, with participants working with the widest range of people possible from across 'the system', in maximum - mix groups of 7-10 people. Huge amounts of data, views and ideas were generated and shared. There was critical dialogue between the 'room' and the 'executive' of the agencies. The executive participated, listened, responded and developed their own thinking which resulted in the production of an action plan by the end of the second day.

The outcome was a wealth of ideas about, and emerging commitments towards, improving, strengthening and learning about the development of local partnerships with communities. The Powerful Partnerships Learning Forum continued the process of learning and dialogue.

The End of the Story?

At the beginning of the twenty-first century the nature of the forces of change demand a radical reconstruction of the way we organise ourselves as a society. The structures that underpin our society, including community and family, and the roles which they play, need to be renegotiated. This is increasingly recognised by all sorts of institutions including Government. However they are uncertain about how to respond. At the heart of this is the issue of right relationship, how we want to live together in the years to come. This is what makes it such a crucial arena for the church. Yet the space for this debate needs to be created. C2M sought to do that. The Spirit is blowing through the world a sense of urgency about the task. I met the same issues being addressed in very similar ways to C2M in Zimbabwe and Pakistan.

C2M was a tiny attempt to model some healthier ways of relating vertically and horizontally, individually and communally, in an excitingly diverse context. The work it undertook played a part in influencing Government policy, especially the neighbourhood renewal agenda. That it had some impact locally is reflected in the fact that the methodology has shaped the Bradford District Neighbourhood Renewal Strategy and its delivery. In this way the thinking and action of the churches and its partners over the past decade has moved from the margins to influence the mainstream.

The work still has a radical edge that is challenging to both communities and institutions. The next few years will show whether the model can work across the whole metropolitan district, creating new relationships between citizens and institutions that transform life for those suffering the greatest poverty and disadvantage.

What C2M has shown is that the challenges that we face together in our society could so easily become opportunities. We need to move from a culture which seeks to blame and scapegoat, to one which acknowledges that recent economic and social change has affected

170

every area of our lives for good and ill, and seeks to redress the price being paid by the most vulnerable. It is our task to enable the processes by which all people may be confident, valued, and empowered members of a more inclusive society made up of interdependent, yet diverse, communities. Of my own branch of the universal Church, the Church of England, I have to ask – is it still interested?

Chapter 12

Helen Reid

Building A Theology Of Being Church In A Multi-Faith Locality
Bradford

This paper draws on the experiences and reflections of Christians living in Great Horton and Lidget Green, Bradford. It tells the story of initiative in building a theology of being church in a multi-faith locality undertaken by the Faith to Faith Project.[72] This initiative began as an opportunity to explore how churches could become involved in multi-faith initiatives in one area of the city of Bradford. The report of its findings is a record of the hopes and dreams, worries and concerns, reflections and thoughts of the people of Great Horton and Lidget Green churches as regards the multi-faith nature of their area. Moreover, it has the potential to become the springboard to further reflection and to action, to the building of multi-faith initiatives in the area.[73]

Great Horton and Lidget Green
The neighbouring areas of Great Horton and Lidget Green are on the edge of the inner city. In recent years, there has been an increase in the presence of other minority ethnic groups coupled with a decrease in the presence of white residents. The ethnic composition of residents is diverse; residents are White, Pakistani, Indian, Bangladeshi and Black.

There is also a diversity of faiths in this area. Residents are Buddhist, Christian, Hindu, Muslim, Sikh and those with no religious faith. Among Christians there is a range of churches, which includes two Anglican Churches, one Apostolic Church, one Methodist Church, one Methodist and United Reformed Church, and one New Testament Church of God.

A Faithful Future Project

The project began with a series of interviews[74] when people were asked about their church and their locality, and their understandings of multi-faith co-operation. In this way, they were asked for information and also encouraged to articulate and reflect on the theology of being Christian in a multi-faith locality.

A variety of people from each of the six local churches were interviewed, including clergy, activists and regular attenders. This range of participants ensured that the project reflected a breadth of church experience and different perspectives.

The paper now turns to what the Christians of Great Horton and Lidget Green said. It begins by outlining the main areas of church activities and then reports on people's views on the future of multi-faith co-operation in the area.

The Churches of Great Horton and Lidget Green

A variety of activities take place at all the churches in Great Horton and Lidget Green. Some are faith-orientated activities, such as Bible Study Groups, and others are community-orientated activities, such as Parent and Toddler Groups. The activities in this latter group may be organised by a church itself or by others who use church premises. The focuses of community-orientated activities relate to concern for children, families, elderly people, health, international aid and homelessness. There is a clear and strong commitment to the locality.

Christians in Great Horton and Lidget Green articulated a range of aims that they hope to achieve through involvement in community-orientated activities. These relate to their religious beliefs and the needs they perceive in community life, and are an integral part of their understanding of Christian and church life. They include living according to their Christian calling, a commitment to mission and evangelism, to develop church life and to play an active part in their community. They form a spectrum of theological understandings of involvement in community-orientated activities.

The local population is changing and becoming increasingly multi-faith in composition. Such a change inevitably affects community life and, therefore, churches' community-orientated activities. One of the ways in which it must affect church life is in the pressing need to develop a theology for being church in a multi-faith locality.

Christian Perspectives On Multi-Faith Co-operation

(Words in italics are quotations from the interview records).

Participants were asked to consider how Christians might become involved in multi-faith initiatives in their locality. They described a range of considerations, which included benefits and difficulties both for themselves and others, and included a clear role for faith in terms of religious beliefs and commitment to the community.

All participants believed that co-operation between different faith, ethnic and cultural groups would benefit the local community. Saying, for example:
The positive outcomes depend on the projects but if there is a degree of collaboration and consultation, it will give possibilities for building a stronger and more effective community.
Also that:
Any organisation that can help towards understanding between the different ethnic groups and ourselves must be of assistance to the community. We tend to talk about 'us' and 'them' but it should be all 'us' really.

Many participants felt that the first step to establishing multi-faith initiatives was preparation and education of those who would be involved, particularly education about the other's faith.
It would help to have a greater understanding of other faiths in the community and their beliefs. A lot of members of the Church don't know what Muslims are all about and think that they believe in something completely different, that there is no common ground.

174

Another said:

We need knowledge of each other's faith. The other faith would like us to have some knowledge about them and I would want them to know something about what I believe in, so there is a basis for talking. Otherwise, you might say something that is unknowingly insulting.

Others, however, suggested that an action approach such as an event or project would be the most effective way to involve people in a multi-faith initiative, saying, for example:

People tend to work better together if there is a project to do, e.g. a drop-in café.

People who took this approach anticipated that discussions about religious beliefs could follow shared action.

My commitment is in working with others rather than sitting around talking about it. The dialogue about each other's faiths comes out of doing things together.

These participants who wanted to be involved in an action project did, however, think that there was a need to establish first a joint understanding of the project and each other's aims. Overall, therefore, participants felt that a mutual understanding of a multi-faith project's aims must be agreed at the outset, whether that project was action or dialogue.

People raised the practical difficulties of establishing multi-faith co-operation. Speaking, for example, of a lack of knowledge of other faith communities and their leaders.

One of the problems is that there is no local authority structure in the Muslim community, there is no mosque in the area. This means it is hard to contact members of the Asian community.

This difficulty may not pose as much of a problem for others who envisaged a different approach to multi-faith interaction. One said,

It might be very, very simple. You start from where the people are. It is about understanding and getting to know who your neighbour is, what their name is, where were they born?

175

There were, therefore, differences of opinion as to the best way to establish interfaith relationships, whether the first step should be action or dialogue, and whether this should be formal or informal.

Participants anticipated that due to existing commitments, it might be a problem to find the resources required to run a multi-faith initiative. For example, given the range of present church activities,
It can be difficult to get people to give up even more of their time when they already have a busy schedule from their own church.
As another participant said:
It requires extra will and energy to work together.
This is particularly true at a time when many churches are struggling to afford the upkeep of buildings and have little funds left for community development.
When resources are scarce, people tend to go along with what they need to do.
Others suggested, however, that a lack of resources might be a motivation for multi-faith co-operation because more could be done with shared resources.
Co-operation would mean the utilising of skills, knowledge and the experiences of a wider group of people. Multi-faith co-operation would show people where groups can work together, joining together to have a collective voice about education, policing, housing and poverty.
Many participants highlighted the issue of limited time and resources, although not all interpreted the effect of this in the same way.

When considering the issue of multi-faith co-operation, some participants focussed on the fact that in Great Horton and Lidget Green, differences of faith allegiance are associated with differences in ethnic background. Multi-faith co-operation would, therefore, mean multi-ethnic co-operation and as a result could build bridges between different ethnic groups in the locality. This was seen as a way of reversing a negative and divisive trend in the community. One said:
There is some fear amongst certain people in [our church] about the increase in the ethnic minority population….A lot of people, if they understood a lot

176

more about other people would find that they didn't have to fear them, so wouldn't have to hate them. One of our biggest problems is people who do not understand and are afraid of what they do not understand.

Another said that such understanding could be achieved through meetings:

More contact with the Asian community will help the members of the congregation to overcome their fears.

There was general agreement that in a multi-faith, multi-ethnic locality, establishing positive relationships between people belonging to different groups would bring social and community benefits.

Some spoke of this aim of developing relationships in terms of a specifically Christian imperative. Recalling, for example, the teaching to 'Love your neighbour as yourself', and saying that they felt they should 'love our Asian neighbours more' and that they felt guilty about their present attitudes. Such attitudes had specific focuses among people living alongside each other. One participant explained the situation saying:

I have difficulty living out a Christian attitude towards other faiths because a lot of local deprivation is caused by particularly Asian landlords acquiring property in the area, renting it out and letting it fall into a state of disrepair. Equally, however, when I talk to my neighbours, some of whom are Asian themselves, they are just as disgusted about it.

In addition to these general issues in the area, one church had recently been the focus of persistent vandalism. This distressed members and one described the situation and his feelings, saying:

There is the problem of some Asian youths misusing church buildings and the yard by doing graffiti, dropping litter and being rude when I ask them to stop. They pick up girls in their cars and bring them to the car park. I find this situation difficult…. This is a personal conflict for me. … I have never been so close to wanting to move out of the area as now; I've been living in the same house for 35 years.

Such events have clearly impinged on people's sense of sacred space and also a sense of violation of this sacred space.

This issue of sacred space is experienced more positively in another local church where there is a large and well-kept garden. During the summer, many local people of different backgrounds enjoy sitting there. People at this church take pride in the garden and are pleased to see others enjoying it too. Saying for example:

The [church] building looks intimidating. However, there are lots of Asians who sit in the garden, so they must feel able to do that.

There was a sense of being able to welcome others and to have that welcome respected. However, at the back of the church, there is a car park that is troubled by car crime, as is typical in the inner city. This means that the experience of being in this particular locality is mixed for this congregation.

Many participants reflected on the theological dimension of interfaith relationships and multi-faith co-operation. They considered what effect working alongside people of different faiths might have on their own beliefs. One said:

One of the fears people might have is 'Does this mean my beliefs will be watered down?'

Not all participants, however, saw difference of belief as a barrier to co-operation. One said:

You have to have an awareness of yourself and your own beliefs but you also have to acknowledge that other faith groups will come with their own beliefs and ways of viewing the world. It's about holding on to your own belief but not being in a position where you cannot work alongside others or understand what they are saying.

In this context, many commented on the distinctiveness of Christianity and how this might affect interfaith relationships. One said:

Your faith is distinctive, it is important to know this but also to know where you stand with gentleness and respect. It is no good being unrespectful [sic] to others.

Some emphasised that the distinctiveness of Christian beliefs meant exclusivity and they were wary of unacceptable compromises that might arise from multi-faith co-operation.

I would not want to compromise the exclusiveness of Christianity when working with any other faith.

Another went further and said:

I believe that the Christian faith is 'intolerably unique' and there is no other way. …I do not want to get together with other faith groups. The Archbishop of Canterbury is wrong in saying we should be meeting people from other faiths halfway. Togetherness can only do so far, 'you can't have bitter and sweet waters coming out of the same fountain.'

There was also the commonly raised statement that Christianity and Islam are both missionary faiths and questions as to how this might affect co-operation. Participants were split quite evenly between those who saw this as a problem and those who saw it as a commonality. For example:

I don't see how the church can work with, for example, Muslims. They are trying to convert people to Islam and we are trying to convert people to Christianity. Ultimately I don't think that you can put the two together.

Another said, however:

We would have more understanding about the common problems we face, we are similar in many ways, we are both missionary faiths.

The crux of the matter for many was whether, through multi-faith co-operation, people were seeking the conversion of non-Christians to Christianity. Some were seeking conversion and said, for example:

There are those who are part of other faiths who need to hear what the church has to say about Jesus. People can be brought up in a certain faith but when they are grown up, they can hear the facts for themselves and make up their own minds.

Others adopted a dialogical approach to acknowledging the religious dimension of working with people of different faiths.

You have to be willing to listen, that is the learning curve for everyone. There has to be a basis of mutual respect…. You should accept them on equal terms and not try to evangelise, although you must still represent your own faith and not try to deny it. We should take on board what other faiths can teach us.

Another said:

179

I wouldn't like to see the Asian community co-opted into Christianity because being a Christian is a personal decision.

For some participants the key issue concerning Christian distinctiveness was not conversion but the integrity of worship. They stressed the importance of separating joint social action and joint worship. One interviewee said, for example, that he would like to be involved in multi-faith co-operation:

As long as there is a distinction that it is not for worship but for social action.

Another stated that at his church:

We wouldn't want to do activities that blurred the distinctiveness of either our beliefs or other faith's beliefs. We would be unhappy with inter-faith worship but we would regard social action or fulfilling a social need as a distinct possibility.

The possibility of multi-faith worship was seen by some as being rejected equally by themselves and by people of different faiths.

I can see links, for example, getting a football team together or something like that. I would draw the line at joint worship. I wouldn't go to worship at the mosque and I wouldn't expect a Muslim to worship at church.

Others did not speak directly on the issues of conversion or worship. They interpreted the distinctiveness of Christianity and of other faiths as a reason to emphasise social and community aspects of co-operation rather than the faith aspect. Their reasoning came across as more social than theological, yet this had a theological basis.

I am the interfaith link for the church and I also have Muslim friends. Everyone seems a bit suspicious of each other's faith, it is a stand-off situation. We don't share beliefs but this isn't a reason not to share other things. There is just a bit of mistrust about what the other is trying to achieve. In social areas, we share common things but we don't try to share the spiritual side of things at an interfaith angle.

And:

[Multi-faith co-operation] would be all right on a social ground. Beliefs can be conflicting and cause division. If it could be about helping each other decorate places of worship or apply for funding together or arrange social occasions, then brilliant!

180

Participants identified a range of benefits Christians would enjoy as a consequence of engaging in multi-faith co-operation. Some spoke of the way that multi-faith co-operation and meeting people of different faiths had matured their own faith. One said:

Working at [a school with a high proportion of Muslim pupils] made me value the spirituality and the discipline in prayer of the Muslim faith, which I feel that the West has somehow lost. Faith is a part and parcel of myself, just as the faith of the children and parents was part and parcel of them. The children taught me as much as I taught them, and they taught me about my own faith, which was the amazing part.

In this way, knowledge of another's faith can highlight and strengthen aspects of one's own faith.

Some believed that multi-faith co-operation could enhance not just an individual's faith journey, but also the collective journey. For example, saying that:

[Multi-faith co-operation] would make the church more real and give it more of a purpose. Those who go to church would get more of an insight into their own faith.

Moreover, that reflection on the experience would be of great value.

Multi-ethnic co-operation would definitely benefit the church, it would mean looking at 'What is a church?' It is the people, who they are and the wider community…[it is about] actually doing what Jesus did.

Another related this to Christian tradition, saying:

It will also help us to see the early Church as it was, to see what the Apostles meant when they were living in a society with Asian religions. We live in a society of different faiths, just as Jesus did. It can make your own faith deeper.

In a variety of ways, these participants identified a refining aspect of living and worshipping in a multi-faith area. They stated the belief that if Christians could rise to the challenge posed by living alongside people of different faiths, their own faith and faith community life would be enhanced.

All participants spoke about the theological dimension of living and working alongside people of different faiths. Such reflection on the

181

context and a Christian approach to it is important. So is the theological dimension of multi-faith co-operation. It may seem like a 'good idea' but Christians require a greater coherence than that if they are to become involved in such initiatives. As one participant explained:

People ask, "Why are we doing it? What is the purpose?"

It is, therefore, crucial to continue to build and refine a theological approach to multi-faith co-operation and, more broadly, of being church in a multi-faith locality.

Building A Theology Of Being Church In A Multi-Faith Locality

During the interview process, participants drew on their experiences as individuals who share in church life and as congregations who are able to draw on a tradition of being church. Their theology also springs from a response to their context on the edges of the inner city of Bradford in an increasingly multi-faith locality. They spoke of an idealism of multi cultural and multi faith harmony with a realistic acknowledgement of the difficulties raised against this by some of the dynamics of inner city life and attitudes to the 'other'. Much of the focus is about 'what we would like to see happen' and 'how we would like things to be' rather than what is happening now and how things are. In part this might be due to the relative newness of the multi faith nature of the area and, given time, the positive focus will be on the way things are.

In terms of theology, participants tended to make a distinction between faith and community; that is between belief and worship, and social needs and activities. In this way, many drew a dividing line between what was acceptable to share with those of other faiths and what must be kept separate. Where inter faith interaction was seen as relating to the 'faith side', then it was predominantly in terms of enhancing commitment to their own faith and to their understanding of others, and not that it would directly affect how they might think theologically.

It is interesting to note that references to 'other faiths' were used almost synonymously with Muslims and also with Asians. Although Asians in the area, and indeed in the city as a whole, might be Hindu, Muslim or Sikh, the majority are Muslim. This is not true simply in terms of numbers but also in terms of the perception of their prominence in the city. The emphasis in the interviews on Asians meant that participants often linked multi faith and multi cultural issues. The emphasis on Islam meant that some participants raised the issue of the mutuality of evangelism and the potential for conversion. Such considerations set distinctive parameters for people's approaches to inter faith interaction.

In their context, God calls the Christians of Great Horton and Lidget Green to engagement with people of different faiths and to think through the issues this raises for Christians. Much of this theology is at an early stage of development and, therefore, it is speculative and exploratory, sometimes uncertain and fearful, sometimes optimistic and positive. It is largely a theology of new beginnings and of good intentions. With time and commitment, it can mature through participation in multi-faith initiatives.

Chapter 13

Peter Atkinson

Modern Communities Of The Exile

Contemporary "Exiles"

The twentieth century has been haunted by the image of the refugee; a stark reminder that military and economic conflict result in the displacement of countless people from all that they have loved and cherished. However, it is not only the refugee who experiences displacement and exile in today's world. Residents of inner cities and outer estates (Urban Priority Areas – UPAs) in prosperous countries including Britain may also be considered to be experiencing some degree of "exile" in that they are excluded from many of the world's goods. For this reason the metaphor of "exile", particularly as found in the experience of ancient Israel in the Hebrew scriptures, may be a fruitful one to explore, especially in relation to the role of churches in UPAs.

In 1950s and 1960s Britain many people found themselves in exile from what they had known as they were moved from former homes and "decanted" into new estates many of which have become the UPAs of the present day. It can be argued that they were "deported" and displaced. Subsequent generations may not have had the same experience. Nevertheless, in some senses, people who live in our UPAs may be seen as exiles which includes the sense of being excluded. If it is argued that exile can only refer to physical displacement from a former place of residence, the reply must be a reminder that the image is a metaphor and not precise. It is also helpful to recall the words of Frederick Buechner, "We carry inside us a vision of wholeness that we sense is our true home and that beckons to us."[75] Some of the negative characteristics of life in UPAs; poverty, exclusion from banking and shopping facilities, struggling schools, inadequate public transport and health provision, fear of crime and high levels of crime, the flow of money and skills out of the area, low self-esteem, limited expectations, a sense of being abandoned and the scapegoating of the poor and unemployed residents for the ills of society with, in some cases attendant guilt; together conspire to increase the sense of exile from that wholeness which Buechner calls "home".

Churches in UPAs may be considered to be enduring a double exile. They share the exile of other UPA residents in living surrounded by a culture which measures human worth by financial wealth and possessions. Walter Brueggemann describes the prevailing contemporary culture as one of "military consumerism" which he describes as follows. "A construal of the world in which individual persons are reckoned as the primary units of meaning and reference, and individual persons in unfettered freedom are authorised (self-authorised) to pursue well-being, security and happiness as they choose." According to Brueggemann, this prevailing culture imposes no limit on the individual's right to pursue such supposed well-being, to consume what is required in achieving that goal, even at the expense of others. The military aspect arises:

> In the conviction that having a disproportion of whatever it takes to enjoy well-being, security and happiness is appropriate and that the use of force, coercion or violence either to secure or maintain a disproportion is completely congruent with this notion of happiness.[76]

In addition to sharing this exilic experience of UPA residents, churches in UPAs are also exiled from the rest of the church which all too often may be imbued with the values and outlook of the prevailing culture described above. (Brueggemann also refers to it as "the empire").

How can such "exiled" Christians be sustained? Where are the theological resources on which to draw? Clearly, ancient Israel's experience of exile is central to any such enquiry. But first of all a brief comment is necessary. Norman Gottwald[77] observes that on the surface the deported Jews were not too badly treated. Rather than seeking to punish the exiles Nebuchadnezzar probably wanted no more than to prevent further revolt. The exiles mostly lived in farming communities with a certain measure of freedom. Some found their way to the capital and got involved in commerce. Some Jews became so prosperous in exile that they were unwilling to return to Jerusalem when it was possible to do so.

The impact of exile, then, was felt most keenly in moral, cultural and theological terms rather than physically or economically. It caused a severe crisis of belief. Israel's faith and the means by which it had been expressed, particularly through the monarchy and the state, had been swept away. Never before had there been such a threat to the way in which the people understood God and themselves. Exile seemed to deny all expectations. Could Yahweh be trusted any longer; was Yahweh the equal of other gods?

"Lamentations", written in the Jewish community left behind in Palestine expresses something of that enormous loss, pain and bewilderment of the Jewish people of that time. Had God intended the ruin of Jerusalem? Has Yahweh got any further plans? They had a deep sense of being deserted by Yahweh but perhaps Yahweh wasn't finished with the people. Perhaps it is still possible to trust this inscrutable God. But they would never trust worldly power again.

The prophet Ezekiel also offered new hope. He helped Israel survive and be renewed by stressing Judaism as a way of life requiring high moral standards and ritual observance with an equal stress on both. Renewal and revision of faith in the light of exile came also through Deutero-Isaiah (40-55) who asserts Yahweh's sovereignty and control of history, and the power of righteous suffering. Yahweh's purpose was universal. The gentile, Cyrus, would liberate the Jewish people who in turn were called to be a light to the nations. The answer to despair was to assert Yahweh's strength.

Brueggemann explores further developments in the faith and practice of the exiles.[78] Faith in Yahweh as creator was renewed and explored – Genesis 1 and 2. The disorder and chaos of exile where there is no temple and no king and where the weak do not get a fair chance leads Israel to appeal to the Creator to counter disorder through the continuing process of creation. Hence the stress on worship in which a sense of order and coherence could be renewed. Complaint was a further response of the people as Lamentations and some of the Psalms bear witness. Some writers like Deutero-Isaiah began to explore the notion of the hiddenness of God (Is. 45: 15). Yahweh may be invisible but that does not mean Yahweh is not present.

Working Through Loss
Given that the exile was a situation of total loss and defeat and that in it people in UPAs may detect echoes of their own losses and defeats, an examination of some of the ways in which the Jewish exiles found new ways of renewing and practising their faith may be instructive for Christians in UPAs. Perhaps the hardest and most profound lesson from the Jewish exile is that Israel learned to exist without its former political and religious structures – the monarchy and the temple; a lesson that should encourage UPA churches.

How then did Israel respond in practice? What were its strategies for survival and renewal? It should be remembered that ultimately Israel did not abandon its faith but came to a more daring expression of it.

Brueggemann[79] suggests the following requirements for coping with exile, drawing on his understanding of the response of ancient Israel:
* the need to grieve
* the need to overcome the sense of rootlessness
* the need to overcome the power of despair
* the need to cope with the apparent absence of God
* the need to recognise and deal with the moral questioning which exile creates
* the need to overcome self-preoccupation.

With Bruggemann, let us look at each in turn.

The need to grieve

Exiles have to face their situation honestly, resisting denial and pretence (Jer. 29: 5-7). Brueggemann speaks of the need for the expression of 'resentful sadness' and for 'communities of honest sadness'. No doubt this is a role already being fulfilled by some UPA churches. Can it be carried out more consciously? Can the sense of being excluded from so much be articulated in UPA churches? Ancient Israel grieved but also protested and complained about the injustice of their exile. Here is a role for UPA churches in their worship and in their engagement with their neighbourhoods. Can they be 'communities of honest sadness'?

In Blackbird Leys, for example, the church may have been fulfilling such a role when the issue of 'joy-riding' was given such prominence in the national press. The church, along with some other residents, resented what it saw as a misleading and unjust portrayal of the area. It grieved because the people on the estate were being stereotyped and misrepresented.

Overcoming rootlessness

Brueggemann suggests that being exiled is like being orphaned. So exiles need to take old habits, customs and memories with them. This may be particularly true for minority ethnic groups in UPAs. It will also be true where there has been large scale new building on an estate with a consequent increase in the number of newcomers whose response may initially be one of lament "by the waters of Babylon" (Ps. 137: 1). There is an important place for remembering as the new community is being built. Brueggemann believes the scriptural equivalent of these old memories are the genealogies. Churches have a role in bearing and articulating these memories through worship and special events.

Overcoming the power of despair

Brueggemann believes that despair is the greatest threat to exiles. Israel doubted God's faithfulness and God's power to save. The crucial scriptural resource here is Isaiah 40-55 which counters despair with four themes:

1. The good news that Yahweh has triumphed over the power of exile, i.e. Babylon's gods and monarchy, so Israel does not have to derive its identity from that discredited regime (Is. 46: 1-4). An implication for UPAs which churches might express is that UPAs find their identity within and not from the society and prevailing culture which marginalises and disables them.

2. A rediscovery of faith in God as Creator (Is. 40: 12-17). Israel is urged to "think big" and "sing big" about the forces of life that are working on its behalf. Worship is the great opportunity for UPA churches to reaffirm this sustaining faith. Creation faith asserts that despite appearances God is at work. How much UPA worship reflects this conviction? Is it more likely to do so than worship in non-UPA churches?

3. Israel is to hear Isaiah's speeches of judgement in which Yahweh disputes the claims of the Babylonian gods. This is a way of re-establishing and putting "backbone" into Israel. How can the gods of our prevailing and excluding culture be exposed and judged? Churches and projects can enable people to find strength and dignity in themselves and each other rather than allowing themselves to be defined by the wider society.

4. The salvation oracles (Is. 4: 13, 14-16; 43: 1-5) use creation language to pull Israel away from being in thrall to the rulers of this age who thrive on despair and instead act as a people heading for home. Acting "as if" means living from an alternative reality. Again, worship focuses and expresses this way of overcoming despair. For an hour or so each week, churches, especially in UPAs, act as though the Kingdom of God had really come. Liturgy becomes a way of creating a new world. How much more meaningful this might be in a UPA where there is a real struggle and so much contradicts human aspirations. But worship in such a context can be a necessary and

almost absurd act of defiance, an expression of hope which is a refusal to accept the status quo. If UPA churches can be communities of honest sadness, they might also be communities where defiant joy can be expressed.

Addressing the absence of God
Brueggemann speaks of the "profaned absence" of God. The temple has been destroyed. The glory has departed. A related feeling today is expressed when people complain that nothing is sacred any more. Brueggemann points out that right wing, popular religion exploits this sense of loss. In searching for answers, Brueggemann looks to what he calls the "sacramental life" of Israel. If God seems absent, might God not become a counter presence to Babylonian profanation through certain observances?[80]

> The features of this so-called "sacramental life" were:
> * Circumcision – which in exile became a metaphor for faith. It distinguishes, marks out, those who receive it from their cultural surroundings. It became a way of resisting the ways in which the prevailing culture tried to label and categorise people.
> * Sabbath observance – emerged as a basic act of faith in exile. Brueggemann sees this as a refusal to be defined by the production system of the empire (Babylon) "so life is regularly enacted as a trusted gift and not a frantic achievement".
> * The tabernacle – which is seen as a means of respectfully localising God's holiness, ensuring that it can be depended on (Exodus 25: 21, 35-40). This may have been a fantasy rather than a reality in exilic Israel, but it still expressed a trust that God would be present in exile.

Circumcision, Sabbath observance and the tabernacle reflect the need of exiles to "touch and handle" things unseen (Hebrews 7-10). Words of assurance are not enough.

If, as Brueggemann suggests, "our present exilic crisis is marked by a technological emptiness that is filled by the liturgies of consumerism and commoditisation", perhaps part of the means of resisting this ideology may be found in contemporary equivalents of obversances developed during Israel's exile.

For circumcision, the clear parallel is baptism. Seen as the defining moment in a person's life and stating that nothing and no one else ultimately tells you who you are, the practice of baptism in UPA churches may have something to teach churches in "better off" areas about where the source of what it means to be truly and fully human really lies.   Again, like UPA worship, baptism can be an act of defiance.

The obvious equivalent to the Sabbath is Lord's Day observance but given the prevalence of Sunday opening this may be a lost battle. There is a sharp tension here for exiles living within the influence of the "empire" and at the same time not being of it. Can common cause be found in UPAs where there may be other faith communities to find a way of asserting a refusal to be sucked into "frantic achievement"? Of course, with high rates of unemployment in some UPAs it might be said that many are not part of that ethos anyway. A real question for UPA churches is how to avoid being "ghetto-ised" which indeed is the effect of the attitude of the rest of society towards UPAs generally.

As for ancient exilic Israel's use of or thoughts about the tabernacle, it may be equally difficult to suggest a modern equivalent but it does point strongly to the importance of "sacred space" which is being recovered in many places and experiences. For some it may be the allotment or the canal side. But a more clearly "named" place in a UPA is essential. Whether church occupies a former shop, a pub, or "traditional" building, the message must be that God is present among exiles.

Moral questioning
Israel's exile completely undermined the old moral certainties which saw a neat relation between behaviour and consequences. The classic response to exile would be to say that exile is a punishment from God

for violating the Torah. The book of Job was the first real attempt to wrestle with these issues. It challenged the view that catastrophe was divine punishment for moral transgression. Such an approach might keep the world morally neat and tidy, but at enormous cost. It also reflects a guilt-ridden mentality. Fault and blame are only part of the picture. Something else is loose in the world, undermining its stability and wrecking its peace.

Against this background, it is not difficult to see that UPA churches have an important role in addressing issues raised by moral confusion. Questions of moral guilt and blame are particularly relevant. The poor, the unemployed and single parents frequently have blame heaped on them for the ills of society. They become scapegoats. How much guilt, if any, this induces in those who live in UPAs may be debatable but churches in UPAs in their worship and pastoral role in their neighbourhoods can enable their members to say "It's not our fault. Our exile, our poverty, our exclusion is the result of the policy decisions of a consumerist economy."

Self-preoccupation
Brueggemann regards this as one of the greatest dangers in exile. It becomes difficult to look beyond self to a greater reality. It is interesting to note in this connection that Viktor Frankl[81] observed as a result of his experience in Nazi concentration camps that generally those who survived were those who were able to look forward.

It is suggested that one of ancient Israel's strategies for surviving creatively and enabling exiles to look beyond themselves was the use of stories of defiance and cunning. The implication is that exiles were encouraged "not to confront their harsh overlords directly but to negotiate knowingly between faith and the pressures of 'reality' ". This kind of story is an encouragement to "hang on" in a world where faith is hardly recognised.

Stories of particular value in this context are those of Joseph, Esther and Daniel. Joseph is clever enough to co-operate with "the empire"

192

whilst at the same time looking out for the interests of his own people. He does not completely submit to the establishment's definition of reality. Esther is about a courageous Jew who outwits the ruling powers. Daniel shows a young man maintaining a distinct identity with its roots outside the oppressive power which has recruited him to its civil service.

Enduring and Emerging

The central point in all these stories is that the leading characters are not totally immersed in the prevailing culture. They remember who they are and who they belong to. Transposing these insights into the present suggests that central to the ministry of UPA churches is the role of enabling people to remember who they are and who they belong to. Exiles need to have their identity affirmed and renewed.

There is much to learn from the strategies of ancient Israel devised during its years in exile. All enabled it to endure and emerge with a faith renewed but transformed and better adapted to a new context. UPA churches can be inspirational foci for their neighbourhoods witnessing to an alternative reality which offers hope. Experience suggests that churches and projects in UPAs which are most alive and most effective are those which are driven by real prayer and have Bible reading and story-telling at their heart. This can be seen as a direct link with the experience of the Jewish exiles, maintaining continuity with the tradition but finding hope in reworking texts and writing new ones arising from their new experience. As communities of honest sadness and defiant joy in the apparent wilderness of exile, it may be that UPA churches can offer much for the wider church on which to draw and put it in touch with the rich resources in the Christian faith's Jewish heritage at a time when it may just be coming to an awareness of its own exile.

There is a mutuality in all of this; a mutuality between UPA churches and the wider church and the church and society. It is exemplified in what must be a key test: "Seek the welfare of the city where I have sent you into exile and pray to the Lord on its behalf, for in its welfare you will find your welfare." (Jer. 29: 7).

Chapter 14

Ann Morisy

The Suburban Challenge
South London

There are two things that authors dread - seeing their book discounted in a sale; and hearing that someone began reading it, only to have put it down after the first twenty pages and never open it again. These twin dreads can mean that authors soft pedal those things readers might find hard to take. I did just that when writing about community ministry.[82] My aim was to get people to buy the book and to read on to the end, by enticement rather than hard challenge, and trying to disarm subtly rather than brutally. However, such tactics are not the stuff of healthy theology. My aim to please stifled an important theological perspective - that of a theology which explicitly challenges suburban living. Making a serious challenge to 'the mainstream' risks biting the hand that feeds me, and risks onlookers inspecting my lifestyle and wagging their heads as they find it no different from their own. Talk is cheap in relation to the afflictions of suburban life and authentic action is hard to find.

On reflection, it proved more acceptable, and marketable, to speak-up on the side of the poor than it did to confront the mainstream culture which forms us so extensively. In inviting my work to be viewed as a contribution to urban theology, my aim was to convince readers that the book was the stuff of drama and passion in a way that was likely to enhance my reputation. In comparison, suburban theology sounds a little sad. Theology derived from Hyacinth Bouquet in 'Keeping-Up Appearances' is hardly the most inspiring prospect, and more than this, it might also be a little too close for comfort for most readers and for the author. For I, like so many others, use my affluence, modest as it might be, to buy security and pleasure. As if in a playpen, I protect myself from the raw and abrasive aspects of life:

- It has become an affront to be cold
- It is unbelievably irksome to have to get up from the couch to change TV channels
- We value the habit of taking foreign holidays supported by tour companies and couriers
- Our reliance on car travel not only protects from inclement weather and the exhaustion of travel, but also spares us the demands of having to rub shoulders with strangers
- Buying 'over the counter' medication to chase away pains and discomfort.

The list is long and very personal – and the implications of such a lifestyle are huge – with powerful repercussions for spirituality and church life. But more than anything, as history will tell, we are moral accomplices in the perpetuation of the extensive and often intense distress of our brothers and sisters in two thirds of the world.

For the vast majority of us in Britain, and in the West as a whole, our experience of life is profoundly at odds with 99% of human history and at odds with the life experience of two thirds of the world's population today. According to Camus when pestilence or hardship confronts us we discover that there are more things to admire in our neighbour than to despise. However, given the protection of the playpen constructed with our disposable income, we habitually ignore or even despise our brothers and sisters, and this has distressing implications for those committed to working for the Kingdom of God as both a present and a future reality.

Added to this, suburban living too easily stifles our hearing and seeing. The seductive tones promoted by marketing executives stop our ears to the message to 'love your neighbour as you love yourself'.

196

How do we represent a God who enters into the harshness of human struggle at a time when people consider the raw and abrasive aspect of life to be an insult to our status as homo sapiens and alien to suburban existence? How do we speak of the self-emptying of Jesus on the cross to a culture in which self-love is considered good sense?

'The Cross' Taken out of Life

The efforts to avoid the cross could not be more concerted than those that prevail in my suburban household. So little of the cross is to be found in our lives, less now than at other times in human history. Whilst we resist engaging in struggle for anything other than our own wellbeing, and habitually avoid any kind of engagement with others, other than those within our own household, we miss the very point of Jesus' presence here on earth and we stifle the manifestation of an incarnate God.

Michael Ignatieff describes the route that he takes to avoid the cross that his neighbours carry. In his book *The Needs of Strangers*[83], Ignatieff begins with a description of those who shop at the weekly market held in the North London street where he lives. He focuses on the elderly people who pick over the second hand clothes on the various stalls. Not only does he perceive their poverty, but he also perceives their isolation. Their children are likely to have moved to the suburbs or further afield, and their new neighbours only stay for short periods before resettling somewhere else.

In the local post office, Ignatieff and the pensioners find themselves in the same queue, and it is here where he sees a parable of modern relationships between strangers... He writes, "Their needs and their entitlements establish a silent relationship between us". He reflects that although they remain strangers, in drawing their pension some tiny proportion of his wealth is transferred to them. He goes on to observe that "They are dependent on the state, not upon me, and we are both glad of it."[84]

Through the mechanism of the state, and its million tiny capillaries, we are able to boast that we are our indeed our neighbour's keeper, even though our neighbour remains a stranger. In this way, we who inhabit the suburbs have contrived to be Samaritan, Priest and Levite - all three at once - to the man who was beaten and robbed on the road to Jericho. It is an extraordinary human invention that those to whom we in the suburbs provide help remain strangers to us. But the absence of such a face-to-face encounter also lessens the likelihood of a transformational encounter.

The aim of community ministry is to increase the likelihood of such transformational encounters. At a superficial level, community ministry can be viewed simply as a means by which a local church can engage helpfully with those who are beset by the raw and abrasive aspects of life. Community ministry also involves inviting others to join with church members to participate in community projects that address issues of local concern and people's specific needs. But to focus solely on engagement with the needs that present themselves is to underestimate the real potency of community ministry. It is a radical act to invite those who are cocooned in playpen living to draw alongside those for whom the playpen provides no protection. Potentially, a face-to-face encounter with those who are poor provides a profound and transformational 'wake-up' call to those who naively dream, shrouded in the Sunday supplements. Community ministry is at its most powerful when it enables those who live in the metaphorical playpen to commit the equivalent of class treason.

Community Ministry in relation to Suburban Life
The difficulty at the heart of a community ministry approach is that of transferring it from an urban environment to a suburban context. The problem in a suburban context is how to identify needs. There most certainly will be needs, but they are likely to be kept private, or their nature is such that pastoral care is a more appropriate response than participative community ministry. The *in your face* hardship,

198

which makes the community ministry model viable in an urban context, is a rare commodity in suburbia.

However, *in your face hardship* is not a rare commodity in our world. Community ministry does not have to focus on the local. It can also promote engagement with issues that are far away. The transformational encounter that is so essential to community ministry may require a flight from Heathrow, not so much for the sun and sea, but to come alongside those who are embroiled in the raw and abrasive aspects of life. This makes for a very different type of package holiday to that which is *de rigeur* to playpen living.

In one of the smarter west London Boroughs, a local GP has joined a colleague who is based in the Philippines. Together they have set-up a micro-credit organisation. The GP goes round his friends, often those linked with his church, inviting them to write a cheque for £100. This sum is then made available to a household in Manila who are reliant on some form of personal enterprise if they are to escape from crippling poverty. The capacity for enterprise does not seem to be in short supply, but the financial capital needed to launch an enterprise is scarce. It is this gap that the GPs friends and neighbours have begun to address in a very modest, but structured way. Each contributor receives a profile of the household and an outline of the venture they are trying to develop. If the household moves into a position to re-pay the loan, that sum is 're-cycled' and made available to another household. Each year the London based GP invites three or four of the west London sponsors to visit Manila with him to see things at first hand, and to meet with the network of households that are linked through the micro-credit scheme.

The obvious way in which this modest micro-credit scheme promotes change for the better is through the provision of otherwise non-existent investment capital to those in chronic poverty. However, the venture also promotes other dynamics that carry positive contributions in the direction of the Kingdom of God. It enables stories of hope and struggle to be carried to suburbia, as well as carrying the potential for transformation through encounter, and does so in a direction that fundamentally reverses the assumed relationship between those from first world and those of the third. The radical nature of this modest venture rests not so much in its overt intention, but in these two latent features.

The significance of such experiences, particularly those that combine the elements of both hope and struggle, in shaping people's attitudes and future options, often goes unrecognised. Where people's lives are story-thin a good story can have a particularly strong impact, and in the isolated households that characterise so much of suburbia, stories that combine elements of both hope and struggle may be thin on the ground. And where there are such stories, they tend to be kept under wraps. People pay a cost for living in an environment that is story thin, because the ability to see ourselves as something more and better than we presently are is dependent on the stories that we have to hand. Stories that speak of both hope and struggle, or speak of an essential genuineness, will not leave us alone. They carry a capacity to change us.

There are many ways in which the micro-credit project generates experiences that have the capacity to change people. I sketch a possible scenario:

> Jim and Sue are invited to a supper party hosted by the neighbours up the road. It's a leaving party as the host and hostess are soon to retire and move to Devon. The conversation during the evening naturally focuses on the freedom that comes with retirement and the scope for leisure and hobbies. Others still in employment can only speak of holidays that are being planned, but in the midst of such suburban conversations, the story that Jim and Sue carry has the capacity to open up possibilities that can shape the choices to be made by the people in that gathering, and ultimately to shape the people themselves.

Some one says that they are thinking of booking a fortnight in Cuba, another comments on the nature of the Castro regime, and yet another talks of the frequent business trips to increasingly entrepreneurial Poland. At this point Sue says that she and Jim are going to Manila next month to visit some of the people in the shanty townships, because they are part of a micro-credit project run by a GP who goes to their church...

The experience that Sue and Jim have had, even before they visit Manila, let alone after - carries the ability to change those who are party to it. Some will certainly respond by writing a cheque for £100, but that will only be part of the dynamic that is set in train by Sue and Jim's story. Quietly, people will ponder whether they too could be party to experiences that are a rich source of genuine stories that go deep and speak of abiding and humane values. They too would like to have a story rich life like Sue and Jim seem to have discovered. The stories that surround us are more important than we realise. Taylor comments that most of us can rise no higher than the stories that surround us, for in the stories we hear we can glimpse our 'potential self' and this in turn informs the choices we go on to make.[85]

Daniel Taylor also suggests that by the simple means of story we can travel across the distances between our separate worlds. He notes William James comments that the greatest gap that exists in the universe is that between one human mind and another.[86] Flying to other planets is child's play compared to crossing the light years between the galaxy of my suburban shaped mind and those who dwell in Bedouin encampments or in the slums of Manila. Story is our best hope for flying over the chasms that separate individuals, races, genders, ages and the myriad of other differences between the children of God.

Stories That Form Us
Story has the capacity to cross the gap between different lifestyles and cultures, and evoke thinking and feeling that lead to commitment. The stories of hope and struggle that are often seeded by those who are beset by the raw and abrasive aspects of life can issue a wake-up call to those of us deluded by the false security of the playpen. This waking-up to our own and others' reality is likely to have the following dimensions:

Our hearts will be moistened
This phrase used by John Donne grows out of the awareness that preoccupation with self-interest hardens our heart. Through the grace of God those of us seduced by playpen existence can, 'by proxy' i.e. through stories of hope and struggle, partake of the raw and abrasive aspects of life, and this transforms our imagination. Compassion begins to flow as we begin to see 'the person' behind the hardship. Though we ourselves may have suffered very little, it is in the nature and power of story that makes it possible for a few moments for someone else's suffering to become our suffering. The root meaning of compassion is 'to suffer with' and it is this process that enables me to care about anyone other than me and my household.

The dignity and stamina of the human spirit may be glimpsed
The encounter with the person living amidst the raw and abrasive aspects of life when combined with hearing his or her underlying story makes clear the choices that they had to make in their lives. The choices that we make reveal the values that we live by and speak of our character. Very often, those beset by the harshness of life communicate an unfettered humility and endurance. Such capacities may seem dated in a suburban world. However, secretly each of us fears that 'character' such as this is worth more than it is credited with. Those who are exposed to the raw and abrasive aspects of life so often display the real, undeniable child of God that is within them, exposing the sham confidence and self regard that lurks within

202

suburban hearts. Dignified behaviour takes on a different hue when it is characterised by the lowliest people

The all-encompassing and subtle nature of sin begins to be recognised
The encounter with the person who is homeless or in poverty also allows the story that underpins their circumstances to be heard and understood. This can lead to a sense within the hearer of 'there but for the grace of God go I', and this is an important step in recognising that blaming others for the circumstances in which they find themselves is a senseless approach. Hearing the underlying story of the person enables the nature of our human plight to be recognised. Once we allow ourselves to be frank about the vulnerability of the human condition, then there is scope for a more informed and mature understanding of the nature of sin. People's underlying story asks for understanding. Such underlying stories tend to make us more tolerant and forgiving of moral failure at the same time that they convince us of the reality and necessity of the moral dimension of life. Taylor comments that a person steeped in stories is less likely to be judgmental, but more likely to realise that judgements must be made.[87]

Furthermore, we begin to acknowledge both the perceptible and imperceptible ways in which each one of us contributes to a predicament that defies human will and agency. Sin ceases to be about personal morality and becomes something far more potent - a force that mires and infects even our best intentions. We begin to see how all of us are caught-up in sin, and not just those whom the conveyors of current morality choose to pillory.

Recognition of the inclination of institutions to organise things for the convenience and benefit of those on the inside
An encounter with those who face hardship (or an encounter with their story) enables the messy particulars of their circumstances to be unfurled, and as a result the limited response of bureaucratic 'legal-rational' organisations is revealed. Despite having been established with the aim of helping those in hardship, their very 'rationality'

based on universal principals and theories tends to side-step so many messy particulars. Inevitably, over time, agencies established to work on behalf of those in need develop so many conditions and boundaries that the help they offer becomes restricted and conditional. But this is not all, the boundaries that are maintained benefit the professional class that administers the agency. The task of supervising the correct application of rules and regulations counts for more than the task of applying such procedures to those in need. Despite our best endeavours our rationally rooted application of care and concern fails to live up to our intentions and our hopes, but has never failed to provide secure and 'meaningful' careers. This assessment is not so much rooted in cynicism as recognition of the nature of structural sin.

Helps people to achieve 'deep literacy'
Deep literacy is the name Paulo Freire gives to the ability to read how power is exercised and distributed.[88] It requires us to acknowledge that our perceptions are not open and innocent but shaped by myriad sources, and in ways that maintain the status quo. There are patterns that underpin our apparent common sense and these patterns repeatedly favour some and disadvantage others. Often what passes as common sense serves a sectional interest rather than everyone's interests, and certainly not the interests of the poorest and most vulnerable.

Deep literacy requires the willingness to question what we think we know, and this willingness brings with it scope for dialogue with those who see and experience the world differently from us. As has been demonstrated, it is the encounter with those who are excluded that carries the transformational capacity, and enables us to see the normally hidden power of unexamined assumptions.

Recognition that all dwell in a continual state of vulnerability
Exposure to the vulnerability of those who have no money to routinely protect themselves from the raw and abrasive aspects of life can enable the more affluent to acknowledge our own vulnerability.

204

There is an invitation at the heart of every story that is shared. It is the invitation "You come too." In this invitation resides the formative and potentially healing power of an encounter with those who know their vulnerability. The veneer of security that money can give gets exposed as just that, it is insubstantial in the face of challenges of the inevitability of sickness and death. In the absence of open acknowledgement of our vulnerability we live with a constant apprehension about what *might* happen. Vulnerability becomes not just a characteristic feature of the poor, but a democratic fact of life. It is through the acknowledgement of our vulnerability that the route to honest thinking and acting opens up before us.

Could it be that our essential orientation to life is a consequence of the stories that form us? If this is the case, then the transmission of stories, and in particular, stories of hope and struggle, becomes a radical force for change as well as a radical basis for theology. Community ministry, because of its emphasis on participation and encountering people with genuine and challenging stories, is a key resource in this process. Community ministry is a powerful tool in both urban and suburban contexts. However, for many reasons, the significance of encouraging suburban people to take-up radical action and reflection has been underplayed. Suburban Britain needs to be taken seriously if an authentic, 'joined-up' and committed theology is to flourish in Britain.

The term 'committed' theology is important, for community ministry is about praxis - action and engagement which provides the material that makes theological thinking a possibility, and even as a necessity. Committed theology is also unafraid of identifying particular priorities around which action and reflection need to focus. The commitment at the heart of community ministry, when it travels to the suburbs, is a commitment to the transformation of suburbia, and it can do this by modelling a committed lifestyle sufficiently attractive to entice people away from the addictive lifestyle of playpen existence. The challenge will be to do this without provoking dysfunctional defensiveness and guilt within those of us for whom playpen living is the norm. However, until the churches of suburbia can offer congregations praxis that coaxes us out of a playpen into engagement with struggle, then suburban churches, as successful as they may appear now, will be judged by history to have been whitened sepulchres.

Chapter 15

Colin Marchant

New Signs In The City

Backcloth

East London is my patch. The London Borough of Newham has been my home and place of work for 35 years.

Back in 1965 the docks began to close, people kept moving out, working class culture still held together. The churches huddled uneasily beneath the blankets of nostalgia (the good old days) and decline. Maintenance or survival were the themes, the "doctrine of the remnant" theology.

In the 1980s there was a noticeable stirring and shaking in the inner cities, shoots of new life, clusters of the concerned, networks, initiatives and new churches, often ethnic or charismatic. Holistic Gospel, social transformation, inner city urban mission, urban poor. Denominational movements like Mission alongside the Poor and Faith in the City were linked with national networks ranging from the Evangelical Coalition for Urban Mission (ECUM) to Christians Organised for Social, Political and Economic Change (COSPEC), Urban Mission was really on the agenda.

As we move into the twenty first century something else is happening. Even as denominational budgets and church interest in Urban Mission falter and contraction is the style across the U.K., new and renewed signals are coming in East London.

Greg Smith's 'Christ of the Barking Road' is a journey down one main road in our Borough. It tells a graphic story and raises the questions.

Documentation is now in the Directories of Religion[89] recently published. Analysis is sketched in 'Religious Trends'.[90]

What is going on? Are there messages or signs? Is God at work in new ways? Can we discern underlying theologies?

New Signs

Signals flash from a spectrum of sources; shopfront presence, changing buildings, numerical growth, diversity, clustering of congregations, creative projects, world faiths and an incredible range of 'visuals'. Shop front 'presence' takes many forms. The Word of God International Worship Centre, Signs and Wonders hairdresser, His Grace Cosmetics Beauty Centre. It is Well (in our city); Amazing Grace has a mini-market and an International Worship Centre, a training, counselling and prayer unit. Buildings are converted! One garage has become the Calvary Charismatic Church, another a Muslim mosque. A clothing store now houses the Glory Bible Church and another shop has become the Sree Narayan Guru Mission.

Growth can be phenomenal. An initial 'church plant' of 40 Ghanaian Christians grows to 700 in five years, across in Hackney the Highway Church claims 5,000 members. New buildings set aside for religion have nearly doubled every decade since 1970 (1970s-19; 1980s-25; 1990s-50).

Diversity is Kaleidoscopic. Colombian Fathers and Coptic Church, Faith Temple Mission and Mayflower, St. Matthew's and Tenillan Prophetic Ministries, Centres, Shops, Churches, fellowships, Missions, Units, Ministries, Chaplaincies, Assemblies and Programmes.

Clustering of congregations is everywhere. Some community centres have 6 churches using their premises. The Baptist Church where I belong has two new churches following on from our morning service and two others use our adjacent hall. World Faiths are with us in strength - 25 Muslim organisations, 15 Hindu, 4 Sikh and 2 Buddhist.

We have 3 Interfaith and 2 Multi-Faith groups alongside the Bahai and Jewish people.

Visible signals flash. Bible-carrying Pentecostalists and white-capped Muslim boys, Buddhist flags and all night Christian prayer meetings, murals and mini-vans, projects and lit-up crosses.

These are signs that are confusing, difficult to code, and hard to document - flows rather than patterns, confusing rather than clear-cut. There are shut-downs and opening-ups, there is a patchiness and shifting. But something is happening. Faith communities, similarities and beliefs are bubbling, co-existing and evident. What is going on? What is behind this? Are there causes and consequences?

Causes And Consequences

There are some obvious causes for the ferment - in East London, we know that globalisation and world faiths and realities for the world is with us, as we co-exist with the world faiths and we connect with global cities. All of these causes have led on to accelerating consequences. Put this alongside the fundamental process of regeneration within a post-industrial district and there is a heady mix.

Over half of the population are black. Caribbean, Asian and African people have streamed in. Immigrants, refugees and asylum seekers carry their culture and faith with them. They have come into a vortex of population change, bringing beliefs and life-styles.

Names, languages and people groups tell the story. Names: Ambedkat International Mission, The Church (World-wide Inc.), French African Church. Languages: Filipino, Tamil, Urdu, French, Punjabi, Kiswahili. People groups: Afro-Caribbean, Asian, and African break down into Jamaican, Barbadian and Trinidadian, Sri Lanka, Filipino and South Indian; Kenyan, Congolese and Ugandans.

Co-Existence With World Faiths

In the Primary Schools of Newham, Muslims (32%), Hindus (6%), Sikhs (4%), have combined with Buddhists and Tavists (4%) to leapfrog the Christian 43%.

More than 20 mosques, 15 Hindu temples and 4 Sikh gurudwaras stand where each faith only had one building in 1978 in Newham. Religious Education in Schools and morality (gambling, deviant sexuality, family) are challenged by the convictions and practice of these faiths. Muslims are missionaries- local minicab drivers speak openly of faith.

Theologies are confronted. For Christians, Jesus is central, salvation is by faith. Second-hand, family 'pass-down' faith is no longer tolerable. There is now a market-place of faith.

Theologies are openly tested. There is a public pragmatism in the size of congregations, evidence of 'signs and wonders', glossiness of advertising, and localised identity for the Christians. There is the Friday prayer stream for the Koran classes, and the fasting festivals for the Muslim.

Little collaboration, some competition, mostly co-existence. But the awareness, the cultures and the tensions are constantly with us.

Becoming A World City

East London was driven by the Industrial Revolution and was characterised by the 'cockney' working class culture. The underlay of white working class culture persists but is now patchy, weakening and moving out to Essex.

We are now part of a World City which has more in common with New York, Sydney, and Sao Paulo than Liverpool, Newcastle or Plymouth. Cultures and communications are the bridges.

With Christian Mission the defining, initial emphasis on incarnation as the root theology for witness and social action is giving way to a flow, spirit filled, Salvationist theology that ignores parish, neighbourhood and denominational boundaries. People movements, culture and identity are the carriers and trustees of faith.

Reverse Missionary Flow

The docks that saw British missionaries 'going into all the world' received in the 1950s and 1960s the Caribbean people who, in the face of racism and rejection, founded vibrant churches. African and Asian Christians have joined them in a wave of church planting and direct evangelism that has spread across East London - and is known in the major conurbations.

Personal faith, preaching emphasis and participatory worship are rooted in Scripture and song. Convulsion and the Spirit are central. Leadership is indigenous, emerging by 'gift' or spontaneity.

Faith has become visible - in the street processions, window posters, local paper adverts, and congregations sitting out onto the pavements. This missionary flow is a 'boomerang' consequence of the missionary movement and the Commonwealth influence. Prominent within this flow is Pentecostalism.

March of Pentecostalism

The statistics are clear. 72 of the 180 Christian congregations in Newham are Pentecostal. More than the combined total of the Anglicans (26), Baptists (13), Roman Catholics (12), Methodists (7) and URC's (3). Back in 1978 there were 6 white and 13 black-led congregations in the Borough - a jump from 19 to 72 in twenty years.

The pace and the scale are overwhelming. 39 of the 72 Pentecostal groups were not known to us in 1995 - but 18 of the 1995 grouping have disappeared! The Calvary Charismatic Baptist Church in Newham has grown from 40 to 700 members in five years and worshipped on 3 sites the city-wide. London City Church

(Kensington Temple) has 12,000 members clustering in scores of language or neighbourhood groupings (one branch began in our local school 6 weeks ago!) and the Highway Church (bestraddling Hackney and Newham) has 5000 members. And those are the mega-churches standing within scores of smaller varied congregations to be found in almost all our neighbourhoods.

We are part of the Pentecostal advance across the cities of the world in the twentieth century. The urban theologian Harvey Cox made his name with *Secular City* in 1966.[91] Thirty years later came his *Fire from Heaven*.[92] The subtitles sketch the journey from 'secularisation and urbanisation in theological perspective' to 'the rise of Pentecostal spirituality and the re-shaping of religion in the twenty-first century'. That re-shaping has begun in East London.

Within this movement are the social factors of identity, culture and language. But there is also the vibrant worship, the personal faith, the spontaneity and the spiritual gifting that reaches and transforms individuals, families and groups caught up in urban transition.

New Networks
Although traditional forms of network persist largely in denominations, Councils of Churches and Fraternals have given way to new associations.

The Newham Christian Fellowship draws together mainly white-led charismatic and evangelical churches 'working together for the Kingdom of God in Newham operating through Leaders Meetings, celebration events, and a Bible Training Centre. At the other end of the spectrum TELCO (The East London Community Organisation) networks 'to unite the voice and power of local community organisations in East London so that we can act together for a better tomorrow'. Breaking across both the political Borough boundaries and the ecclesiastical dioceses, parishes, circuits and synods this network links with other faiths, community groups and social agencies.

Regeneration And Renewal

Beneath the signs of ferment there is another profound process. Regeneration and renewal is going on deep within the life of the community.

Newham has gone through a double cycle of growth. It has known the full industrial revolution of fields to factories to brownfields, of villages, overcrowding and urban. It is now accelerating into a second cycle of regeneration. The physical regeneration of the old Docklands, development of 'brown field' sites and the renewal of communications in the Limehouse Highway, Docklands Light railway and the Jubilee Line have followed each other. High profile 'signs' like the Dome, Canary Wharf and the Thames Barrier surround Newham while the London City Airport sits like an ungainly cuckoo sharply within it. The massive changes in housing and roads, the removal of landmarks, and the population exodus has ploughed up both the physical and social environments.

There has been a matching regeneration within spirituality. At one level renewal is taking place within the long established churches and the agencies and programmes that spring from them. At another level new faith communities and networks are rooting into, and springing from the social matrix.

Signs of Renewal

In Newham many of the main line congregations are growing in numbers, confidence and initiatives. The Newham Group of United Reformed Churches have increased in membership, started a new church, and service community action projects. 500 clients in seven years have been equipped for work in the 'Shoulder to Shoulder' project; 250 individuals approached the Breakthrough Advice and Advisory Service in the first six months.

Over against the national picture of overall decline the Newham picture of half the churches increasing, a quarter constant and a quarter in decline is accompanied by other significant trends:

- 'Only a small handful of Christian congregations are numerically dominated by the over 50s.

- 'Only a quarter of the groups have a full-time paid religious leader'.

Church buildings are another barometer. Expansion, adaptation, reclaiming and multi-usage are the indicators. Some buildings once abandoned by the established churches have been clawed back by the new churches - the Glory Bible Church has completely renewed the large two-storey clothing store which itself was the former Baptist, Barking Road Tabernacle. Others have changed ownership - the old Jewish synagogue is now a Muslim mosque.

Many have taken over premises - the Harmony Church advertises its site above the High Street Argos. An Independent Church has refurbished a redundant Anglican building. Site noticeboards include a variety of tenant congregations; most have one or two. Some have five or six. Closures, once so frequent, have virtually ceased.

Agencies birthed in the Victorian hay-day are coming alive again. All the YMCA centres in Newham shut years ago but now The George Williams Training College has come to Canning Town as a 'centre for studies in informal and community education' and neighbouring centres appoint chaplain and workout mission statements. Dr Barnados began work in East London and now have their CANDL Project (Church and Neighbourhood Development in London) in Hackney, established in 1988 to work with children and young people and to train local church groups.

Even the Christian Socialist Movement has known renewal! Although Newham had the first Labour MP in Keir Hardie and the first local council in 1899 at West Ham faith presence in the political world has never been as strong as today. The present CSM group walked down the Barking Road with Greg Smith - including an M.P. and two councillors. They are witnesses to all that is happening.

Monastic Orders first came to Newham in the late eighteenth century. *Hidden Lives*[93] published in the closing months of 1999 tells the story of the opening of the Anglican Franciscan house to the wider community and the growing of the 'helping hands' project. Institution has moved into a creative opening phase living by the Franciscan dictum- 'Preach often, sometimes using words'. Other Orders like the Roman Catholic Colombian Fathers, have come 'to reach out in Partnership beyond the boundaries of church structures where religious and cultural pluralism meet with poverty'.

Here the incarnational Kingdom theology supports the value of the individual and the significance of prayer.

It is something of a 'double whammy'. The incoming forces of globalisation, a multi-everything society and in particular, the march of Pentecostalism coincide with the consequences of massive physical and social regeneration.

Patterns are being both re-arranged and augmented, some aspects are being clarified but the final picture is still emerging. Something is happening in East London - documentation and description precede understanding and assessment. The future is emerging and it will be continuity and change as the people of God work at being both authentic and appropriate in 'glo-cal' society.

Chapter 16

John Vincent

From Testimony To Testament

"This is That"

What is the testimony of our stories which begins to create theology? What are the lines of the 'Testament' which can be discerned arising from the testimonies we have heard?

We may observe immediately that this is Testament created in the midst of the urban world, by disciples living out their discipleship, and, especially, asking themselves before, during or after their practice, how their commitments and experiences fit in with aspects of the Christian way recorded in scripture, tradition and theology. Sometimes, this is done consciously and intentionally, as when Peter Howard's co-workers at Frankie's ask:

> What do we make of all this?
> What connections do we make?
> What sociological analysis is there?
> What theology can we do with our experience?

He could have added, What theology have we already done in our experience? For the Testament, the story, built up by these different testimonies, is one of 'Word in Action' or 'Action as Word'.

Theology done in the Urban context is essentially theological practice, rather than the much vaunted 'theological reflection'. The theology, the Word of God, the divine reality, has been in the practice – before it, within it, alongside it, after it. In the scripture, the stories and words only occur after the happening, the action, be it action by God, by Jesus or by disciples. First the action, the practice, the happening.

Then the story, the witness, the testimony. And then, as a way of making sense of it all, the conclusions, the elaborations, the globalisations, the meaning-makings, the theology, the doctrine.

Especially, the theology arises out of and comes through the actions that the people get involved in which recall biblical actions. One element in this is clearly the ways in which certain texts or passages of scripture sometimes suddenly appear relevant, or even attain a contemporary re-coining or re-enactment, in specific incidents or events, or to meet certain challenges. Just as the New Testament claimed that the activities going on in the earliest church were to be described as "This is that which was spoken through the prophet" in the Old Testament (Acts 2: 16), so the Urban Testament today says "This is that which was spoken of in the Old and New Testaments".

Thus, at St Chad's, Wood End, Steve sees the desolate streets, boarded up houses and stripped trees, and sees the desolation left by the locusts of Joel 1: 4; or he sees the invading hordes of vandals and sees the marauding lions of Joel 1: 6-7. And Brian sees the depleting numbers on the estate, fleeing the city, and is 'upheld' by Jeremiah buying the field at Anathoth (Jer. 32: 7-8); and comes to believe that even in this place "will be heard the sounds of joy and gladness" (Jer. 33: 11).

At Denaby Main, the closure of the coalfields is likened to the destruction of Jerusalem and the Temple (Jer. 52: 17-18). Only a memorial tower remains. Jane Thomas, wondering what to do with the tools in her garden shed, discovers "See that you finish the work you have begun in the Lord" (presumably from 1 Chron. 28: 20).

I shared this with the others. We agreed that none of us were aware that we were doing anything "in the Lord" – more of a good idea really.

217

But the group finish their "good idea" with biblical stories and expectations – including the title "Highway" which they get from Isaiah 62: 10.

At Wood End, among the St Chad's people, it is "urban theology" as "people of faith and experience, talking together about what God requires, and accepting the implications and consequences". And "What God requires" is seen in:

> What does the Lord require of you
> But to do justly,
> And to love kindness
> And to walk humbly with your God? (Micah 6: 8).

Among the Highway group of Christians at Denaby Main, it is "risk, prayers, mutual support, and reliance on God and each other" – and responding to "feed my sheep", summed up in:

> Christ has no hands but your hands, to do his work today;
> Christ has no feet but your feet to lead folk on his way
> He has no voice but your voice, to tell them how he died
> He has no help but your help, to bring them to his side.

What are we Saying?
Sometimes, the movement goes from a piece of the biblical or theological tradition, which triggers off the memory, so that a contemporary phenomenon appears to be like it. In Newton Heath, the model of "Christian presence", is based particularly on the Christian doctrine of incarnation and upon the concept of discipleship as being "salt" and "light" and "leaven" in the world. The Gospel concepts determine what the practitioner sees in the contemporary scene. The contribution of Christianity, says Derek Purnell, is invariably "redemption and lift". But the problem is that Church members take these to mean "redemption and leave", so that the inner city churches are constantly denuded of their own products and their potential or actual leaders. But true disciples remain.

218

Derek Purnell thus interprets Jesus' parable of the kingdom as yeast (Mt. 13: 33):

> We must mix into the local culture, as the yeast mixes into the dough, and we must live out our Christianity in that context, just as the yeast dispenses its own life on the surrounding dough.

In the story of Frankie's, it is the acting out of the practice called forth by the situation, its needs, and the new demands and attitudes called for among the group of helpers involved, which provoke the biblical and theological naming. Following a hunch, and led by others starting a venture, the untrained helpers stumble into their project, make mistakes, and find unexpected blessings. Then, looking back, they see how their practice has in fact embodied pieces of the Gospel story of Jesus – good news for the poor (Lk. 4: 18), pitying people without a shepherd (Mk. 6: 34), creating a sheepfold (Jn. 10: 7ff), lifting burdens (Mt. 11: 28), sharing feasts (Mt. 22: 3ff), using meagre resources (Mk. 6: 38ff) and being "foolish people" who confound the wise (1 Cor 1: 27), but yet entertaining angels unawares (Heb. 13: 2).

The list, of course, is not an agenda for running a youth café, or a strategy for doing a Gospel project. It is a reflection on theologically coherent practice, in the light of unexpected "namings" after the event.

The ecclesiastical scenario exposed by Chris Baker is all too familiar. The major denominations, each moving more and more into a mutually recognisable top-downwards power structure, impose "bold experiments in church design, ecumenical integration and team working" which merely mirror the secular context. Whereas;
In the heavily planned and regulated environment of the new city, what is needed from the churches is maybe not more of the same, but something more subversive – open, chaotic, small, intimate.

219

Consequently, the new base, The Well, is a mixed community of adults and children sharing a large house, exercised with a mission which is a mix of hospitality, peace and justice, partnership with others, and exploring spirituality and faith through art and creativity rather than word. It is "chaotic, unstructured, spontaneous, small-scale". And it manifests a few Gospel signs. What more is the "church" supposed to be?

Ann Morrisy observes how far the physical, financial and neighbourhood mores, "the Playpen", she calls it, of suburbia produce a theology of compliance, of self-centredness, of "the cross taken out of life". Love of neighbour is catered for by the state, and personal contact with strangers is avoided. This situation is broken into by the experiences of a local GP going to the Philippines and setting up micro-credit. Such "radical actions" expose people to new experiences, and their stories help to change others. Suburban churches need to "offer congregations praxis that coaxes us out of a playpen into engagement with struggle". A striking new vocation is surely here for inner city and housing estate congregations – to provide suburban Christians with opportunities for radical personal and bodily discoveries, which will start creating the new experiences which will become new stories of transformation.

Discerning the Gospel Story
Greg Smith indicates the disarming pluralism both of Christian groups and of ethnic and faith communities, and recalls the many books – and theologies – which are "guide books or street maps offering control over the urban environment". He goes on:

> As urban theologians, we have learned to be much more modest, and just put our stories alongside Bible Stories, and get people to talk about it.

So, his five "Gospel signposts" to support and speak from his "Christ of the Barking Road" turn out to be not places or specific incidents, but journeys, passages, movements from one place to another, "roads" along which new revelations appear.

The "signposts" are strange, unexpected, fraught with surprise and threat and peril. The Jericho Road (Lk. 10: 25-37) has the faithful saved by the foreigner; the Jerusalem Road (Lk. 19: 23) means prophetic protest and politics against God and Causes; the Emmaus Road (Lk 24: 13-35) exposes unknown companions and revelations; the road to Africa (Acts 8: 26-30) opens up to us the black disciple; the Damascus Road (Acts 9: 1-9) demands conversion to the city.

Geoff Curtiss's account brings together the two decisive guiding themes of urban theology as described in this volume. First, and as an immediate impetus, it is Gospel stories of Jesus which lead to picking up this issue or that, certain methods, assumptions and "stands" – and even to choosing "partners" or "target groups". "Give them something to eat" (Mk. 6: 30), "When did I see you hungry?" (Mt. 25: 31ff), "Let the children come to me" (Mk. 10: 13ff), "Who are my brothers and sisters?" (Mk. 3: 31ff), "Don't put a lamp under the bushel" (Mk. 4: 21ff), "Go and buy the field" (Mt. 13: 44), "A hundred fold now" (Mk. 10: 29ff) – all these Gospel slogans and vignettes become springboards for action, mission statements for policy, suggestive comparisons for disciples seeking their way.

However, Curtiss also indicates that there is a second impetus, derived from larger biblical traditions. Here, he builds on the biblical call to Justice, in classic texts like Psalm 82: 1-4, the prophets Micah, Jeremiah, Isaiah, Ezekiel, and the requirements of the Torah. Micah 6: 8 and Isaiah 58: 2-10 appear again, as does the tradition of the Jubilee in Leviticus 25: 36 and Luke 4: 16-20.

So, says Geoff, the practices of urban mission follow. "On behalf of God, we have fed the homeless together and slept on the floor together" – but also supported the development of Community Based Police, and Broad Based Community Organisation. Justice takes us beyond the immediate Gospel actions of Jesus into taking on the

221

principalities and powers, and seeking to establish new and more just corporate and civil structures and policies.

Both are necessary, we may conclude. The street level Jesus practice is part of God's justice. And God's justice is the final aim of all Gospel street practice.

Discerning Bible Themes

The testimony of John Summers describes a journey made by not a few urban practitioners. Beginning with an evangelical theology, he finds himself asking, "Why is this not working? Why does the barrier between the Church's version of the Gospel and what can appear as good news on the street, remain so great?" John discovers liberation theology and the base ecclesial community, and learns that the biblical good news is discovered on the street, and becomes credible in small neighbourhood groups of "mini-ekklesias". Lk: 4. 18-19 is not to be 'spiritualised', but taken literally, as real "good news for the poor and liberation for the oppressed", which is "heady, dangerous and revolutionary stuff". And the people outside the church become part of a new form of the church, a Christian community of the Base, of the neighbourhood, of the ordinary people.

In Bradford, Elaine Appelbee sees in the present-day church's insensitivity to urban issues, a contemporary counterpart to the people of Israel, as seen by the prophet Isaiah. She points out how Is. 58: 1-12 provides a step-by-step process whereby Israel then and contemporary churches now can move from insensitivity to realities, persistence in irrelevant and unacceptable worship and religious disciplines, and failure to discern the significance of their actual practice and actions. Only through initially perceiving these realities can they come to a time of repentance which is a radical reformation of their ways, especially in their attitude to the poor, which alone opens the way to acceptance by God and material blessing to their community.

Here, a specific biblical passage becomes a paradigm for modern practice. The discernment has been made that the two situations of Isaiah's time, and of the contemporary city, are comparable in decisive ways – the poverty, the victimisation, the offence of religious practice, the failure to secure or practice real change. And the solution, it is suggested, is similar too. Only a radical, total change in practice can alter either the condition of the poor or the acceptability of the worship and practice of the would-be believers.

The views of church people in Bradford, quoted in Helen Reid's survey, prove to be very specific to the issues of multi-faith areas. The attitudes of tolerance to non-white and non-Christian communities, and interest in working with them, would be repeated in most mixed race inner city areas. In this sense, the presence of a new situation and of new people in fact evokes from Christians some of the basic attitudes of faith – respect for others, love of neighbour, belief in a Creator God, regard for religious practices – which, while part of the general beliefs of Christianity in Britain, are brought to the surface only because of the new situation and its challenges.

The oft-quoted words of St Francis used by Colin Marchant, are relevant: "Preach often, sometimes using words". The "incarnational, Kingdom theology is that of more and more Christian groups". Colin's dramatic account plots not only the demise of the "straight" churches, but also the enlivening presence of new influences, coming from new people from outside Britain, bringing their ethos and vitality to renew even the old denominations at times.

Such a theology and mission practice finds itself alongside the growing non-Christian faiths in our inner cities. In places, the Christians slowly sort out their confusions and discover a few new directions, as in Helen Reid's account. Elsewhere, as Greg Smith records, open conflict and rival claims inevitably emerge. Indeed, the multi-faith situation is generally now felt to lead to a quickening of faith consciousness on the part of some Christian groups. For long, they had rested in a presumed "Christendom" or at least "post-

223

Christian" situation. Now, the lively presence of other faiths actually results in the Christian churches around becoming a bit livelier themselves.

Theological elements are inherent in many current issues – healthy communities, sustainability, quality of life. The search for truly inclusive policies, for organised care, for proper government, are all theological concerns which relate to the heart of Christianity. Theology is in the practice. The focus on community provides a chance to combine the pastoral and prophetic, to live out the story, to practice the 'how'. The local focuses how relationships of justice can be established on a larger scale. The "how" questions are the questions of value, which Geoff Mulgan of DEMOS regards as "the starting point for any credible politics".

So the theology arises from the practice, and the practice drives along and reveals the theology. Thus Ian McCollough writes of the Denaby Main Ecumenical Group:

> At different stages, that which was interpreted as an action to be done "out there", led to an awareness of the need for similar transformation in themselves and others, to be faithful in putting the Word into action, and in the development of their own incarnational ministry and understanding.

We shall turn in Chapter 21 to an attempt to make sense in theological terms of this theology of practice which the testimonies and stories have witnessed. We shall seek to answer the question, what *kind* of theology? What are the distinctive marks of the scripture and theology evident here?

Meantime, I want to point out some elements in the stories which particularly concern the character of the churches which are visible.

The Future Shape of Urban Churches

The churches of the future in these areas, according to our essayists, will look rather different from the present churches there, and even more from the typical suburban or town centre churches which are not there.

Nerissa Jones bears witness to a liturgical community on her estate which has a weekly Eucharist, which might be very similar to an Anglican Eucharist anywhere in England, but for the decisive difference of real, local, human, experience-based, congregational, participation, and reflections of the life and culture of the worshippers. John Summers sees the future in "smaller neighbourhood eucharistic communities on the model of the Base Ecclesial Communities". Indeed, one can readily see how any denomination, including Anglican, which seeks to be present in its parish's deprived areas, would need to be present there in an indigenous, culture-related, bottom up form, as determined by the people actually there, both disciples and wider community. The Highway group, described by Ian McCollough, has many of these aspects, appropriating God and the actions of God for its own work.

Derek Purnell's model of the oikos congregation belongs to the same genre. The difference between the oikos community and the contemporary "House Churches" is that the oikos community, like the Base Ecclesial Communities, remains a neighbourhood congregation, remains small, and remains in people's houses. No attempt is made to "grow" into larger assemblies, necessitating public halls or church buildings. The seed of the congregation in the house replicates itself or indigenously grows authentically in other house contexts. But it does not become a larger congregation or take over neighbouring house congregations.

Nearly 20 years after *Faith in the City*, it may well be that the pre-ecclesiastical, non-traditional congregations we have described might well indicate precisely the "truly indigenous Church in the UPAs" which the report hoped might at last arise.[94]

225

Certainly, the continuing presence of small religious residential communities as told by Peter Baker and Colin Marchant indicates a significant element, continuing the revival of community house living of the 1970s, for example in the Iona and Ashram Communities.[95] Certainly, there is a significant return to the church in the home, not simply evident in the House Church movement and the evangelical Community Churches - another story not told here - but also in the grass roots congregations described by Derek Purnell and John Summers. Colin Marchant perhaps holds out new hope for the future when he describes Newham mainline congregations as mainly under-50s, only a quarter with a full time religious leader, and with church buildings of wide variety.

This growing and chaotic pluralism is the opposite of the orderly "growing into unity" which Peter Baker finds so debilitating. Likewise, "Inter faith dialogue" remains an academic enterprise which does not come naturally or of necessity in situations where all religious groups find it exhausting enough to "carry on", and to keep their own communities in some kind of shape in the threatening environment all around. Church unity and inter-faith dialogue seem the luxuries of middle-class, settled congregations, rather than the necessary bread and butter of survival experienced by the churches reported upon here.

The future of Christian communities in inner cities and housing estates may follow any of the lines indicated here. The direction of project development in alliance with major city partners is here only described by Geoff Curtiss from the USA. But it is the route pursued by many British entrepreneurial Christian faith communities - the Furnival in the Sheffield Inner City Ecumenical Mission is an outstanding recent example.[96] Again, the contemporary cities in which 'Broad Based Organising' has been developed are not reflected in our stories, though there are many who 'swear by it'.[97] At the same time, new street-level faith communities, along the lines of the Base

Ecclesial Communities described by John Summers in Plymouth, come into existence, occasionally assisted by local denominations.

There are very few non-congregation-based enterprises like Touchstone in Bradford, described by Elaine Applebee and Helen Reid, and they depend on strong initial outside funding and denominational preparedness to support an extra-congregational agency. I have recently proclaimed the message "Every Project a Congregation, and Every Congregation a Project" as a way not only of making possible inner city projects, but also of giving new life to inner city congregations.[98]

The development of post-denominational, "people's" churches and faith communities is not reflected here, and is at present a fragile new growth, hailed by Derek Purnell, John Summers and Peter Baker in very different ways. "Church" in most places still means a local presence of one of the major denominations, usually in a special ecclesiastical or other building.

How long this will remain the case, only the future will tell. In the accounts of Greg Smith and Colin Marchant, the traditional denominations are only holding on in enormously depleted strength, while many other indigenous and culturally varied congregations and communities grow and thrive. In this sense, as other inner cities "catch up" with the East End of London - if they do, we will see a growth in all kinds of alternative, Pentecostal and other Christian communities in the future, alongside many other non-Christian and post-Christian faith communities.

Part Two

Reflections and Discernments

Chapter 17

Andrew Davey

The Practise Of Theology And The Urban Future

The Task and Scope of Urban Theology

What is so significant about urban theological activity? What is the nature of this activity we call urban theology and how might it contribute to the future of our urban areas?

We are constantly reminded that our world is an urbanising planet. Over half its 5.2 billion people live in urban areas many in the new mega-cities of Africa, Asia and the Americas where new forms of the urban experience impact on millions of people on a daily basis. In the UK there is talk of urban crisis - provincial cities find whole swathes of housing abandoned, while in the South East a bitter war is fought over the use of brown or greenfield sites to meet the burgeoning demand for housing, much of it for smaller or single person households. Among the urban poor in inner or outer housing areas much has not changed as third and fourth generations find themselves with few prospects for rewarding and secure employment. Racism remains an invidious player in these areas, alongside violence and the not so clandestine traffic in drugs and small-arms.

Urban theology or urban theological practice comes from communities and individuals familiar with much of this from daily experience. Understanding this present, speaking of it, where the reality is sometimes denied, involves speaking from a context that is multilayered, interconnected and globally connected in ways that urbanologists of even fifteen years ago could not conceive. As a contextual theology that is concerned with this reality of the world in which we live, those who are engaged with urban theological practice must reconceive its dynamics, its scope and its constituency.

If all theology, as a form of human production, is contextual then almost all theology must be urban - coming out of those urban academic institutions the university and seminary. But their context of activity is rarely acknowledged and rarely does such activity attempt to change the setting in which it takes place.

Urban theology that is engaged and committed must be part of the movement that is associated with liberation theology as it takes as its subject, its defining concern and draws its authority from the communities of the poor. That position must attest that it is orientated towards change, towards *a different future* for those who find themselves in poverty, excluded or the victims of racism and violence. That *different future* cannot be a ghetto vision but must encompass the whole of the urban project - because that different future has implications for all that live in our cities and our urbanising world.

Urban theology must of its essence be praxis-orientated, trenchant, impatient, observant and engaged within the reality of life in those communities that for want of a better phraseology have become known as 'urban priority areas'. It must have a vision of how the future must be different and be committed to finding some of the mechanisms to make that a reality.

As the prophet said:

> The philosophers have only interpreted the world in various ways; the point is to change it.[99]

The scope of urban theology encompasses the concerns of an urbanising world and the condition of the Christian presence and witness therein. It is rooted in struggles of the poor to shape and own their communities - be it the physical environment in which they live, the civil arrangements, or the *ecclesia* which they form around the scriptures and the Eucharist.

Urban theology is a task that concerns and belongs in those communities. It is the process into which disciples bring their experience of their struggles so that through the mutual activity of perceiving, reflecting and engaging, an alternative future may emerge. Theology will inform all parts of that cyclical activity often described in its most basic form as *see-judge-act*.

Urban theology is not just the task of the theological specialist but of the whole community as theologians. Those traditionally identified as theologians - priests, ministers, lay-leaders etc. - will find themselves drawn in to resource the community - informing the process of judgement, recording the process, reflecting and discerning alongside others.

South African theologian, John De Gruchy describes the ordained minister as a practical theologian with the central tasks of discernment and leadership, enabling the community to ask, and discovering with them, 'What does God require of us there and now?'[100] Answering this question implies a commitment to struggle and participation, with the minister becoming a 'resource' for the local church. Urban Theology is theology asking that question from a particular context/location, asking that question so the future may be different.

Answering that question will involve developing what Paulo Friere calls *deep literacy*: understanding the forces and factors that shape the context, entering a dialogue with others, in similar contexts (maybe scriptural, maybe spatial), entering a dialogue with others who have an interest in that urban future (planners, urbanologists, architects etc.). Answering that question may result in a struggle with those who see the situation differently, who have a different answer. Urban theological practice and writing must involve a mutual, informed reading of the signs of the times. The communities that engage in

231

these tasks will often have knowledge that supposed experts lack, experts who view that community as the object of their profession. Urban theological practice will involve engaging with reports and policy initiatives that emanate from government and think-tanks, probably in preference to those that come from church bodies.

Informing Urban Praxis

Enabling such deep literacy among those who are shaping the urban future is the concern of the Australian writer Leonie Sandercock in her book *Towards Cosmopolis*.[101] Sandercock is concerned with the vocation and praxis of the urban planner and writes to challenge the ideological and epistemological assumptions of much planning theory and practice in cities that are undergoing rapid social and cultural change. The monolith cities of planning theory (or much of the urban theology and theory that informed *Faith in the City* fifteen years ago) have little in common with the urban populations that are emerging shaped by migration and new minorities with their multiple layers of expectation and activity. Globalization is a local, community phenomenon; the world city is not only defined by its financial and technological connections but through the diversity of its inhabitants. Pluralism poses the greatest challenge to the practice of planning, with its enlightenment and modernist assumptions, which has led to socially and ethnically polarised cities where planning is primarily capital led, concerned with grandiose projects. Sandercock criticises the false assumption that either planning or architecture can be practised from a politically neutral standpoint way above these concerns; and declares the need for planning theory to be informed by the struggles and aspirations of ordinary urban people alongside the new possibilities provoked by post-modernism, feminism and post-colonialism.

Sandercock dissects the attempts of planning theory to impose and define the spirit of urban communities from the top-down, with appeals to ill-defined notions of 'public interest' and 'civic welfare'. The demands for new types of space on a human scale must force a re-assessment of how planning and architecture are discussed and exercised. Urban space must be negotiated through layers of economics, culture, religion and identity. In the new city the planner's work must be informed by a new literacy based on the willingness to learn, listen and dialogue with the communities whose lives are being moulded. In the end, however, it will be those subjects who must shape the cities of the future.

The human dimension of the global city is where people can learn to live with each other, concerned with the quality of life and its sustainability, where negotiation plays a full part in the process of transformation. Those negotiations must recognise the difference in and draw on the richness of those layers if the city is to have a future, if it is to move towards *cosmopolis*.

Cosmopolis is 'a post-modern Utopia…a construction site of the mind, a city/region in which there is genuine connection with, and respect and space for the cultural Other, and the possibility of working together on matters of common destiny, a recognition of intertwined fates.'[102] Her vision of *cosmopolis* offers possibility to the planner, demanding a paradigmatic shift away from the assumptions of the modernist city towards alternative epistemologies found in communities of diversity, struggle and hope.

> Local communities have grounded experiential, intuitive contextual knowledges which are often more manifested in stories, songs, visual images and speech than in typical planning sources. Insurgent planners need to learn and practise these in other ways.[103]

For planning to be ethical 'the public interest' must be deconstructed and replaced by Sandercock's new paradigm of negotiation, practised with discretion and imagination.

Theologically there is obviously common ground between Sandercock's vision of *Cosmopolis* and the biblical concepts of *koinonia* (solidarity/participation) and (to use what remains a problematic patriarchal phrase) *the kingdom*. Both are concerned with the practice of new, defiant patterns of social relationships that draw on the ideal-already-but-not-yet. That is 'on earth, as is in heaven'. As with *Cosmopolis* we are dealing with that which 'can never be realised, but must always be in the making'.[104] These notions demand an inclusivity in the communities that are initiated, an affirmation of those excluded by other communities and a reordering of resources. Utopian? Yes, but with feet firmly on the ground.

This is all mediated and sustained in what liberation theologians have taught us is *praxis*, where experience and theory, reflection and action combine, are subject to the critique of marginal communities for whom change is a matter of life for death. *Praxis* demands an ideological underpinning, matched by personal commitment. For example, put the words of the Argentine philosopher-theologian Enrique Dussel alongside the vision that emerges from Sandercock:

> Praxis is the actualisation of proximity, of the experience of being proximate, for one's neighbour. Praxis is the experience of constructing the other as person, as the end of my action and not as means. We are dealing with a relationship of infinite respect.[105]

Sandercock is ultimately concerned with the *praxis* of the planner, reawakening a sense of action synonymous with change. It is a matter of profession and vocation through which a new way of creating robust and sustainable urban communities must emerge. Solidarity is critical; from solidarity the critique will emerge; '…the most promising experiments in insurgent planning have involved mobilised communities forging coalitions to work for broad objectives of economic, environmental, social and cultural justice, and in the process resisting, engaging with and participating in the state.'[106]

Sandercock's passion and conviction about how cities are and what they might become come through clearly. There are some omissions and at times the argument stumbles. There is still work to be done on how the economic base of the city can interact with the communities that surround and depend on it. Yet Sandercock's is an audacious challenge to all those whose professions are bound up with shaping the world's urban future - planners, architects, community workers, and urban theologians. Are the services, the solidarity and the critiques we offer really concerned with the possibility of community and hope in such new and dynamic incarnations? Sandercock's final paragraphs sets the agenda:

> I dream of a city in which action is synonymous with change, where social justice is more prized than law and order, where I have a right to my surroundings and so do my fellow-citizens; where we don't exist for the city but are wooed by it; where only after consultation with us could decisions be made about our neighbourhoods; where scarcity does not build a barbed-wire fence around our carefully guarded inequalities; where no one flaunts their authority and no one is without authority; where I do not have to translate my 'expertise' into jargon to impress officials and confuse citizens. (...) I want a city where my profession contributes to all of (this)....where city planning is a war of liberation fought against dumb, featureless public space as well as the multiple sources of oppression and domination and exploitation and violence; where citizens wrest from space new possibilities, and immerse themselves in their cultures while respecting those of their neighbours, and collectively forging new hybrid cultures and spaces.[107]

Could we want less as theologians?

Addressing the diversity we encounter in urban society must challenge the way our theology negotiates and speaks alongside and within the diverse, competing, conflicting cultural claims on the future. The Catholic writer Robert Schreiter considers this to be a

235

primary task in the creation of a European contextual theology. The future that theology struggles for must involve an equitable access to the basic means of human life – housing, employment, education, medical care; accompanied by recognition of diversity, respect of difference and the creation of meeting points for co-operation and communication.[108] Like Sandercock he considers the lucidity of process to be a key factor – 'theology must in all forms be intelligible to its communities, but also in forms commensurate with how meaning is being shaped in contemporary society'.[109] To be appropriate to the new locally diverse and globally connected society that is emerging, theology must develop a base that includes among its tasks the creation of 'a utopian horizon for cultural inclusion and transformation.'[110]

Although not solely addressing the issues of urban settlements, Schreiter's challenge is to engage with the processes, movements and policy trends that are shaping our national and regional future. It is to bring into the communal arena a vision that goes beyond self-interest and advocates those who have no voice as the location of power, a vision drawn from the negotiated and remoulded space of urban communities. Regeneration initiatives will be a critical arena for engagement as they are often not the good news for the poor, particularly those from excluded minorities, they claim to be, but are rather orientated to the needs of local governments and developers. Imagining a different city, a different future, will mean that we have to engage with the epistemological assumptions of those who are in the vanguard of urban and social policy.

There is a need to rediscover the potential of urban life, its vibrancy, diversity and conviviality the possibility of interaction and community. Those engaged in urban theology must be active in the laying the foundations of new communities built on the people's visions[111] as part of the healing, redeeming and transformation of our neighbourhoods and cities, and our urbanising, globalising world.

So what might envisioning a different urban future mean in Britain at the end of the 20th century? What forms of change might we engage in - and which should we stand against?

Seeing the Future Differently
At the end of June 1999 the Urban Task Force, set up by the Deputy Prime Minister and chaired by Lord Rogers, produced their final report entitled *Towards an Urban Renaissance.*[112] In its report the Task Force attempts to look at how urban decline might be halted through design, the use of derelict land and strategies for a sustainable urban environment. By identifying the strengths and positive side of urban living the Task Force hopes to identify the strategies through which urban living can attract people back to the cities as places of environmental quality and vibrancy, that are well managed and economically viable.

There is much in the report's pages that achieves those aims and should be the cause for excitement among those who desire the renewal of our urban areas. Design, planning, and land reclamation do need the types of incentive envisaged by the recommendations. The establishment of an Urban Renaissance Fund and the designation of 'Urban Priority Areas' (the Church of England should have copyrighted that phrase after *Faith in the City*!) hold great promise if they are to be part of the forthcoming DETR urban white paper. But there are also gaps in this vision, blindspots that maybe indicate the haste with which the report has been conceived and published.

The challenge to consider the issues facing different groups of people who make up the urban populace[113] is not addressed in the final report. Are there assumptions here about the population that is to be attracted back to urban living that remain unstated? Elsewhere in the report there seems to be a complete absence of a recognisable human dimension to the cityscape in the diversity and activity that most city dwellers experience on a daily basis.

Although there is much about cities as cultural powerhouses, nowhere in the report do we encounter ethnic and cultural diversity as a major contributing factor to the positive side of life in major cities. The independent study commissioned by the Task Force, *But would you live there? Shaping attitudes to urban living*[114] leads the way on this. The importance of community, identity and soul were stressed as important elements in making areas attractive to live in, though the examples given - Lavender Hill, Camden Market, Bristol's Clifton - are not the places of strong multi-cultural identity. Similarly there is nothing about the social exclusion and racism that many minority communities experience, which is very much part of their negative experience of the urban environment. I would include in this criticism the failure to draw on the well-documented struggles of minority communities to engage in urban renewal through housing associations, SRB and local economic strategies. To ignore the diverse nature of our major cities can only imply a limitation of concern and vision for the future of our urban areas. There is nothing in the Task Force's report about the negotiated nature of urban space, the multi-layered nature of a place's identity and soul, or about the human cost of regeneration.

For example, you will not find the Elephant and Castle in the Task Force report. For many years now the Elephant has been a by-word for the failure of urban development sixties style. It constitutes a shopping centre that lurches from sludge green to pink to red, vacant government offices, a scary maze of subways and the larger slab blocks of housing on the New Kent Road. A recent *Guardian* article spoke of 'a brave new plan to put the heart back into London's dreariest intersection' with Southwark Borough's Director of Regeneration looking forward to a 'new landmark in urban and environmentally friendly design: a development that could be seen as exemplary, world wide'.[115] Yes, one has to admit that the area fails in many ways, but like the Urban Task Force if one only looks for design failure one is missing what is happening in the human dimension of our cities. Stop at the Elephant, even dare to park your car, and walk through the doors of the shopping centre. At first you may be struck by the limitations of size compared to more recently designed malls. But walk further in and you discover a lesson in globalisation and minority community enterprise. A Latin American café, accompanied by a number of stalls, make the first floor a key meeting place for a community that came to London as refugees in the mid-seventies. Alongside you will find a sari shop, a West Indian building society, a West African Pentecostal bookshop, a black newspaper office, a Turkish Bank. In the market that occupies the centre forecourt you will find a Nigerian snack bar, a diversity of music stalls, hair and cosmetic products, and distinctive foods. These businesses serving the disparate population that lives within walking distance or passes through this transport hub on its way to other parts of South East London make the Elephant a global intersection. Maybe the most significant spaces in the centre are those taken by the new communications businesses offering low cost telephone calls around the globe, fax and e-mail facilities, as well as cheap flights, ensuring that at least some of the benefits of globalisation are open to those excluded from its other manifestations. As a cultural intersection the Elephant works. There may be questions about the economic sustainability of the space these businesses occupy, but no design thresholds or planning incentives could have provided the space in which this activity has emerged. All of this is a far cry from the cultural identities represented by the likes of Camden Market. The inevitable regeneration of the Elephant will disperse this unplanned enterprise, which may, or may not, remerge in another failing business quarter waiting 'regeneration'.

To use the Elephant as a parable of the multi-layered processes we encounter in the contemporary city poses critical questions concerning the assumptions of the Task Force's work. Is it possible to reshape and repopulate our urban areas solely by the imposition of planning, management and environmental controls? What other forces are at work - in residential areas, as well as commercial environments like the Elephant? Does the Task Force provide an adequate critique of the visions and movements that conceived the design of the Elephant and numerous other prize-winning developments of its time? Or does it succumb to the same assumptions? What is to be learnt from the way in which the urban population has expropriated and reshaped such space for its own ends? In *Justice, Nature and the Geographies of Difference*, David Harvey writes:

> The difficulty with so-called "high-modernism" and the city was not its "totalling" vision, but its persistent habit of privileging things and spatial forms over social processes. It presumed that social engineering could be accomplished through the engineering of physical forms.[116]

The Task Force does seem to dismiss genuine observation and analysis, it has little to say about involving citizens in the reimagination of our urban areas. The European and North American examples which are cited are not placed in the wider economic and social contexts of those societies or of the global movements that contribute to urbanisation. David Harvey again:

> ...urbanisation [is] a process (or more accurately, a multiplicity of processes) producing a distinctive mix of spatialised permanences in relation to each other. The idea that a thing called the city has causal powers in relation to social life is untenable. Yet the material embeddedness of spatial structures created in the course of urbanisation are in persistent tension with the fluidity of social processes such as capital accumulation and social reproduction.[117]

It would be wrong to suggest that the Task Force report pursues solely a civic realm of lottery funding, bureaucracy, cafes and loft-conversions. The acknowledgement that sustainable development in suburban communities and small towns is as much part of urban policy as the traditionally targeted decay of the inner-city is vital. But there is another significant population group that the report fails. The

240

imbalance in the Task Force's emphasis on the centres of cities from the perspectives of both design and population leaves many estate dwellers out in the cold. Outer estates have distinctive characteristics and needs, and cannot be grouped with the estates that overlook the inner-city skyline. A strategy for outer estates is critical if the *urban renaissance* is to impact on all areas of urban living. These estates may not be players in the greenbelt vs. brown field debate, but the residents of these areas are as entitled to collaborate in an approach to good design, management and environmental regulation as those who will return to the city centres, to the cafes and imaginatively designed townscapes.

Citizenship, which the current government seems so keen on, implies participation in the destiny of our cities. Urban living must be negotiated and a framework for that developed. Yet in areas of social and economic disadvantage, local consultation is given hardly a passing nod. The report fails to identify how those who have previously been excluded from imagining the future of their home area can be involved as key stakeholders. Making urban living an attractive option must involve working with those who know the positive and negative through daily experience. Similarly the report fails to consider the cost of regeneration to the individual and community. Upgrading an area has social consequences, as established residents find themselves squeezed out with property prices accelerating, and local amenities and services adapt themselves to higher income groups, as the current home price boom in London is proving.[118]

Those responsible for conceiving the Urban White Paper and for taking its recommendations further must look beyond the well designed facades of the riverside to the people who make up the diverse communities in their shadow, and the marginalised estates beyond them, if they are to develop a vision for an *urban renaissance* that offers possibility of inclusion, participation, identity and soul in our urban areas.

A Theology That Will Engage

It is quickly apparent that the rhetoric of urban planning and policy is littered with theological concepts and phrases. Alongside Sandercock's visionary discourse we can place talk about regeneration, renewal and renaissance. All this seems fine until one looks at how these terms are used across a broad stretch of opinion.

Regeneration may be associated with radical notions of social justice and ecological sustainability, the hope of new forms of community. But as Rob Furbey, from Sheffield Hallam University, reminds us, regeneration came to the fore of urban thinking through a radical-right wing agenda, with its appeal to individualistic understandings of Christianity.[119] Margaret Thatcher said in 1988: 'We can only build a responsible, independent community with responsible independent people'.[120]   Just as in certain forms of evangelical religion regeneration in British cities was needed because there are those who are unregenerate and unrenewed. I'm afraid that there are ideological strands within New Labour's approach to urban policy that are firmly rooted in this. (A similar view stands behind the rhetoric of social exclusion where the responsibility for exclusion is placed firmly on the excluded themselves.) The vision that is offered is always the only option. There is little room for negotiation, for compatibility, adaptability or accommodation. Dissension or difference are not options.

Spatial coercion is a strong biblical theme. Exile, dislocation and exclusion are critical experiences from which the people of God seek liberation, not regeneration or inclusion. The importance of place that can be shaped, trusted and storied is an essential part of the Biblical tradition's preoccupation with land and belonging. Space becomes place only when there are stories and hopes lodged there. The experience of exile and captivity is the experience of coerced space in contrast with trusted place.[121] Liberation happens when access to the resources and process through which belonging becomes a relationship with the place, rather than with social or political forces that enslave, impoverish, or debilitate.

Theological engagement with the greater urban debates should lead us to instigate new approaches to our urban environments that will give all residents a sense of home; a stake in its future, as they begin to control to their own destiny; a sense of safety; a sense of trust, in those who have been traditionally portrayed as experts - in planning, architecture, social policy, community development; (this applies also to the Church); a sense that they are part of and can contribute to the shaping of the future as equal partners, not as junior partners at a token consultation, or because they have been included or regenerated on someone else's terms.

If we take seriously our dialogue with others concerned with the issues raised concerning the shaping of our urban areas, I believe we will find a possibility for a truly *negotiated settlement,* which draws on the human resources -experience, hopes, aspirations, energy- that are located in the life of urban communities. Beyond the physical environment, we must be aware that local urban change is interconnected by the social, technological and economic changes that are global processes. As we address the realities of the local context we must not be afraid to seek their connectivity with complex issues and systems as we find ourselves in new, often bewildering territory. To engage with and shape our urban future(s), it is our responsibility as Christian disciples to be laying the foundations of urban theological practice that is aware and adequate for the task to which we are called.

A revised and expanded version of this material is published in *Urban Christianity and Global Order (SPCK 2001).*

Chapter 18

Michael Northcott

The Word In Space: The Body Of Christ As The True Urban Form Which Overcomes Exclusion

Introduction

Twenty years ago the Archbishop of Canterbury's Commission on Urban Priority Areas were asked to deliberate on the kinds of theology that emerged from the churches' presence in the city. Although they had much to say about the social and economic conditions of the cities of Britain and the 1980s, and about the church in the ordering of its ministry in urban priority areas, when it came to theology they took the view that systemisation was not possible. There were so many local theologies in the city that they felt that they could not do justice to the diversity by writing a theology of the city. When he invited me to participate in this series of seminars Peter Francis suggested that I attempt to systematise some crucial themes in urban theology and I'm glad he did.

I understand the meaning of system as applied to theology in a particular way, and a way which is informed by interaction with reflection upon urban society in the human sciences. The secular disciplines conceive of the urban form in holistic and systemic terms. Murray Bookchin for example views the city as an ecosystem, a class system, an economic system and a social system.[122] For Bookchin the dilemmas of the modern city and in particular the alienation between the ghetto and the suburb, are the consequence of bad practises such as long-distance commuting in private cars and modern urban planning. The practices are bad because they lack an adequate ethical account of the nature of human community. If the city is to be more than a function of an economic system then, Bookchin suggests, we need to reformulate the systems which make up the modern city around the abiding qualities of human association and the human spirit, and in particular the need for community.

Like Bookchin, Jane Jacobs was concerned that the outcomes of economic, bureaucratic and political processes in urban life had resulted in the death of the modern city.[123] She contrasts the trafficked and alienated throughways and impersonal canyons of modern cityscapes with the more urbane people-sized city streets of predecessor eras. She reminds us that the city is made for people, not people for the city. People, local people, are the best governors, creators and designers of city neighbourhoods. She also perceives how city streets where the residents' eyes are on the street are much safer than streets where the eyes are in the air in apartment blocks. The human element in design is something that city planners are only now recovering as an important feature of crime prevention and making cities safer for their residents.

While Jacobs and Bookchin both suggest the imperative of refocusing the design of cities upon human community and the nature of persons, neither can name the origins of the secular reversal of people and urban form which characterises the modern city because both work within the canons of atheist modernity. Philip Bond identifies the problem of modern aesthetics and design as a theological problem at root. The move towards concentration on form in modern art, which is also reflected in modern architecture and urban design, is indicative of the loss of a belief that the reality of nature is a meaningful *given* which human representation in art and the built environment reflects and to which it responds: 'the actuality of the world is stripped of any integral goodness, beauty or truth that it might once have been thought to disclose, because for this era *what* is does not convey what should be and what should not'.[124] The demise of the Christian vision of the world as divine *creation* sustains a break between the real and the ideal, the material and the moral. And this break informs modern art and design such that the modern aesthetic is devoted to representation of the forms of human perception and reason rather than the divinely given and sustained natural order which informed art and the design of the built environment, including particular medieval cities, in predecessor eras. The alienation between the fragile and personal shape of human bodies and human communities – their natural created character – and the built environment of the modern city is thus a physical representation of the modern denial of God and the atheist attempt to generate material reality from an entirely immanentist foundation.[125]

The extent to which the modern metropolis and its economic systems is a locus of growing and destructive maldistribution of the gifts of God's good creation may also be read in the light of the substitution of the demise of transcendence, understood both aesthetically and morally, and the turn to immanence in modern social order. The alienation between the metropolitan economy, its urban material forms, and the ecological systems of the earth can be explained in the same way. The authoritative sages of modernity – Hobbes, Hume, Locke – discounted the possibility that the prior order of nature had any moral or transcendent significance, and modern industrial societies are constituted by systems of production, exchange and consumption which fracture and fragment solidarity and sociality in human communities of place, and which endanger the very physical structure of the world on which human flourishing ultimately depends. This is nowhere more evident than in the degraded environments in which most low-income communities are located in the world's cities.[126]

In this essay I propose that the social and ecological alienations of the modern metropolis can only convincingly be challenged and superseded by a reappropriation of the meaning of Incarnation in the Christian tradition. The foundational claim of this tradition is that in the Incarnation of the Word in the space and time of creation the God who made the world has vindicated its promise as the gift of a loving God who wills its good. The material condition of life after the redemptive Incarnation, Crucifixion and Resurrection of Christ therefore involves participation in the love of God, and this recognition is central to a Christian theological reversal of modernity's divorce between the material and the moral. This recognition also provides a theological framework for the reconnection of the aesthetic, ecological and economic shape of urban life with the Christian attempt to recover the spiritual significance of ethical life in communities characterised by justice and love.[127]

Space and Alienation in the Medieval and the Modern City

Ever since Jesus Christ wryly observed that "foxes have holes and birds their nests but the Son of Man has nowhere to lay his head" (Matt 8: 20) Christians have had an ambiguous relationship to place: as the writer to the Hebrews put it "Here we have no continuing city" (Heb 13: 14). The first worshipping spaces of Christians were rooms, often knocked together, in private houses rather than consecrated buildings, and although the Jewish Christians were settled in one place, the mission to the Gentiles was conducted by the restless St Paul whose biography as the Gentile Apostle is one of continuous and arduous journeying. Christians came to consecrate buildings, and even basilicas after the conversion of Constantine. But these acts of consecration are ambiguous, for Christians believe that God is 'everywhere' and that in the light of the Incarnation of Jesus Christ within creaturely space and time, all space, and all time, are consecrated, in continuous relationship with the Creator who is known in the form of the Incarnate Word.

Richard Sennett argues that this sense of 'spiritual dislocation and homelessness' undergoes a transformation in the theology of St Augustine, and in particular in his vision of the earthly and heavenly cities set forth in his City of God.[128] Augustine's vision of the inner life is opposed in certain crucial respects, Sennett suggests, to the life of the senses such that sense experience, and the outer world of action, are unreliable as pathways to God without the correcting light of *theoria*, of seeing with the inner eye of conscience and the Spirit. Sennett sees this inner-outer dualism as the source of 'the Christian's tragedy' for although experience of the outer world of physicality, bodies and sense perception is necessary for faith, only the light of inward spiritual experience can enable the Christian to interpret sense experience truthfully: "the very act of believing would deprive a person of the ability to make sense of the scenes of life outside".[129]

Sennett suggests that his division between inner and outer, explains the shape of medieval Christian cities such as Seville and Canterbury. These cities were designed as places of sanctuary and shelter but they also presented a sharp distinction between the chaos and violence of the life of the street and the immense solidarity, clarity, complexity and beauty of the cathedral and its environs. In the medieval city secular space is marked by disorder, both physical and moral: the jumble of buildings, the labyrinth of streets is a 'secular zone' in which neither charity nor order may be found. In the sanctuary on the other hand the sacred centre of the city takes refined form, 'the place where the Word ruled'.[130] In the Cathedral the senses may be trusted to lead the eye through the cruciform shape of the building and the ascending tiers and arches of the Gothic interior to the very bottom of heaven. But, Sennett suggests, this making of sacred space from profane left the rest of the city to the primal forces of greed and violence, a place of 'moral amnesia' and this dualism between inner and outer marks Western urbanism to this day.

In the work of Walter Benjamin we find a more materialist account of alienation between interior and exterior in the modern city. In his monumental *Arcades Project* Benjamin finds that the theological interiority achieved by the medieval cathedral cities is refocused in the aesthetic of the modern city on the domestic interior.[131] The nineteenth and twentieth century bourgeois interior is a new and distinctive place in urban civility where individuals and families fashion an escape, a refuge, from the city of machines, of manipulation and of the masses. The domestic interior is marked by collections of significant objects and becomes a place of escape from the brutal and anonymous exterior of the industrial commodity form. The interior is also marked by a private morality – a morality of face to face relations, of nurture, care and civility – which is different from

248

the morality of contract, consumerism and capitalism which mark the public spaces of the modern urban form. Benjamin reads interior decency as the refusal of justice in the public space, and interior design as pointing to the home as place of display for the objects of the collector, the *flaneur* who is captivated by the fetishised commodities purveyed in the glass arcades – the precursors to the modern malls – in the nineteenth century cities of Brussels, Paris, Leeds or Manchester, but who does not see their origins in the suffering of the controlled masses and of the colonial peoples whose lands and labour are fuel to industrial accumulation and consumption. For Benjamin this focus on the interior, on order and control, the arrangement of objects of production in the Arcades and in domestic interiors contributes to the reproduction of the exterior as empty space, where space expresses a relational and moral vacuum as in the wide boulevards of Paris. In this symbiotic relationship of interior and exterior in nineteenth century Paris, Benjamin saw the reproduction of the alienation which is intrinsic to the division of labour and the class system which marred, and still mar, the social experience of the modern city.

When we revisit the earliest forms of urban theology in Britain, in the light of Benjamin's reading of the alienation between inner and outer in the nineteenth century city, we find a rendition of precisely this division in the life stories of the early Christian socialists. John Ruskin and William Morris resisted the brutality and ugliness of the modern industrial city because they saw the exclusion of beauty and truth as an offence *both* against transcendence, or what Sennett calls interiority, and against humanity in the form of working people, idealised by both Ruskin and Morris as rural artisans who had been excluded from their ancestral villages and common lands, and corralled in urban slums, workshops and factories. Their loss of economic independence accompanies the loss of craft skills and aesthetic sensibility, their participation in industrial manufacture reduced to alienating service to the machine. Seen in this light Morris's attempt to reform the aesthetic of urban living is much more significant than its bourgeois outcome of interior design for wealthy churches and homeowners. Morris tried to put into effect in his workshops his belief that ugliness reduces the dignity of those upon whom it is imposed because it also rejects the sublime in the order of nature as refracted in the skill of the craftsman in transforming natural materials into useful and beautiful objects.[132] Ruskin was to describe the theological significance of the consequent turn to the domestic interior, the home, as follows:

> This is the nature of home – it is the place of peace: the shelter, not only from injury, but from all terror, doubt and division. In so far as it is not this, it is not home; so far as the anxieties of the outer life penetrate into it, and the inconsistently-minded, unloved, or hostile society of the outer world is allowed by either husband or wife to cross the threshold it ceases to be a home; it is then only part of the outer world which you have roofed over and lighted fire in. But so far as it is a sacred place, a vestal temple, a temple of the hearth … it is a home.[133]

As J. K. Galbraith contends, this quest for domestic sanctuary in the midst of public squalor and social injustice is redoubled in the post-industrial cities of Britain and North America.[134] In Britain the urban rat population has increased tenfold with the privatisation of drains and water, beggars and litter jostle in doorways and subway stations while people avert their eyes from the disorder of public spaces on their journeys from their increasingly over-designed homes to constantly made-over office, restaurant and retail interiors. The designed interior cannot redeem the inequality and social exclusion fostered by the corporate and governmental embrace of the borderless global economy. Indeed, as Sennett suggests, the "perverse consequences of the search for refuge in secular society" are "an increase in isolation and in inequality".[135]

Faced with the aesthetic duality of spiritual or moral interior and functional and amoral exterior in the post-modern city, and the material exclusion which is the economic basis of this dualism, a

250

theological aesthetic offers a crucial corrective, for it presents the relation of material and spiritual as something which is intrinsic to being, and which is rescued from Fallenness and futility in the Incarnation and Resurrection of Christ. Whereas Sennett suggests Christian orthodoxy is an inherently tragic ideology which sets up a necessary duality between inward and outward, a fully Incarnational orthodoxy posits the redemption of the material created forms of matter and of human bodies viewed in the light of the redeeming Word made flesh in material space and cosmic time. An orthodox theological critique of the aesthetic of the modern city will however need to challenge the divide in theology between the inner world of conscience, religious experience and love between persons, and the outer world of contract, of industrialism, of usury which liberal Christian ethics designated as an intermediate realm where Christians must balance justice with power and love with influence. In a post-liberal and orthodox perspective, the abuse of power, the systematic domination and exclusion of one social group by another, and the aesthetic forms in which these problems are writ large in modern cities, may be described as the outcomes of idolatry, and in particular of the sovereignty in modern thought and modern social forms of disembodied reason, and hence of that which is not God, and not worthy of worship.[136] Viewed in this light, the extensive social exclusion which emanates from structural unemployment and the low-waged McDonaldised labour markets of what are sometimes called 'post-industrial' societies may be seen as the inevitable outcome of the devotion of arcades, malls and production systems to the fetishism of commodities and luxury; as Benjamin so powerfully put it, the "ennoblement of technological artifice through the aesthetics of fashion and style achieves a spiritual dominance in the institutions of the modern urbanite".[137]

The roots of the alienating economic functionalism of public spaces in the modern city, and of social exclusion which is its most tragic aspect, are then theological and spiritual in essence. The turn of European civilisation after the Renaissance towards immanent forms of sovereignty, and the attempted recovery of classical patrician architecture and landscape to valorise them, eventuated in the internal colonial conquest of the peasantry, their associations and their common lands, a process which Britain embraced with greater rigor than any other nation. The British people have been the longest urbanised of any nation but the distance between the Enclosures and the Clearances and the present day does not erase those acts of violence and injustice by which self-sufficient rural communities were evicted and either criminalised as homeless or disciplined as factory workers or as the poor of the parish, by cash greedy and self-styles 'aristocrats' and their representatives in Parliament. Centuries after the Enclosures Britain retains one of the most unequal patterns of land distribution of any nation, developed or developing, and the corralling of the 'excluded' into polluted and ugly urban estates, and the walled enclosures of large country houses and estates, are the geographic as well as symbolic forms that social exclusion still takes.

It was against the enforced eviction of agricultural communities from their ancestral lands that the early Christian Socialists protested when they sought to reinvent the qualities of rural work and artisanship in Victorian England, and to exalt the rituals of craftsmanship over the coercive reductionism of machine minding. John Milbank argues that the thought and practices of the early Christian Socialists provide a continuing source for the critique of the coercive maldistribution of space in contemporary capitalist societies. They point us towards an understanding of what Milbank calls 'complex space', by which he means societies characterised by complex networks of intermediate groups and associations. Unlike Sennett, Milbank contends that the medieval concept of space as the body of Christ offers a radical and orthodox alternative to the modern alienation between private order and social immorality:

> The church as a whole was not an enclosed, defensible realm like the antique *polis*, but in its unity with the heavenly city and Christ its head, infinitely surpassed the scope of the state, and the grasp of human reason. At the same time, what was fundamentally the same excess

could be glimpsed in the single person and the Christian association (monastery or guild) whose activities are legitimised by the quest for salvation, not by human law.[138]

Milbank reconnects spatial aesthetics with the Christian Socialist understanding of justice. In contrast to Sennett's claim that alienated space is the intrinsic outcome of the Christian and Augustinian understanding of secular and sacred space, Milbank sees the alienating spaces and social exclusions of modernity as the connected consequences of the attack on associations, including religious associations, which the emergent nation states of Europe sustained in the pursuit of the Enlightenment ideal of the liberty of the sovereign individual and the fraternity and equality of which the State, and not religion, was the true guarantor.[139] The Enlightenment fostered the concept of 'simple space' in which both the sacred and the associational are marginalised. Simple space is open on the one hand to domination and coercion by the state and the private corporation and, on the other hand, simple space sustains the private morality of the individual as consumer, as home-builder, as lover, friend or parent. 'Complex space' offers a more integrative understanding of being which rests upon the relation of God to the material in the Incarnate Word, and upon the gift of the social as the body of Christ which is the spiritual form of the church after the Ascension. In the body of Christ, polarisations between inner and outer, individual and corporation, love and fairness, are potentially overcome. Socialist and market-orientated societies both stand in need of judgement and completion by a social Christology which sees the incarnation as creating new possibilities for social space against both the private individualism and the coercive public corporatism of modernity. And social Christology at the same time provides an aesthetic as well as an ethical critique of the maldistribution and the maldesign of space in the modern city:

> Without 'community', without its self-sustaining affirmation of objective justice, 'excellence', and

253

transcendental truth, goodness and beauty, one must remain resigned to capitalism and bureaucracy. This, I think, has often been a socialist (less frequently a Communist) claim and it is clearly an inherently religious one. And by that I mean that it is inescapably Platonic, Judaic and Christian.[140]

Alongside his misconstrual of the orthodox Christian inheritance, Sennett's account of the medieval city is flawed in another respect, for it lacks a description of the association and guild system through which the sacred space of the body of Christ represented by the cathedral in stone imbued the social body of the medieval city with a leaven of moral purposiveness and order. The public space beyond the cathedral was not all as immoral and barbaric as Sennett supposes, no more than the public spaces of modern cities are as just and compassionate as the post-Enlightenment story of moral progression would suggest they should be. Milbank links the medieval practice of association with an emphasis on meditation. This social enactment of mediation designated, and designates, the material and aesthetic, as well as experiential, forms of the continuing relation of God to God's creation which is both affirmed in the Incarnation and Resurrection of Jesus Christ and reconstituted in the life of the Spirit which Christians call participation in the body of Christ.

Resisting Spatial Exclusion in the Body of Christ

In the light of this Incarnational account of aesthetics, materiality and space, we may read the alienated ordering of contemporary urban space – inclusion and exclusion, public squalor and domestic order, ugly functionalist aesthetics on the street and shrines to beauty in designed interiors – as consequences of the modern project to style social forms independently of the moral, aesthetic and ecological constraints of divine wisdom as set forth in the created order. It follows that the economic and aesthetic ordering of material space in the modern city is not a matter of religious or moral indifference but, on the contrary, of central importance to Christians, churches, local

254

congregations and also to the managers of church pension funds and investments.

Sasskia Sassen and Manuel Castells have theorised the increasingly delocalised global economy and its effects on metropolitan communities in both Northern and Southern hemispheres. One of its principal consequences is that the geography of inclusion and exclusion in the global economy changes: the former colonially constructed duality of 'highly developed and less developed countries' is now a duality which occurs within both colonial and post-colonial economies:

> The intensified inequality … represents a transformation in the geography of centre and periphery. They signal that peripheralisation processes are occurring inside areas that were once conceived of as 'core' areas – whether at the global, regional or urban level … The condition of being peripheral is installed in different geographic terrains depending on the prevailing economic dynamic. We see new forms of peripheralisation at the centre of major cities in developed countries not far from some of the most expensive commercial land in the world.[141]

The move of the 'less developed' or 'dependent' economic periphery into the centre of the Western cities occasions the crisis in urban governance which is manifest in the high levels of juvenile crime in the *banlieu* of French cities and the drug addiction problems of peripheral housing areas in Edinburgh, Glasgow, Liverpool, Manchester or London, as well as those in New York, Washington DC, or Rio de Janeiro. Corporations seek to manipulate this crisis in order to extract from governments or city authorities grants and tax breaks for their decisions to locate in particular urban areas, or not to relocate elsewhere.[142] But against the corporate and academic advocates of globalisation who contend that the new global economy is essentially delocalised, Sassken argues for the continuing significance of cities as locales in the context of globalisation. They play a strategic role in globalisation as 'command points, global marketplaces, and production sites for the information economy'.[143] Large corporations cannot in fact exist apart from the urban communities that provide their informational and labour resources.

In the light of the increasing domination of the global by transnational corporations, who are therefore the principal agents of economic inclusion and exclusion, Sassken's analysis is suggestive of a new politics of regionalism which relocates governance in urban centres and in the local communities of place which make up those centres. Thus a project to recover some of the political and economic power devolved by nation states onto corporations in the last thirty years becomes central to addressing the problems of social exclusion. Narratives of social exclusion which avoid the more systematic critique of the economic character of social exclusion, of the relationship between social exclusion and capital accumulation in a global corporate economy are fundamentally flawed, untruthful, even immoral. These narratives focus on certain symptoms – high crime rates, poor housing, delinquency, inappropriate skills, labour market inflexibility – which are said to occur in particular urban communities, and which government or church funded projects can therefore alleviate or reverse. This dominant narrative of social exclusion in the United Kingdom is one which Christians must reject. Social exclusion, socially excluded communities may manifest a culture of poverty. But the social conditions which have fostered this culture are largely extraneous to the agency of the individuals and communities which manifest this culture. There is an inextricable relationship between the culture of poverty and the cult of the irresponsible, delocalised, profit-maximising, tax-evading global corporation. Politicians who speak of globalisation and its inevitability rarely refer to the principal actors in this global social process – the corporations. However the same politicians frequently speak of the agency of the poor in creating the conditions for their own exclusion.

256

The focus on individual agency, and the refusal to admit the agency of the corporation, and of governments, in constructing globalisation and its new geography of centre and periphery, inclusions and exclusion, is rooted in a false ontology according to which the individual atomised self – as student, consumer, worker, saver – is seen as the principal motive power in human societies and human destinies. As Seyla Benhabib and other feminist philosophers argue, the modern construction of the individual as solitary agent involves a refusal of the situation of the agent in material and communal networks.[144] Christian orthodoxy understands these relational networks as features of created order – spiritual, ecological and social: they are part of the given conditionality of being creatures in God's creation. Moderns imagine, and are encouraged to believe, that they construct themselves and their social and material circumstances. The global economy is a particularly problematic example of the pathological consequences of such an understanding of the human condition. Charles Leadbetter talks about the new knowledge economy as an economy which lives on 'thin air'.[145] However the people who staff call centres, the machines which they service, the electronically manipulated currency flows of the world, all these are in fact highly dependent upon the material world, and they have significant impacts upon real biophysical life communities of persons and of other species. There is no money economy or informational economy which is not also situated in the material world of fragile bodies, of limited space, of finite ecosystems.

Biblical accounts of the divine origin of the material creation point to its character as gift, and highlight the dangers of treating creation as human possession. The modern idea of absolute ownership, which was first applied in the sphere of land – much of it stolen from peasants in predecessor agrarian communities – is the economic correlate of the sovereign individual. A false ontology generates a false conception of economy. In the Old Testament social and environmental exclusion are understood as the consequences of human greed and idolatry. Isaiah explains that the Israelites are exiled from the promised land because they had rebelled against God who gave it to them, because they worshipped idols, and because they abandoned social justice and the other laws of the covenant:

> See how Yahweh lays the earth waste,
> makes it a desert, buckles its surface,
> scatters its inhabitants,
> priest and people alike, master and slave,
> mistress and maid, seller and buyer,
> lender and borrower, creditor and debtor.
> Ravaged, ravaged the earth,
> despoiled, despoiled,
> as Yahweh has said.
> The earth is mourning, withering,
> the heavens are pining away with the earth
> The earth is defiled under its inhabitants feet,
> for they have transgressed the law, violated the precept,
> broken the everlasting covenant.
> So a curse consumes the earth,
> and its inhabitants suffer their penalty,
> that is why the inhabitants of the earth are burnt up,
> and few men are left. (Isaiah 24: 1-6).

Social exclusion, and exclusion from the beneficent environment of the Promised Land are viewed as consequences of rebellion against God, of idolatry and economic injustice. Abandoning true worship, the leaders and landowners in Israel had also abandoned injunctions in the Torah which restrained inequality, banned usury and prevented slavery through the Sabbath and Jubilee laws which released people from unpayable debt.

In our own society idolatry and rebellion against God are also clearly implicated in social and environmental exclusion. This rebellion is manifest in the refusal to recognise the creation as gift of God, and the moral duty which this giftedness entails to share its fruits equitably between those now living, and to steward them carefully for those yet to be born. It is also manifest in an economy whose

258

accounting mechanisms allow its most powerful agents to discount the social and ecological costs of global production and exchange systems.[146] At the root of the practices which constitute social exclusion is a false ontology, a false conception of being. As Miroslav Volf suggests we 'colonise the life-space of others' we 'join house to house' and 'add field to field, until there is room for no-one in the land' because 'we want to be at the centre and be there alone, single-handedly controlling "the land" '.[147] In this perspective social exclusion is primarily a theological and spiritual pathology, arising from the actions of excluders and the systems they sustain and which sustain them: 'exclusion can entail cutting of the bonds that connect, taking oneself out of the pattern of interdependence and placing oneself in a position of sovereign independence'.[148]

In the time of Jesus those who were excluded were designated 'sinners', outcasts, persons who, because of their trade, ethnicity, gender, disability or disease, were considered to defile those around them. These people were cut off from the religious and social life of their contemporary Jews. If they went to the Temple they had to go when it would be empty. They could not eat at table with their fellows nor invite them into their homes. In response to this exclusion, Jesus not only challenged the false spirituality of those who did the excluding, he also embraced the sinners: 'by embracing the "outcast", Jesus underscored the "sinfulness" of the persons and systems that cast them out.'[149] The response of Jesus to exclusion was not just to name the sin of exclusion but also to rename and remake those who had been excluded, challenging the 'deadly logic of the "politics of purity"'.[150]

The Micropolitics of the Mystical Body
In the early church the logic of exclusion is challenged in the micropolitics of the body of Christ where those who are weak, or whom the world regards as dishonourable, are given a higher place (1 Cor. 12: 23), where Jew Greek, slave and free are united together by one spirit (1 Cor. 12: 13), and those who were once 'no people' become 'a chosen race, a royal priesthood' (1 Peter 2: 10). At the core

259

of the church's response to social exclusion in the first century, and in the twenty-first, is the practice of sacramental worship in which Christians are reconstituted, renamed, not as sovereign individuals or as outcasts – excluders or excluded – but as members of a community subject to the sovereignty of God. In the Eucharist Christians experience their reconstitution as members of the one body of Christ. In the Eucharist Christians rediscover the character of all created things, including that which sustains human life, as gift in the transformation of bread and wine. This *location* of the new creation, the new community, in the celebration of the Eucharist has important spatial implications. As William Cavanaugh suggests the Christian understanding of space is focused on the 'localisation of the sacred in the Eucharist host'.[151] The Eucharist and the local church together constitute 'the contemporary performance of the historical body, the unique historical event of Jesus. Christians are the *real* body of Christ and the Eucharist is where the church *mystically* comes to be.'[152]

However at various moments in the history of the church this crucial aspect of local performance is lost with the consequence that the idea of the church as the mystical body is delocalised, and its spatial and political significance – as challenge to the existing order of material and social relations and as promise of a new order – is diminished. As Cavanaugh points out, the new scholastic theology of the Mass, and of priestly authority in the late Middle Ages, reached a point where the Pope as head of the church claimed dominion over ecclesiastical property which was formerly invested in local Eucharistic communities.[153] This perverted ecclesial practice of dominion laid the foundations for coming secular assertions of the powers of *this* world in the emergence of the market economy and the nation state as the twin loci of authority and power in the modern world, and the loss of transcendence. In the last 300 years the Church of England has also undergone a process of delocalisation. This has partly come about as a consequence of the break-up of rural communities and the relocation of their populations in towns and cities. In response to this relocation much of the wealth of the rural parishes ended up in the hands of the Church Commissioners as large Rectories and Glebe

260

lands were sold off. The ecclesiastical economy in some ways then has mirrored uncritically the very processes of exclusion and accumulation which underlie and precede present-day experiences of social exclusion. In this context the creation by the Church Commissioners of a series of temples to consumerism – large shopping malls built as speculative developments by the Commissioners – in England and Scotland, such as the St Enoch Centre in Glasgow and the Metrocentre in Gateshead with funds amassed from local parishes and congregations is ironic as well as tragic. As it turned out these development projects were not managed in ways which rendered good returns. But more significantly the investment of the formerly localised wealth of the church in temples to consumer fetishism is a revealing indicator of the extent to which the modern church partners rather than critiques the idolatry and false ontology of the sovereign individual which reproduces social exclusion in the contemporary global economy. As Cavanaugh suggests:

> The unfaithfulness of the church in the present age is based to some extent precisely on its failure to take itself seriously as the continuation of Christ's body in the world and to conform itself, body and soul, not to the world but to Christ (Rom. 12: 2).[154]

In Christian history the mediated space of the local body of Christ has given rise to ecclesiastical polities and at times to public polities which express, albeit partially, the intentionality of giving space to the weak as well as to the strong. Christian Socialists have highlighted the significance of intermediate associations such as the Guilds which stood between monarch or baron and household, and between the local economy and the inter-city state trading economy. As we have seen modernity has led to the attenuation of such associations as significant political and economic agents. But the local Church when it is true to its calling to a non-status politics continues to suggest to the world the moral and theological imperative of the dispersal of social, political and economic power. This dispersal is though not u-topic in aspiration or form. While it is true that the place of the church is first and foremost its eternal home, for the church constantly receives its being as the body of Christ as the gift of God rather than as its right,[155] nonetheless the church still exists in space. The church does not simply concede space to the nation-state, nor for that matter to the global economy.[156] Nor can the church accept the distinctions between politics and religion, or between economy and culture, which are imposed by the false ontology of modernity. In the body of Christ, which is made known in the Eucharistic bread and wine, Christians find a visible sign of the suffering which Christ underwent to redeem the material world. As Cavanaugh suggests, the space of the body of Christ, constituted by the Eucharist creates:

> spaces of resistance where the Kingdom of God challenges the reality and inevitability of secular imaginations of space and time. "God shows what is low and despised in the world, things that are not, to reduce to nothing things that are" (1 Cor. 1: 28).[157]

Resistance to those processes of delocalisation which remove governance from local communities and metropolitan areas and confer it on faceless and place-less corporations will involve a more systematic critique of the consumer society and of globalisation, and their effects upon ecological and human flourishing than has hitherto been offered by mainstream churches in the West. It will also involve a reinvigoration of efforts by the church to invest in the local economy as an alternative to the global. In my essay 'A Place of Our Own' in *God in the City* I describe various ways in which local churches have been involved in efforts to reclaim land and housing and land for urban agriculture for local people in low-income urban communities.[158] Church involvement in the establishment of credit unions and of local exchange trading schemes (LETS) are indicators of alternative approaches to reinvigorating the face-to-face and local economy in our cities. And the many artistic and associational projects which have been sponsored by churches in areas of social exclusion, often with the support of the Church Urban Fund, witness to the continuing mission of the church to sustain other than economic forms of human flourishing both aesthetic and associational.

If the Church is truly to challenge exclusion however, it must also, as Volf suggests, be a place where excluded *embrace* the excluders and excluders the excluded. Exclusion is, as we have already recognised, a function of agency, individual as well as social, and it rests in a false, that is sinful, ontology of the sovereign individual, whether the individual person, or the collective personhood of the nation state, the corporation, or the global market. Volf makes the extraordinary claim that 'the will to embrace the unjust precedes agreement on justice'[159] and exemplifies this claim in an examination of the injustice described in the third chapter of the book of Acts whereby the widows of the Hellenist Christians were not being cared for as the widows of the Jewish Christians. The Apostles resolved the problem by setting apart Hellenist Christians to perform the community's care to both Hellenist *and* Jewish widows. As Volf comments:

> Representatives of the injured party have been appointed to take care of *all* the widows, their own as well as those of the injuring party. Justice was to be pursued by inverting perspectives and seeing the problem through the eyes of the wronged.[160]

If churches in Britain are genuinely to challenge social exclusion by seeing it 'through the eyes of the wronged', they not only have to ensure that their own investments, pension funds, buildings and internal organisational structures promote local ownership, local control, local community over the global. Their constituent congregations also have to find ways to enable and encourage their members to bridge the divide between excluded and excluders, a divide increasingly expressed not as hate but as indifference in a global economy in which unskilled, under-educated people are not so much under-rewarded as redundant. The typical metropolitan

Anglican Deanery or Methodist circuit often carries within it the kind of extreme social and economic divides which mar contemporary urban Britain. Such organisational units, or their ecumenical equivalents, are the obvious place for genuine dialogue, inter-communion, and solidarity to be established between excluders and excluded. A new focus on this kind of dialogue in which the spiritual disease of exclusion is faced on the part of both excluders as well as excluded would be a powerful witness to a genuinely spiritual approach to the roots of the problem, and an effective means of resisting the force of governmental rhetoric about the agency of the excluded.

It was an unfortunate irony of the Archbishop's Commission Report on Urban Priority Areas that having lamented the polyphony of theologies which its members encountered in the city, they failed to see the extent to which the criticism of modern capitalism in its metropolitan form entails a spiritual and theological critique of the conditions, structures and processes of the modern economy which give rise to the maldistribution of the riches of God's creation. The early Christian Socialists, particularly those who were of an Anglican persuasion attested to the Incarnational significance of the material conditions of life in the modern economy. Despite the rhetoric of the information economy, the condition of the excluded, the 'underclass', in Britain today requires an equally vigorous appropriation of the tradition of Incarnational social thought, and of its implications for aesthetics, economics, and community. St Paul recognised that it was the rich who threatened the integrity of the Eucharist when they ate their fill while the poor remained hungry in the church at Corinth (I Cor. 11). The Apostle demanded that the offenders themselves were excluded until such time as they changed the conduct. As Cavanaugh suggests, St Paul's approach means that Eucharistic worship involves a discipline; 'discerning the body' means discerning judgement, naming sin as well as performing reconciliation.[161] In this perspective the parish Eucharist can never be a civic ceremony in the divided cities of Britain but must rather be construed as the 're-membering' of the body of Christ Incarnate in the church, in resistance to the exclusions of the secular.

Chapter 19

Ian K. Duffield

Urban Theology: Location, Vocation, Action

For the last eighteen years I have been involved with what might be called advanced training of ministerial practitioners. The degrees of Master and Doctor of Ministry are postgraduate research programmes with a focus on practice. These programmes have been pioneered in the UK by the Urban Theology Unit in Sheffield, initially through its relationship with New York Theological Seminary and then under the auspices of the University of Sheffield. It has been a fascinating experience - as a fellow practising minister - to mentor, tutor, and supervise a wide range of people in this programme: lay and ordained, male and female, parish and non-parish based, belonging to a range of churches wider than the word ecumenical normally conveys.

The programme begins with each person analysing carefully their own particular ministerial location (from a small neighbourhood to an area reflecting district or national responsibilities) with a group of selected 'local' people. The facts are important, and candidates on the programme are encouraged to investigate their reality thoroughly through both formal and informal methods. Alongside this, candidates are encouraged to reflect with their people on possible biblical resonances or parallels with their situation. What emerges is that each person's situation is unique, even if it betrays clear similarities to other situations both present and past. Normally, the invitation to identify imaginatively with the biblical text is found to be difficult. Perseverance, however, can produce biblical passages, themes, conflicts or personalities that can provide suggestive insights into the current situation that is being explored.

Within each person's situation, in the light of biblical work, a specific and urgent problem in ministry is identified by the candidate working with others as something to which they feel called to respond. When the problem is clearly and precisely defined it then becomes the focus for a significant practical project in ministry. This project is carefully planned with attention paid to clear strategies to achieve the change or transformation that is required. The project in ministry is undertaken according to the worked-out specification, evaluated, and written up. This then becomes the focus for further research which leads to the production of a thesis.

Although this way of doing theology cannot be regarded as easy, it provides a working model for doing theology. Such theology begins with location and seeks to discover the particular vocation of a group of believers within it. This is done through reflection on the Bible and the tradition from which people come. Some correlation between the realities of the situation and the realities of faith is investigated. If this is not to be sterile it has to become theological practice. Doing theology moves from this reflection on reality to action within the location to seek some change or transformation within the reality in the light of biblical or theological understanding. Such action (a planned project) can then be reflected upon itself. This is not dependent upon the success of a project. Furthermore, given that history changes and moves, the situation that someone is in requires continuous reflection and analysis, precisely because it refuses to stay still.

Location
From the foregoing it is clear that the key question is, 'Where is theology done?'. In other words, what is the context or location in which theological reflection takes place? This question is critical because we are so dependent upon where we stand, and who we stand with. The influence of our environment and our social world is great. So much of what gets called theology, is more truly 'white theology', or 'bourgeois theology', or 'status-quo-serving theology'. Unless someone deliberately chooses another location than that of

the suburbs, of the academy, the church, and the successful society, then theology will be in captivity to the ideals, pursuits and values which exclude so many in our society and world.[162]

Theology begins with location.[163] It is within a particular context and experience that theological reflection takes place and is moulded into shape. In Britain that dominating location is the urban, whether people live in cities or not. But it is those who live, work, and act on the raw edge of the urban reality who are in the most prestigious context for doing theology - urban theology.

The city, in our day, presents the most dangerous and creative place for theology, for it is there that the dynamics of our social system are seen most clearly. University Theology tends to sit above the city - with consequent dangers of detachment, remoteness, and sterile objectivity. Church Theology tends to sit within its own enclave - with the consequent dangers of retrenchment, aloofness, and irrelevant thinking. Urban Theology sits within and alongside the city - with the dangers of being swamped by the pressures, going with contemporary trends, and neglecting the tradition.

Urban theology cannot be done by those who will not accept the location and the dangers it poses. It is boundary theology, [164] for it is done on the boundary, on the margins of life. If we define the location more precisely, it is the boundary between rich and poor, between church and non-church, between indigenous and migrant, between employed and unemployed, between local communities and political parties, between people and bureaucracies. To say that urban theology is boundary theology is not to imply a tight-rope walking act, a fence-sitting posture, or a neutral theology. It is to say that the realities of the urban are most clearly seen in the interfaces between rich and poor, and so on. Urban theology has its location amongst the poor, the people, and local communities, although it is never submerged by them. It has to walk the boundary and face realities from their perspective, from the bottom.

Vocation

If theology begins with location, it can only continue through vocation.[165] Location by itself can be barren, although many of us can testify that vocation came to us through location - the call of God reaching us precisely because of where we were standing. Vocation describes God's grasping of us, calling us to discipleship, giving us both vision and task. Thus urban theology is no impartial reflecting on the Christian tradition, but rather a radical call from God to reflect with the people in the midst of decay and despair. Without vocation we will not shift our location to live, or work, or act with those who bear a disproportionate burden of our urban society. Without vocation we will not be able to sustain living on the boundary where such theologians can be misunderstood by everyone as 'do-gooders', meddlers', or 'betrayers'. People in the inner city and outer housing estates are rightly nervous and suspicious of urban theologians: What are such people after? Can they be trusted? When it comes to the crunch who will they stand with? What ulterior motives have they got? Are they just getting material for a book? Are they trying to fulfil some inner personal need to be needed? Any of us who dare to call ourselves urban theologians had better be clear about these matters, for poor people will suss us out, non-church people will suspect us, political activists will try to nobble us, academics will dismiss us, church leaders will be anxious about us, and our families will not understand us. Without true vocation it will all be short-lived, like that corn which grew quickly but because it had not got deep roots withered and died when the sun came out and scorched it.[166]

Reflective Thinking

If in some way we have answered the question where theology is done, we can delay no longer in tackling the question of how theology is done. The question itself suggests that theology is a process, and this is particularly true of urban theology. It is not an internal academic debate which is characteristic of University Theology, or an internal debate about church/creed/Bible as with Church Theology. No, it is a dialogue with people, place, and power.

269

In urban theology the authorities are often local people with deep knowledge of their situation, or oppressed people with specific understanding of the culture and mechanisms of oppression they face. Such theology often begins in a group of people reflecting on themselves, their lives, and their struggles. The particularity of people, the particularity of place, and the particular power issues provide basic elements for doing theology.[167] But theology does not come to fruition without reflection. This process of thinking about experience involves story-telling, detailed analysis, and exploration of external or underlying forces. As such, theology is a kind of thinking.

For such thinking to become creative rather than depressive, other elements are required in the process. So much wrong thinking takes place generally. As the Buddhist tradition reminds us, "right thinking" is a pillar of religion and life. To dwell on bad experiences or oppressive situations is to run the danger of not doing theology at all and, far worse, to engender a despairing or violent culture because of such an underlying sense of social impotence. Some so-called activists/revolutionaries seem to take this as their model. This path is not only dangerous - literally - it is also disrespectful to the people. It is fundamentally dehumanising, for it fails to engender the courage for life within each one of us, and the sense of humour which maintains life and, as spiritual writers inform us, 'keeps the devil at bay'. Urban theologians fail in their task if they limit the people's reflection to their situation, and that only in its oppressive mode. Thankfully, the humour of the people surfaces and triumphs often over such sterile approaches, or else apathy is adopted as a strategic response to such negativity.

Right thinking demands that other stories are told to off-set, or set alongside those which dominate and oppress: local stories of triumph, of successful struggles, of faithful predecessors, of humanity transcending defeat. And not just local stories. Christians have a stock of stories from their history and their writings. But there is so much within the Jewish-Christian traditions. Where do we turn? Where are the stories, themes, examples, faithful ancestors for us where we are? Where have believers faced similar struggles, syndromes, and structures?[168] What clues, or inspiration, or guidance can we find from within our corporate spiritual history? From that highly diverse group of writings we call Bible, what is the word that speaks to our social context and human condition here and now?

Action

The reflective thinking that theology is, brings together and attempts to correlate the particular situation and struggle of the people now, with the words, action, and vision of different places and other times. The purpose of such thinking is to think rightly, but not in a narrow, restrictive sense, as if it all goes on in our heads. However, an amazing amount does go on in our heads, and determines how we see situations and respond to them. And much of the ideology that we have been fed, or been socialised into, handicaps our perceptions of ourselves and others, and restricts our capacity for action. Thus to 'think rightly' is liberative and moves towards the freeing of others. Right thinking and right action belong together.

Theology which is not confined to academic or ecclesiastical circles, but is theology rooted in the urban, will always move towards action,[169] if only because it has come from action in the first place. Something has already happened, been experienced, struggled against which has led to thinking, reflection, and hence theology. Urban theology thus assists the articulation of both understanding and response to the situation. Not understanding alone, as if we can really understand something, truly become aware, and then not act. To truly understand, to be fully aware, leads to action.

Urban theology - because it takes the current situation with all its complexities, structures, and ambiguities seriously - can begin to frame relevant, practical and systemic action. Urban theology - because it takes our corporate spiritual tradition and history with all its plurality, paradigms, and visions seriously - can suggest alternative, prophetic, and sacrificial signs; and point us to spiritual

271

resources for sustaining action, living with failure, and avoiding the temptations of success. Thus urban theology is not so much written as done. It goes on whenever groups of Christians and others reflect on their situation and struggle in the light of their religious tradition, and live active and committed lives as a consequence of that reflection. Urban theology is thus a continuous activity - and will be carried on differently in each particular situation, as it takes the particularities of that place and its people seriously.

Correlation

If we look more closely at the theological method of urban theology we find that it is a method of correlation. This has similarities with the theology of Paul Tillich, although for him it is a relating of theological answers to existential questions, where the questions tend to be personal and psychological.[170] As I have written elsewhere:[171]

> For urban theology such existential concerns and questions with ultimacy are seen within a social and communal context. The deep questions are forced upon us by social pressures, political struggles, economic forces, and our experiences-in-community. Theology is dialogue between these 'life and death' problems which arise out of our social existence and the Jewish-Christian tradition to which we belong.

There is a real dialogue, where the tradition is shaped by the actual experience, and the deep questions of communal existence are articulated in the light of the tradition. Out of this process of correlation genuine Christian action is identified. This is what is expected from urban theology: theology which speaks to real situations and moves towards action to change, transform, or liberate those social situations in the light of how God has worked with the People of God in the past; theology which is reformulated and developed out of the urban experience. As such it is a form of contextual theology.

Urban Theology and Contextual Theology
At this point, it may be helpful to clarify what is meant by the expression 'urban theology' in relation to other more familiar expressions, such as contextual theology and liberation theology. What is the relationship between these terms.[172] Clarity would be helpful, otherwise confusion can abound as one person, or a variety of people, can use the same term in contrasting, if not contradictory ways.

There are many forms of theology which are designated by broad titles, such as neo-orthodox theology (e.g. Karl Barth), neo-thomist theology (e.g. Eric Mascall), process theology (e.g. John B.Cobb, Jr), modernist theology (e.g. Paul Badham). Such titles seek to describe the direction or style, so as to distinguish one form of theology from another. That is what titles do. They can only be broadly effective as there is often great debate within each form. Nevertheless, such distinctions are helpful in organising the diverse range of theological offerings.

To speak of contextual theology is to say two things, at least:

1.   all theology, every form of it, is contextual whether it recognises the fact or not;

2.   theology should be engaged in, in a deliberate contextual way.

In one sense, therefore, it is correct to say that 'all theology is contextual theology'. But if terms are to be useful and say something, this quite common statement needs to be recognised as a   three-quarters-truth. All theology may be contextual theology, but not all theology recognises itself to be contextual theology. Indeed, some forms of theology have positively proclaimed themselves to be non-contextual. More traditionally, theology has perceived itself to be mere explication of the givens of scripture and/or church tradition (whether patristics, reformation, or tridentine). Such deductive

273

approaches to theology cannot easily perceive themselves to be contextual. Hence, to advocate contextual theology is to expose such theology to its contextual, and therefore, socio-historical formation. It is to declare that theology is inevitably prejudiced, in that it serves some particular current stance or project.

When urban theologians speak of contextual theology they are more particularly referring to the open and up-front designation of theology as biased. It is advocacy of theology done - openly, explicitly, unapologetically - from a particular context and for that specific context. Contextual theology, therefore, is way of talking about *theological method.* When doing urban theology, it is important to begin with one's actual social context in all its particularity and specificity. In that sense it is a form of inductive rather than deductive theology. Hence, such theology moves beyond the mere explication of the givens of scripture and/or church tradition and seeks to dynamically relate them to the givens of specific sociocultural story, socioeconomic context, and sociopolitical history. This is a dialectical encounter.[173] In terms of theological method context is *primary,* but such context does not exist on its own. Such context, in all its mundane reality, has to be correlated with the biblical and theological tradition.[174] It may thus be more accurate to talk of 'the contextual method of theology' rather than, the more familiar, contextual theology.

Obviously, there are various explicit forms of contextual theology which adopt this basic method. In this sense, contextual theology is *prior* to urban theology, or describes the family to which urban theology may be said to belong.

To speak of urban theology is to say two things, at least:

1. urban theology is one explicit form of contextual theology which adopts that basic theological method;

2.   urban theology is the most appropriate form of contextual theology for the dominating urban context of modern Britain.

In contrast to many other forms of theology, urban theology is open and up-front in acknowledging a particular socio-historical and economic context for the doing of theology. Reflection on the realities of modern Britain, where the vast majority live either in an urban environment or are subject to an urban agenda, justify the creation and use of the phrase 'urban theology', even if it may appear uncongenial to some. To do theology in modern Britain necessitates the doing of such theology. Otherwise, theology is being attempted in a vacuum, or in some de-contextualised way. Hence, urban theology is the most appropriate form of contextual theology, here, now, in this time, in Britain. Presumably, those who speak today of postmodern theology are advocating a similar claim, in that the presumed cultural shift from a modern to a postmodern culture entails the doing of theology within that contextual situation. Whatever the usefulness of such an endeavour it appears to be secondary, in that all kinds of cultural change are part and parcel of the urban context which require analysis and understanding. In other words, any perceived cultural shift is but one part of the current context and is set within the wider frame of our urban society.

To focus on urban theology is to take seriously urban realities, and in particular the urban communities we have learnt to call 'urban priority areas'.[175] The bias of urban theology is not against the rural but towards those who suffer disproportionately the effects of urban life, i.e. those whose main social experience is that of poverty, marginalisation and, what is currently termed, social exclusion. Indeed, some of these people may live in what we term rural areas. Nevertheless, the overwhelming majority of such folk inhabit the inner city, ex-mining villages, and large outer social housing estates. These are the people who are bearing the burden of industrialisation, modernisation and, more recently, the high technological revolution. It is such people and their situation which can act as a 'window' on to the realities of the whole of our society. In other words, urban priority areas are seen to be the clue, 'the tip of the iceberg', from which it is best possible to view the whole of urban Britain. So urban theology designates a *primacy* to the people of urban priority areas and is, furthermore, at the service of praxis. In this sense, urban theology is also *'practical* theology'.

Urban Theology and Liberation Theology

To speak of urban theology is not only a particular way of doing theology but also a way of advocating priority to and activity alongside the victims of Britain's urban social project. Presumably, it would be possible to claim to be doing urban theology without such commitment and in the service of the 'engineers' and managers of social and technological 'progress'. However, if a contextual approach to theology is adopted thoroughly at the micro as well as the macro level then such a so-called urban theology would not survive the experience and realities of the poor in our society. Therefore, it is important that urban theology remains committed to contextual method. Hopefully, the distinctiveness of the designation, urban theology, assists in this. It is also important that urban theology is a committed theology and, as such, continues to have a fundamental commitment to those at the bottom of urban society, in conformity with the teaching and practice of Jesus. In terms of such a commitment and practice, urban theology may be regarded as a form of liberation theology.

To speak of liberation theology is to say two things, at least:

1.   liberation theology is a committed form of theology which makes use of the basic theological method of contextual theology, whether in Latin America, South Africa, or Asia;

2.   liberation theology is committed to the practice of liberation as the most appropriate theological form of the gospel message in the context of all those who are poor, excluded or enslaved in some way, whether amongst the

276

economically poor, women, black people or ethnic minorities.

The primary reference of liberation theology is third world contextual theology that has developed in response to the harsh realities of oppression and segregation in Latin America, South Africa, and Asia. But it is also possible to include similar developments in the first world such as, black, feminist, and womanist theology. In seeking to learn from their experience it then begins to become possible to envisage British Liberation Theology. Such a theology would, obviously, be closely related to what we have previously described as urban theology.[176] Just as urban priority areas in Britain can be seen as the best location for understanding our society and doing theology within it, so also it is possible to regard Asia, Latin America and Africa as the best location for understanding our world and doing theology within it. It thus becomes imperative to learn from their experience, to hear their perspective, to be challenged by their theological critique of our societies and our theologies. This is not to treat 'liberation theology' as a mere subject or topic for academic study alongside other historical forms of theology (as is often done in the university). It is to regard liberation theology as *the* formative theological influence in the world today, whether this is fashionable or not. Similarly, within our society it becomes important, also, to hear the voices of feminist and black theologians who are able to speak more directly to our dominant white, male, middle class setting.[177]

Contextual theology, urban theology and liberation theology, are not so much subjects to be studied as ways of understanding and doing theology as praxis. This might be termed 'practical theology', but any theology which begins by learning the deposit of faith and then seeks to 'apply' it, or moves in a straight line from theory to practice, is not a true understanding of practical theology from within the perspective of liberation theology.

Often, theology remains fundamentally deductive, whereas urban and liberation theology are primarily *inductive*. Hence, the importance that needs to be given to direct experience and learning from it. In one sense this is an 'action-reflection' model of research. Reflection on one's own practice or on social, as well as personal, experience is fundamental to contextual theology. As a method of doing theology it entails taking fundamentally seriously the actual reality in the world with which one is confronted. This requires detailed observation, statistical research, and critical analysis. As the primary datum this then becomes the subject of disciplined theological reflection. In so far as this takes place in the context of modern Britain, particularly (but not exclusively) within urban priority areas, then it may be called urban theology. In so far as it leads to theological reflection which utilises scripture and tradition in the direction of praxis on behalf of the poor and marginalised within that context it may be called liberation theology.

Perhaps it is now possible to understand how it is possible to use, and often interchange, the terms contextual theology and urban theology and liberation theology. This sequence of terms focuses the current theological task in Britain, and also the key ministerial educational task.

Theology and the Primacy of Social Location
To do urban theology is to begin self-consciously and intentionally with social location - to give it primacy in theological endeavour. Of course, the urban reality and experience is diverse. Some people's experience of the city is one of privilege and affluence; others experience solid work and community. Nevertheless, the reality of urban life is exposed by those at the bottom of the city who pay the price of the city's mode of production, who pick up the tab for the social 'organisation' of cities, and who are at the 'fag end' of globalisation.

Cities are magnets. They promise much - and by the concentration of resources enable so much to happen. Cities can be exciting places through such concentrations of power, wealth, and opportunity. However, cities inevitably fail to live up to their promise for all of their members. The social location of the city cannot be fully understood or known apart from the experience of those who become excluded from its promising, flourishing 'topping'. This is where doing urban theology begins. And this is where it ends too - or begins again!

Chapter 20

Stuart Jordan

Urban And Liberation Theologies: Towards A Dialogue

The Way In

The attempt to script a dialogue between urban and liberation theology began as a journey long before it emerged as a written exercise. For myself, Latin America, its churches and emergent theology have been a recurrent interest for many years, initially sparked by a year's teaching post in Colombia in the early 1970s and renewed by various return visits to the continent since. Meanwhile a decade of ministry among multi-racial Methodist congregations in inner London coincided with a research project on the reception of liberation theology in the UK – with the result that the concerns and insights of liberation theology and the immediate demands of urban ministry have in practice regularly been juxtaposed.

An authentic synthesis between the two, however, has always proven elusive due mainly to those factors which have often been identified as inimical to the genesis of a British liberation theology: not least the sociological profile of most British churches and the lack of any clear 'historical project'.[178] A commitment to empowering local leadership and to reclaiming the liberative elements of the biblical tradition kept the possibility of dialogue alive, but the practical discrepancies of local context and agendas were formidable. The process was further inhibited by the recurrent tendency to re-brand so many diverse activities as liberation theology, in a way which often risked blunting the latter's most distinctive critical functions and reduced it to a mere cipher. In the meantime, of course, liberation theology has itself undergone significant developments, evolving into many different forms on a global scale and subsequently being required to engage in critical self-examination in the wake of the new political realities of the last decade.

At the same time an increasing interest in urban theology revealed how wide a range that label has come to denote. It embraces at least four distinct modes: the reflection of individual urban practitioners;[179] the gathering and facilitating role of such agencies as the Urban Theology Unit; the national church's more systematic attempt to harvest its urban experience, exemplified in the *Faith in the City* process[180] or the Methodist *Cities* report;[181] the wider discussion about urban mission and ministry which draws on global experience.[182] That very variety itself invites further reflection – otherwise, as in the case of liberation theology, urban theology too might be applied to so much that it ends up denoting very little.

The essential task addressed here, then, is to explore the basic orientation of these two theological movements. It is not primarily about classification: is urban theology a proper manifestation of liberation theology? That question invests liberation theology with a normative status which is neither justifiable nor appropriate. Nor is it an attempt to validate urban theology by reference to liberation theology since no such validation is necessary: urban theology can only be judged on its own terms as to whether it is appropriate or not; faithful or not; liberating or not. What emerges instead, when the two movements are brought into dialogue, are several points of convergence on the one hand and a number of questions for clarification on the other.

Points of Convergence
Whatever the differences between urban and liberation theology may be, there are clearly also a number of key points of convergence.

Firstly, both are self-consciously *contextual* theologies. Liberation theology embraces its 'preferential option for the poor' not only as a political act or moral imperative but also as the means of engaging with the issues of God's self-revelation in the contemporary world. In so doing it rejects the claim that the prime focus of theology is abstract universal truth. It acknowledges that its own context, like any context, is partial and limited but recalls that those constraints are shared by the incarnation itself - which is seen not merely as one doctrine among others, but rather as God's chosen method.

Similarly urban theologians consciously embrace their own urban contexts. They do this not only out of pastoral solidarity with local congregations and communities, but also out of the conviction that engagement with this place and these people will bring them close to the promises and challenges of the gospel. This is where biblical stories and symbols can resonate in new ways within a framework of urban experience. This is where ministries of hospitality and the inevitable invitations to engage with local issues provoke and enable serious reflection on the meaning of Christian community. Clearly there are fundamental contextual differences between liberation theology and urban theology. Such differences, however, do not undermine the common commitment both make to take their own context seriously as the prime and determinative locus for theological reflection.

Secondly, for both theologies the issue of location also implies a statement about *commitment*. They are not only *there*, they are there *for a purpose*. Liberation theology's 'preferential option for the poor' clearly states its intent and consequently shapes its priorities and self-understanding. This is partisan theology that eschews any theoretical claims to neutrality. In similar vein, while many different congregations may be part of the urban tapestry, urban theology only emerges from those who make a conscious commitment: from those who choose to engage in solidarity with the urban context in order to seek its transformation and renewal.
Liberation theology speaks of, and is driven by, the intolerable nature of suffering - from which liberation must be sought. It has been a channel – sometimes the only available channel - for articulating the 'voice of the voiceless'. In 'seeking the welfare of the

city' urban theology similarly protests against any suggestion that urban deprivation is inevitable, let alone acceptable, and keeps alive an alternative vision of human community which it tries to embody, if only in parabolic ways. Indeed a process such as *Faith in the City*, in its own way also provides a rare opportunity for urban voices to be heard, presented and amplified within the public realm.[183]

Such engagement becomes the raw material, the first stage, for theology – which is why liberation theology describes its task as 'critical reflection on praxis'. It is why it always resists the notion that it is a theology *of* or *about* liberation – claiming rather to be theology done from a commitment *to* liberation. In the same way urban theology is not at all the same as a 'theology *of* the city'. Such a theology can too easily elevate – or rather reduce the city to the status of a symbol or theme, and involves no inherent commitment to engage with the urban reality as it is.

Thirdly, both theologies embody a *holistic* understanding of the gospel. Despite all the claims of reductionism made against liberation theology, from its very inception Gutiérrez defined three integral aspects of liberation: liberation of the individual; liberation for participation as subject of one's own history; liberation from oppressive structures.[184] Similarly urban theology engages not only with individuals but also with civic structures and public policies. In the recent *Urban Theology* reader, to take but one obvious example, the chapter on sin includes items on housing and crime – while other chapters relate to issues of equality and justice, work, power and powerlessness. These are the concerns that impact on and shape urban communities – issues too against which the adequacy of theological language needs to be tested.

At an earlier stage of the dialogue with European theology Gutiérrez offered the oft-quoted insight that whereas European theology has primarily addressed the non-believer, liberation theology addresses the non-person.[185] Whereas the gist of that distinction still undoubtedly holds true for much first-world theology, it is significant that urban theology often finds itself addressing the non-believer who, especially if trapped in the vicious multi-generational circles of so much urban deprivation, may also increasingly bear the marks of the non-person as well.

Fourthly, both theologies claim to be alternative paradigms to the dominant theology, rereading the tradition from the perspective of the poor, the grass-roots, the 'underside of history'. Liberation theology, as an act of reflection, arose out of the recognition that the inherited theological tradition and its embodiment in ecclesiastical structures had left the poor of Latin America as spiritual orphans, denied access to rich heritage of biblical and theological resources that might have empowered them in their struggles. Hence the new project sought both to expose dominant, alienating theology and to reclaim the liberating dynamics of the tradition as tools for social transformation

This task was elaborated in various ways: it adopted a hermeneutic of suspicion that challenged claims of theological neutrality; it contrasted the alienating effect of philosophical dualism with the biblical emphasis on history as the place of God's own revelation; it reclaimed many neglected strands within scripture, not least the insistence that knowledge of God is intimately related to the doing of justice; it asserted the priority of orthopraxis over orthodoxy – controversial claims which were opposed most actively by the institutional Church when embodied in the conviction that the true church is the church of the poor and needs to be 'reinvented' from this base.[186]

By contrast urban theology, as an alternative theology, operates on a more restricted and less polemic map. Partly that is because liberation theology has already rewritten some of the ground rules and rediscovered fundamental biblical paradigms: some wheels simply do not need to be reinvented. Partly it is because of the differing ecclesiological realities – not least the depth of alienation from the churches in many urban contexts. That fact determines the urban mission agenda which is itself often transmuted into a search for credibility: can new forms of authentic Christian activity or presence be devised in our cities that will enable others to overhear 'the reason for the hope that is within us'? (1 Peter 3: 15).

That search for credibility often seems to exhaust urban practitioners to the extent that the potential for urban theology to offer alternative paradigms is frequently undermined. Certainly much of the 'global mode' seems more ready to elaborate strategies and biblical models for reclaiming the city than it does to examine the theological assumptions on which they are based, although its confidence in those assumptions may reflect the evangelical origins of many of its exponents. Sometimes the autobiographical stories which are told or collected, poignant as they often are as testimonies to human courage, compassion or creativity, all too often stop short - affirming for example a renewed experience of urban transcendence without examining the implications of such a claim. Alternatively, even when it is recognised that stories by themselves are not enough, there is a temptation to impose an overly systematic solution on the material.[187]

At this point in the comparison the contextual differences of liberation and urban theology are paramount. One of the most striking achievements of liberation theology, for example, has been its power to use the symbolic universe of biblical imagery to motivate and to sustain hope even in the face of the most brutal political and economic oppression. The scale and urgency of that task required more differentiated discussions to wait. The language used, moreover, did not need to be validated or justified within communities that were comfortable with a traditional religious framework. The task, as Sobrino describes it, was to engage with the 'second Enlightenment' of Marx rather than the 'first Enlightenment' of Kant[188] - with first Enlightenment questions of interpretation and meaning often being by-passed in the process.

Urban theology, by contrast, is required to engage with both forms of Enlightenment simultaneously! The *context* requires issues of social justice to be addressed, new visions to be elaborated and motivational dynamics to be unleashed. Meanwhile the *culture* ensures that questions about the meaning and credibility of faith claims won't go away. So a double task emerges: to articulate a theology of protest, aspiration and hope in response to *social* alienation in a language which at the same time avoids the dangers of *religious* alienation.[189] The combination may be achievable, but it requires a greater awareness of the challenge, and perhaps a greater level of self-criticism, than is sometimes evident.

In conclusion to this section we note some words of José Comblin writing from his contemporary Latin America experience and reviewing 'the changing context of liberation theology':

> Today social liberation is taking place in the city; that is where all the great social problems are concentrated. It is in the city that one can conceive of a civic activity at a time when political activity is becoming ever more impossible. The true community is the city with all its levels of participation and all the complexities of its structures.[190]

Which tends to suggest just how close the points of convergence might actually be.

Questions for Clarification
Alongside these four points of convergence there are a number of questions to be addressed to urban theology from the perspective of liberation theology's own experience - with a view to inviting further clarification of the project.

1. What defines 'Urban'?
Early in its development liberation theology was criticised from within Latin America for its narrow focus on socio-economic categories. Where were the women in its analysis of a continent

which has given the rest of the world the very terms 'macho' and 'machismo', and what of the native indigenous communities, who had been marginalised by race as well as by poverty? Increasingly liberation theology has broadened its analysis and as it moved beyond Latin America one of its strengths has been its ability to offer a fuller analysis of reality and to show the inter-relatedness of different forms of oppression. In the process, however, such a broadening may have blunted liberation theology's sharp focus and encouraged a descent into relativism: we all need liberating from something.

In terms of urban theology the problem translates into the question: how narrowly should we define urban? How much of the urban experience is to be included? Urban theology has emerged predominantly from those working in the inner cities or, perhaps more accurately, in 'urban priority areas'. That is undoubtedly where the issues of urban existence are at their sharpest but such issues cannot be seen in isolation. Urban commentators, for example, increasingly assume a framework dictated by the multi-layered process of globalisation. Does urban theology also need to broaden its scope to this extent so that the analysis it offers is more adequate and comprehensive, or would such a development risk losing the sharpness of its specific focus?[191]

2. What price Pluralism?

Latin America is a huge continent embracing enormous religious variety, as well as geographical, social, economic or political diversity. As a result early debates within liberation theology about the role of 'popular religion' often reflected very different experiences, from the more overtly religious contexts of Peru [Gutiérrez] or Brazil [Boff] to the relatively secularised context of the southern Cone [Segundo]. The issue revolved around the extent to which such religious manifestations could serve the process of liberation or how far it was an irredeemably conservative force.

Within our situation the factors are of course very different. Yet if we have often assumed that 'British urban' only implies tiny remnants of disciples in a secular wilderness we need to recognise that that is no longer the whole story. The East End of London has not traditionally been a very fertile ground for the churches, but the recent Directory of religious groups in the Borough of Newham has almost 300 entries.[192] These are not all Christian by any means, but many are, and among them large and flourishing congregations that reflect that other face of globalisation: the presence in our midst of significant Christian communities from all over the world. The urban scene, not least the inner urban scene, continues to change. The dynamic Christian presence in many cities is increasingly represented by members of black independent churches. There too are focused first-hand experiences of racism and of social and economic exclusion that both expose and illustrate the nature of urban existence for many. The differences of spirituality and theology between such groups and those who have traditionally expounded urban theology are many. The question is therefore raised as to how purist - or how pluralist - an urban theology can now afford to be?

3. What must be done?

Liberation theology has experienced seismic shifts since its inception in the late 1960s. During the first half of its existence it had to face both political and ecclesiastical repression. In the latter half it has seen the emergence of more tolerant democratic regimes – politically if not ecclesiastically – which has significantly changed its role as a vehicle of resistance. Having adopted and defended a clear socialist option, the collapse of the Eastern bloc has derailed its historical confidence. Most recently – in Latin America at least - the significance of the base communities has been undermined both by the systematic appointment of a more conservative church hierarchy and by the aggressive expansion of Pentecostalism which has attracted many of their members.

In the wake of such changes it is instructive to note which elements of liberation theology have retained their fundamental importance. In

288

recent essays surveying that process and tracing the trajectory of liberation theology into a new millennium Gutiérrez and Villa-Vicencio – from Latin America and South Africa respectively – each identify the same two key concerns.[193] Firstly, in a world increasingly dominated by unfettered market forces, a commitment to economic justice and an understanding of the processes which resist it remains a priority: in a simple but telling image from Exodus 22:26, Gutiérrez asks 'Where will the poor sleep in the world that is emerging?'[194] Secondly, there is a continued need for a spirituality which empowers the poor, for a mysticism which holds 'historical solidarity' in tension.[195]

The urban context focuses and represents so many issues and aspects of contemporary living, each of which might justifiably demand our attention and concern. But that very vitality and complexity could cause the energies of urban theology to be diffused and ineffectual. Is not a more focused and strategic, response required and could these undergirding priorities of economic justice and an empowering spirituality provide helpful lodestones for us too? Or will the St Deiniol's project enable more urgent tasks to emerge?

Chapter 21

John Vincent

New Faith In The City

Faith Born out of Practice

So we ask, what is the Theology which comes from the Testaments and the Discernments of our stories? And what does it all add up to for Christianity, for the City, and for the future?

From the point of view of Christianity itself, I believe that it is hard to exaggerate the importance, and even the singularity of what is here. In this chapter, I hope to indicate the grounds for this, and then to look out more widely on the basis of it.

What comes through the stories is a whole ethos which may or may not be described in theological terms, but is informed consciously or unconsciously by some of the central dynamics of the Christian story. It is as if the little companies of believers see themselves as being personally called, not just to be believers and to maintain the service of worship and right belief, but even and much more, to be those who share the mystery, the tragedy and triumph of being Jesus practitioners, God actors, Spirit led project workers. They are not practitioners or actors or project workers in the rather technical sense in which those words are sometimes used in Christian community work circles. They are people who, personally and in groups, see themselves as people called to be significant players in the lives of their communities, at times as pioneers and foundations for fragile, experimental efforts at providing a service for others, at other times just being there as the shoulder to cry upon, the long-stayer who doesn't move out, the faithful neighbour who is there when needed, the upright person who holds to their principles and to whom others turn when integrity and reliability are needed.

Certainly, *Faith in the City* was right in recognising that "The authentic Christian faith towards which common belief must be nurtured"… "can be expressed and achieved in a variety of styles and idioms – by imaginative story-telling, as much as by expositions of doctrine".[196] We would now have to add that the UPA Faith is not merely "informal, spasmodic and expressed in totally non-technical and highly accessible language".[197] We would now have to say that the faith we have discovered is not in fact any of the ten elements which the Report members found "greatly strengthened" in themselves.[198] Rather, the distinctive element, which now needs to be recognised by the whole Church as well as by the UPA Christians, is a new recognition of the dynamic of Gospel practice present in situations of stress and extremity, which seem noticeably absent from churches and Christian experience elsewhere. This is the "pearl of great price" that seems to be the heart of the faithfulness of these urban disciples.

Discipleship to Jesus lies as a determinative but not always named element in all this. Discipleship to Jesus is more a basic assumption lying behind the practice, than a constant reference point. Yet the assumption is decisive. It is assumed that the Gospel stories can be taken up as interpretative or confirmatory or inspirational by the local Christian people, as if they were already about them. They are like the disciples of Jesus, or about the work of the Kingdom, or involved in the community of church, so that the words and stories from Jesus and the disciples are, quite naturally, available as a resource for their self-understanding, support and corporate self-interpretation.

At times, a particular biblical context and historical situation is seen as reflective of, and thus valuable for, a contemporary urban phenomenon. So Peter Atkinson describes the classic out-of-town council housing estate as a place of "exile", and then turns to the accounts of the exile, and the comments of recent writers on it. And, says Peter, some of the strategies visible in the biblical stories and teachings can help us in our "communities of exile". So grief (Jer. 29: 5-7), lamentation (Ps. 137: 1), overcoming despair (Is. 46: 1-4), facing God's absence, dealing with moral confusion and with self-preoccupation all become ways that contemporary people can work through their "alienation", and develop coping mechanisms and prophetic "defiance and cunning".

At other times, some contemporary development or situation or argument triggers off the Christian consciousness that the Christian storehouse contains a story or a tradition, a truth or an assumption, that is "like" the contemporary element, and so can be used to probe, explicate, critique, support or judge it – or perhaps, best of all, engage in sympathetic but discriminating dialogue with it, so that its potential for constructive interpretation or mutation is probed, or its potential for human or community growth in wellbeing is facilitated. Thus, in Andrew Davey's piece, Leonie Sandercock's vision of a new pluralistic "cosmopolis", or David Harvey's critique of "privileging things and spatial forms over social processes", evoke elements in theology of resonance and provocation.

Michael Northcott argues that the phenomena of urban deprivation and social exclusion can only convincingly be challenged by a re-appropriation of the Incarnation, which signifies that "the God who made the world has vindicated its promise as the gift of a loving God who wills its good." "The material condition of life therefore invokes participation in the love of God", so that the material and the moral are conjoined. Likewise, the "aesthetic, ecological and economic shape of urban life", is reconnected with "the Christian attempt to recover the spiritual significance of ethical life in communities characterised by justice and love".

Michael's conception of incarnation follows Augustine's "City of God" in which there is order, like the "immense solidity, clarity, complexity and beauty of the cathedral and its environs", separated from the chaos, greed and violence of the secular world outside.

Building from New Paradigms

So, Andrew Davey finds Leonie Sandercock speaking of the new urban future as a pluralistic cosmopolis necessitating genuine bottom-up involvement and decision-taking by local communities.

> Local communities have grounded experiential, contextual knowledges which are often more manifested in stories, songs, visual images and speech than in typical planning sources.

The old top-downwards planning paradigm – whether of theologians, church leaders, journalists, politicians or planners, needs to be replaced by a new paradigm of "negotiation, practised with discretion and imagination" (Davey). This certainly fits into our stories, which often describe working with others, participating in wider partnerships, developing secular as well as theological strategies, and learning from people in very varied community groupings.

Such a paradigm has common ground with biblical concepts of koinonia as solidarity/participation, and of the Kingdom – "new, defiant patterns of social relationships that draw on the ideal already-but-not-yet" (Davey). It is something that "can never be realised, but always be in the making" (Sandercock). Experience and theory, reflection and action combine, and are "subject to the critique of marginal communities for whom change is a matter of life and death."

Thus, all the pieces of our collection invite attention to new paradigms whereby Christians get their theology together on the back of their mission.

The paradigm of Urban Theology is the response and fruit of discipleship and mission within the urban environment. It relates the realities of urban experiences to the scriptural and theological storehouses of faith.

Part of Urban Theology's "newness" proceeds from three basic realities and intentions:

1. **Location**. Urban Theology is a reflective theology based on a particular context, that of the city, and, particularly, the inner cities and housing estates. Thus the location of the theology gives it a specific social, cultural and political context and "feel".
2. **Intentionality**. Urban Theology proceeds from commitment. It is a feet, hands and heart theology first, and only then a "head" theology or a book theology.
3. **Primacy**. Urban Theology is a theology from the prime context for Britain today. The vast majority in Britain live in an urban environment or are subject to urban agendas. Other theologies have to take place within the environment of the urban.

Urban Theology has usually emerged at the end of urban practice, the fruit of urban Christians, people held together in a particular location, with a particular intentionality, who want to use Christian faith as a way to deal with some of the key issues of our time. This is the new paradigm of Urban Theology.

The Promise of Urban Theology
Where Urban Theology stands in relation to other theologies is an ongoing interest. Clearly, Urban Theology belongs within the general area of Contextual Theologies. The relationship between Urban Theology and Liberation Theology engages Stuart Jordan and Ian Duffield. There are decisive elements in common. Stuart names contextuality, commitment, holistic understanding of the Gospel, and a clear perception of being "alternative paradigms to the dominant theology". Ian names Urban Theology's character as contextual, committed to the gospel of liberation, and committed to the poor, excluded or enslaved.

In some ways, this volume itself indicates the beginnings of a movement of Urban Theology into the directions which Stuart Jordan hopes for, notably globalisation, pluralism, and spirituality. Andrew Davey, Michael Northcott and Geoff Curtiss see the urban as both urban priority area and global city; and the prizes and problems of pluralism are the theme of Colin Marchant and Greg Smith. The specific question of urban spirituality was not addressed at St Deiniol's except in a group sharing on urban worship. But if spirituality is something like "what holds us together as people in Christ where we are",[199] then many of our contributors here are writing about spirituality. And the specific search for an "urban spirituality" as reported upon elsewhere turns out to be liberation spirituality.[200]

In the typical contemporary congregation, the weekly readings of the stories of the Gospels often only provide glimpses of a curious world or at best an invitation to some kind of "spiritual" reading of the stories. One contribution of the Church's urban disciples is to say that this curious world is not so curious to us. We seem to have things going on that make sense in the light of the Gospel stories – and the Gospel stories make sense to us because of things going on around us here, in church, in community, in people. We thus have "material" readings, not spiritual ones.

I have illustrated this in my recent book, *Hope from the City*. I ask a question which I can only repeat here:

> If these stories were told
> of certain odd and controversial events,
> taking place in dark, unnoticed and unexpected places,
> long ago, on the streets of Galilee and Judea,
> What odd and controversial events,
> taking place in dark, unnoticed and unexpected places,
> today, on the streets of our cities,
> might be felt to be
> in the same world as the biblical ones,
> and thus perhaps become also
> new parts of the ongoing divine sagas?[201]

295

The almost instinctive process visible in many of the stories here recorded is carried out in systematic form in urban ministry courses. There, the process is of situation analysis, bible /gospel analogy, problem identification, and mission discernment, followed by project development, execution, monitoring and critiquing. This is the process referred to by Ian Duffield, who sees it as a "working model for doing theology".

The crucial element is what I am finding myself more and more calling "theological practice". The crucial theological element is not in the preconceiving, as classic theology thought. Neither is the crucial theological element in the contemporary "theological reflection". The former claims that the area of practice is merely that of "putting into action" what the already agreed and received theological "truths" dictate or open up. The latter assumes that theology has not decisively influenced things that have happened, but only comes in as "reflection" on them. "Theological Practice" places the theology as core and reality of the practice, not just preparation for it or reflection after it.

"Theological practice" still awaits a contemporary systematics. It is an implication of a theology created by Incarnation. Incarnation does not dictate theological pre-requisites or preconceptions, which then determine practice – the classic view. Neither does incarnation allow a post-event mental activity "reflection". Rather, incarnation decisively determines the God-reality and the God-event – the God-practice or "God-walk".[202]

The Future of Christian Theology

Theology is the stage of harvesting, of bringing realities into one place. Theology is when you make an overarching interpretation of your realities, a framework for understanding, a "plausibility structure" (Peter Berger), something which you can hopefully operate with as a way to support yourselves and your colleagues and to communicate to others.

Theology is whatever gets you through the night. Theology is the "Aha!" moments of insight during or after particular unexpected happenings. Theology is the bag that you put the pick-and-mix into – the pick-and-mix of the contemporary smorgasbord of ever-multiplying phenomena of the contemporary pluralistic scene of Jesus-faithful practice in a secular world.

Theology is always the end product of struggle. It is the work of people on the edge of existence, trying to grab stories, myths, paradigms, patterns, models, heroines, heroes, sagas, truths (perhaps from scripture) which might have in them the same fire, and incomprehensibility, and violence, and unacceptableness, and bliss and insight and giftedness, as the realities that, daily, now burst through their doors, or batter at their windows, or confront them in the street, or slowly dawn on their blinded sight at the end of the day, or strengthen them in the long night watches, or catch their breath at an end-of-the-road discussion in the church council, or burst out with reality and significance at the parents-and-toddlers club.

All Theology is harvest. Urban Theology is Urban Harvest. It is the bringing home to those who have worked at them, the crops, the fruits, the grains, from what has been growing through the long hot summers. It is the Harvest Thanksgiving - the celebration that not only have some seeds been sown, and grown secretly, and produced plants and leaves, but that at the end of the day there are some fruits. The fruits can even be brought back into the barn of the Church wider, and celebrated by those who have not worked to produce them, who are yet welcome to rejoice at them and share them.

So that, like all Theology, Urban Theology is new pieces of contemporary witness, testimony and discernment, ending in new theologising. David Ford and Laurie Green describe this process:

> The 'grip' of the urban situation and the 'grip' of the
> gospel cry out for a wisdom that engages the reality

of both, and this community wisdom helps to shape and in turn is shaped by Christian theology. The Christian community acting together can carry diverse experiences in its wisdom, and can take from this great treasure house of experience and wisdom such treasures as will help it in each new context within which it operates. This distilled Christian wisdom, experienced and carried within the Christian community, is the 'tradition' of the Church, born of its experiences of doing theology in various contexts.[203]

Finally, then, we take back our "fruits" and set them within the Church's ever-expanding storehouse of theological elements, paradigms and models. What have we got? Where do we contribute our new pieces for the ongoing theological search? What "Doctrines" achieve new mutations here? Incarnation? Discipleship? Kingdom? Soteriology? Death and Resurrection? Vision? Koinonia? New Jerusalem?

Of course, each theological "truth" has different versions in different theologies. The actual meaning to be applied to Incarnation emerges as crucial for Urban Theology. Clearly as Stuart Jordan says, incarnation "is seen not merely as one doctrine among others, but rather as God's chosen method".

There are two ways in which incarnation is important for urban theologising. In the first place, there is what arises spontaneously from many of the stories - an identification of Christian workers and disciples with aspects of Jesus' own ministry and mission. Especially here, Jesus' origins, his home town, his family, his disciples, invite comparison to the people and situation of the cities. There is an "Urban Hearing of the Gospel", which finds Jesus "at home" there.[204] Jesus' chosen disciples, his chosen places of mission, the "outcasts" to whom he ministers, the political and civic enemies he challenges - all of these are points of comparison and identification. This tradition manifests itself in many of the stories from urban practitioners within evangelical, catholic and radical traditions.[205]

Beyond this, incarnation becomes a term for the sanctification of the created world, the placing of the Body of Christ within the human race as such, so that the "building up of the body" is at least in part involved with and at times co-terminous with the wholeness of the body of humanity, corporate and politic. This is essentially the view of Michael Northcott. It is also the underlying theology of many church people in the inner cities and housing estates, who belong to more "catholic" traditions.

These two streams unite in the spirituality of many of our contributions, though there is more explicit reference to the first than to the second. Either way, the urban re-coining of Incarnation is a striking example of the way that the contextual experience of Christians in specific times rediscovers and reformulates a specific aspect of Christian theology. We may imagine that other aspects of Christian Theology may be lying dormant, or at least inexperienced or not seen in any contemporary manifestation.

The future of Christian theology will and must depend upon such contextual rediscovery, re-coining and reformulation.[206]

New Faith for New Times
Ann Morisy raises some very serious questions about the contemporary suburban dilution of the Gospel in the churches of Britain today. Her conclusion is that only radical new practice and experience will create the "conversion" necessary for a rediscovery of full Christianity. None of the writers apart from Ann raises the question of whether and if so, how, suburban Christians - the vast majority - can participate in the rediscovery of Christianity at the urban grass roots which this book celebrates.

Equally, we as theologians believe that we have practical and conceptual "goodies" which can help social analysts, planners, politicians and citizens, not only when provoked by some new situation, but also when primarily provoked by pieces in the biblical - theological traditions themselves. Ian Duffield thus speaks of "biblical passages, themes, conflicts or personalities that can provide suggestive insights into the current situation which is being explored".

Hence, Peter Atkinson with *Exile* and Michael Northcott with *Body of Christ*. Both begin with an analysis of a piece of biblical-theological exposition and then see in the contemporary urban realities elements of resonance and reprise.

Churches in UPAs, says Peter Atkinson, endure a "double exile" - geographical, being far from the centre, and cultural, being excluded from the wealth of society in general, and the rest of the church. In fact, a new way of bringing insight and interpretation into contemporary experience results, as contemporary people learn from their spiritual forbears in the Hebrew Scriptures, how "the absence of God, and moral questioning, and self-preoccupation, can be met."

Michael Northcott sees the alienation of the "fragile and personal shape of human bodies and human communities" produced by the modern built environment. From within the Christian tradition of Body of Christ, he seeks to draw both analogies and spiritual realities into the service of the re-incorporation of the fragmented body politic of the modern city, to secure a new wholeness, reciprocity and sustainability.

This re-creation of theology within the urban, of course, has its problems. Problematic "questions about the meaning and credibility of faith claims won't go away". Stuart Jordan observes:

> A double task emerges: to articulate a theology of protest, aspiration, and hope in response to social alienation in a language which at the same time avoids the danger of religious alienation.

Urban theology has to establish itself as legitimate not only in terms of the constantly volatile urban situation, but also in terms of theology in a constantly changing religious situation.

One recent writer in a book on Urban Theology states:

> One of the primary questions for an urban (priority) theology is whether it can begin or be done by those who are only passing through, in one way or another.[207]

Our answer is "No". Our book amounts to a plea that, for a start, theologians and church leaders, at least, should begin working from the bottom, start listening to their foot soldiers and pioneer corps, the people who work in the kitchen and on the streets. They would then become part of a rediscovery and even re-creation of the core drama of Christian faith, which began with the kitchen and the street, the working folk and tradespeople of Galilee or of the early church communities, and then builds up from there.

Noticeable, too, is the more or less complete absence of theology as "the great truths" or "the revealed doctrines". If the Sunday liturgy had spoken in any way (as it well might) of a God of power, or of might, or of Lordship, there is little or no indication of it here. Indeed, the classic truths of the Trinity, or of the God of love, or of providence are missing, or at least not articulated. Not surprisingly, it is assumed that there is no point in praying "for those in power", as it is they who are the perceived enemies of the common people. The great churches of the cathedral or the city or the suburbs might assume that they have some natural affinity with the powers, or people in authority, and expect them to be "on the same side", or even that the churches should be their collaborators. But that is not the assumption of the congregations described in this book. And a God made in the image of the powers (whether civil servants, politicians, social workers or ecclesiastics) has no witness here.

Rather than as a community colluding with the forces and powers of society, the urban churches emerge as communities which have found that calls to Gospel faithfulness and practice place them, whether welcome or not, as the critics, and sometimes the opponents, of all powerful people. This is especially true of the church leaders in the parent denominations, or the councillors or the social workers or police (there are exceptions, of course). Typically, all are "they" and "them". They are not "us". And if "they" presume also to think that they belong to the Christian "cause", then the burden of proof lies with them. Certainly, the Gospel stories and values and dynamics which are seen to be at work in the urban churches, appear to be mightily different from, and even at odds with, the stories, values and dynamics of everyone else outside, including the churches.

Faith for New Times must begin with both the realities and the testimonies of the city. It may be that precisely here, where all old expectations, establishments, hegemonies and "rules of law" have largely disappeared, some elements of new faith, not dependent upon any of them, are beginning to emerge.[208]

A New Vision of Urban Living
The final section of the Government's 2000 White Paper which led to the November 2002 Urban Summit, states "a simple vision which is at the heart of this White Paper" (2.37).

> This vision for towns and cities is part of the Government's overall strategy for tackling poverty and social exclusion and fostering economic growth in a way that benefits all citizens. Throughout this strategy there is a recognition that social, economic and environmental issues are interdependent – and that failure to act effectively in all of these areas leads to polarised cities that cannot succeed in the longer term.

"A new vision of urban living" is put forward, of towns, cities and suburbs which "offer a high quality of life and opportunity for all, not just the few."

1. People sharing the future of their community, supported by strong and truly representative local leaders.
2. People living in attractive, well kept towns and cities which use space and buildings well.
3. Good design and planning which makes it practical to live in a more environmentally sustainable way, with less noise, pollution and traffic congestion.
4. Towns and cities able to create and share prosperity, investing to help all their citizens reach their full potential, and;
5. Good quality services – health, education, housing, transport, finance, shopping, leisure and protection from crime – that meet the needs of people and businesses wherever they are.

It concludes, "This urban renaissance will benefit everyone, making towns and cities vibrant and successful, and protecting the countryside from development pressure."[209]

However, the evidence coming from our volume and my own experiences at the Urban Summit[210] and on the Sheffield Burngreave New Deal for Communities Partnership Board would suggest immediately that we have a contribution to make to the debate about any such "vision". The people about whom we have written already have attitudes and policies on all the points of the Government's 'Vision', which suggest alternative proposals.   Point by point, we would respond to the White Paper's "Vision" rather differently:

1. At present there is great scepticism about local government and local leadership. We need courageous experiments in well-resourced local neighbourhood government.[211] Is there willingness to change at this level?
2. The physical appearance and structure of buildings needs vastly greater investment not in initial design and reconstruction, but in

303

the ongoing, weekly, costly, labour-intensive care and maintenance of them. Will finance be diverted from over-paid, temporary, incoming experts, and spent on under-paid local maintenance workers? Incoming money must *stay* in the areas.

3. Experience shows that desirable environmental improvements in deprived areas can only be made at the cost of inconveniencing suburban and commercial through traffic. Would politicians support this? Again, maintenance at the grass roots level is also needed.

4. In the economy of the future, shared prosperity if it were taken seriously might well be only at the expense of lower standards for the rich. Are we prepared for this? When is Government prepared to offer models for this?

5. Good quality services in all these departments must be organised, administered and delivered within the deprived neighbourhoods themselves, to help build up local self-regard and improve the actual reception of such services at the local level. Are power-holding prestigious professionals willing to move their offices, if not their homes?

Our witnesses would suggest that if an "urban renaissance" is to "benefit everyone", it has to begin with changing the reality and the experience of those in the most deprived areas, from the bottom up. There is no "trickle down". One day, there might be a "trickle up", from the bottom, as new ways of more appropriate living are discovered in the places of present non-success. This is the alternative "vision of urban living" our stories look towards, building on the local people's own successes and strengths, and building up a new "renaissance" from the basis of the present realities, not from some outside dream. There is resurrection where there is death.

Faithfulness in the City
In December 2002, six of the writers of this book, with six other urban "theological practitioners", met again at St Deiniol's for the fourth week-long, now annual, Urban Theology Collective. All the essays were available for scrutiny, comment and occasionally improvement.

We talked long and hard about our title. "Faith from the City" led on to "Treasure in Urban Vessels" – which is what we have, though it sounded cosy. So we settled on "Faithfulness in the City". The word "faith" so easily becomes mere "belief", or even "convictions", and encourages phrases like "having faith" or "holding on to faith". What we have seen in our stories is rather more the witnesses, the *martyria*, of contemporary disciples, and "faithfulness" seems the right, if mundane, description. It is both "faithfulness" as the phenomenon of being "full of faith" as shown in practice; and also "faithfulness" as the long-term survival and authenticity of individuals at the sharp edges of society.

In December 2002, we also looked, somewhat critically, at ourselves. We reflected that the churches alone have labelled our places "Urban *Priority* Areas", though we as the workers there did not feel that the church afforded us any "priority", certainly not as theologians! Indeed there is a degree of impertinence in all authentic Christian theology-making – much less vision-making. Yet the originating dynamic of vision in the Old or New Testaments derived from the dreams of the downtrodden, the protests of the persecuted, the mindsets of the martyrs. And, whatever else may be observed concerning our stories, they witness to sudden, unexpected, momentary, but still persistent, gut-level and constantly reinforced identifications of ourselves with the originating characters, locations and commitments of our scriptural and theological forbears. They witness to our *faithfulness*, at very least, to that tradition.

So, at our Collective, we discussed possible images for ourselves and our work. "At times, it feels like a fire brigade service, with liturgical services on the side". "Sometimes, we rejoice that there's less "religion" where we are". Occasionally, we have more grandiose delusions – that we have bits and pieces of actuality which can only be described as "a retake of primitive Christianity," as "minimal, essential Christianity," even as "witness to what God is doing", or

305

"being part of the thin red line of the apostolic succession of radical discipleship down through the centuries".

However, we also reflected that, unavoidably and properly, there is a fragile character about it all. The bits of treasure – and they are only bits, even if of treasure – are held in very easily broken "pots of clay", very makeshift "earthen vessels". There is a kind of foolishness about it all, a crying in the wilderness, a Don Quixote tilting against windmills, a singing the songs of Zion in a strange land, or crooning spirituals of freedom under the slave-master's whip. Perhaps only when you allow yourself to be put in a situation where there are no other ways to speak about your experience, no other grounds for legitimisation, no other authority for your actions, do human beings in fact have resort to, or have need for, biblical tales, or theological insights. We have actions beyond our theologies. We are doing things whose theology is not yet articulated.

In the end, we want to say: This is how it is with us. We do not want to be goldfish bowls – so don't come and visit us for an afternoon. But we do want to be provokers – so come and give us bits of your lives, and see whether anything happens to you like has happened to us.

Appendix I:

Books And Resources

Bibliography

Loyde H. Hartley, *Cities and Churches. An International Bibliography*, (Scarecrow, 1993).

Global Analysis & Theology

Analysis

Sheridan Bartlett et al., *Cities for Children: Children's Rights, Poverty & Urban Management*, (Earthscan, 2000).
Manuel Castells, *The Information City*, (Blackwell, 1989).
Manuel Castells, The *Information Age: Economy, Society and Culture: Vol. 1: The Rise of the Network Society*, 1996 (2nd ed. 2000); *Vol. 2: The Power of Identity* 1997; *Vol. 3: The End of Millennium* 1997, (2nd ed. Blackwell, 2000).
Manuel Castells, Ida Susser, eds., *Castells' Reader on Cities and Social Theory*, (Blackwell, 2001).
David Clark, *Urban World / Global City*, (Routledge, 1996).
Mike Douglass & John Friedmann, *Cities for Citizens: Planning and the Rise of Civil Society in a Global Age*, (John Wiley, 1998).
John Eade, ed., *Living the Global City: Globalization as local process*, (Routledge, 1997).
John Eade & Christopher Mele, *Understanding the City*, (Blackwell, 2002).
Herbert Giradet, *Gaia Atlas of Cities*, (Gaia, 1996).
Stephen Graham and Simon Marvin, *Splintering Urbanism*, (Routledge, 2001).
Peter Hall, *Cities of Tomorrow* (Blackwell, 1996).

Peter Hall and Ulrich Pfeiffer, *Urban Future 21, A Global Agenda for Twenty First Century Cities*, (E&FN Spon, 2000).
INURA *Possible Urban Worlds. Urban Strategies at the End of the Twentieth Century,* (Birkhaüser, 1999).
Engin F. Isin ed., *Democracy, Citizenship and the Global City,* (Routledge: London).
Richard Le Gates and Frederick Stout eds., *The City Reader,* (Routledge, 1996).
Andy Merrifield and Erik Swyngedouw eds., *The Urbanization of Injustice,* (Lawrence and Wishart, 1996).
William Mitchell, *City of Bits,* (MIT Press, 1996); *e-topia. urban life Jim but not as we know it,* (MIT Press, 2000).

Open University
Doreen Massey, John Allen and Steve Pile, *Understanding Cities* (3 vols.): John Allen, Doreen Massey and Michael Pryke, *City Worlds;* John Allen, Doreen Massey and Michael Pryke, *Unsettling Cities: Movement /Settlement;* Steve Pile, Christopher Brook and Gerry Mooney, *Unruly Cities? Order/Disorder,* (Routledge, 1999).
Also study guide: Christopher Brook and Kathy Pain, *City Themes,* (Open University, 1999).

Michael Pacione, *Urban Geography,* (Routledge, 2001).
Richard Rogers, *Cities for a Small Planet,* (Faber, 1997).
Leonie Sandercock, *Towards Cosmopolis,* John Wiley 1998; ed., *Making the Invisible Visible –A Multicultural History of Planning,* (University of California, 1998).
Saskia Sassen, *Globalization and its Discontents,* (New Press, 1999); *The Global City: New York, London, Tokyo,* (Princeton, 2nd ed., 2001); *Cities in a World Economy,* (Pine Forge, 2nd ed., 2000); *Global Networks, Linked Cities,* (Routledge, 2002).
David Sattherwaite,*The Earthscan Reader in Sustainable Cities,* (Earthscan, 1999).
Allen J. Scott ed., *Global City-regions,* (OUP, 2001).
United Nations (UNCHS) Global Reports on Human Settlements: *An Urbanising World,* (Oxford, 1996); *Cities in a Globalising World,* (Earthscan, 2001).

John Urry, *Global Complexitiy*, (Polity, 2003).
Petra Weyland & Ayse Once, *Space, Culture and Power – New identities in Globalising Cities,* (Zed, 1998).

The Shape of the City (historical, cultural and theoretical analysis)
Ash Amin & Nigel Thrift, *Cities. Reimagining the Urban,* (Polity, 2002).
Ian Borden, Joe Kerr, Jane Rendell, *The Unknown City-Contesting Architecture and Social Space*, (MIT Press, 2001).
John Eade and Christopher Mele, eds., *Understanding the City*, (Blackwell, 2002).
Susan Fainstein and Scott Campbell, eds., *Readings in Urban Theory*, (Blackwell, 1996).
David Harvey, *Social Justice and the City,* (Blackwell, 1973/83)*; Justice, Nature and the Geography of Difference*, (Blackwell, 1996); *Spaces of Hope*, (Edinburgh University Press, 2000).
Peter Hall, *Cities and Civilisation,* (W&N, 1998).
Jane M. Jacobs, *Edge of Empire. Postcolonialism and the City*, (Routledge, 1996).
Rem Koolhaus et al., *Mutations,* (Actar, 2001).
Andy Merrifield, *Dialectical Urbanism,* Monthly Review 2002; *Metromarxism,* (Routledge, 2002).
Joseph Rykwert, *The Seduction of Place*, (Weidenfeld & Nicholson, 2000).
Richard Sennett, *The Conscience of the Eye -The Design and Social Life of Cities*, (Faber, 1990); *Flesh and Stone -The Body and City in Western Civilisation*, (Faber, 1994).
Edward Soja, *Postmetropolis: Critical Studies of Cities and Regions*, (Blackwell, 2000).
Aidan Southall, *The City in Time and Space*, (CUP, 2000).
Sophie Watson and Katherine Gibson, eds., *Postmodern Cities and Spaces,* (Blackwell, 1995).
Sophie Watson and Gary Bridge, eds., *A Companion to the City,* (Blackwell, 2000); *City Reader,* (Blackwell, 2002).

Urban theology & ministry in an international perspective

Ray Bakke, *A Theology as Big as the City*, (IVP, 1997).

Andrew Davey, "Globalization as challenge and opportunity in urban mission. An outlook from London" in *International Review of Mission*, (October, 1999).

Andrew Davey, *Urban Christianity and Global Order: Theological Resources for an Urban Future*, (SPCK 2001/Hendrickson 2002).

Laurie Green, *The Impact of the Global: An Urban Theology*, (New City UTU, 2000).

Bob Linthicum, *City of God, City of Satan - A Biblical Theology of the Urban Church*, (Zondervan, 1991); *Signs of Hope in the City*, (MARC USA, 1996).

Bruce J. Nicholls, and Beulah R. Wood, eds., *Sharing Good News with the Poor*, (World Evangelical Fellowship / Paternoster Press, 1996).

Tesunao Yamamori, Bryant Myers and Kenneth Luscombe, *Serving with the Urban Poor*, (World Vision/Marc, 1999).

The cities of the south

Jo Beall ed., *A City for All – Valuing Difference and Working with Diversity*, (Zed, 1997).

Rod Burgess et al. eds., *The Challenge of Sustainable Cities*, (Zed, 1997).

Alan Gilbert & Josef Gugler, *Cities, Poverty and Development - Urbanisation in the Third World*, (OUP, 1992).

Josef Gugler ed., *The Urbanisation of the Third World*, (OUP, 1988).

Robert Potter & Sally Lloyd Evans, *The City in the Developing World*, (Longman, 1998).

Africa

Patrick Bond, *Cities of Gold, Townships of Coal: Essays on South Africa's New Urban Crisis*, (AWP, 2000).

Aswin Desai, *We are the poors*, (Monthly Review Press, 2003).

Alan Mabin and Susan Parnell, *Urban South Africa*, (Blackwell, 2002).

Anthony O'Connor, *The African City*, (Hutchinson, 1983).

Aylward Shorter, *The Church in the African City*, (Geoffrey Chapman, 1991).

Latin America
Phillip Berryman, *Religion in the Megacity: Catholic and Protestant Portraits from Latin America,* (Orbis, 1996).
Alan Gilbert, *The Latin American City*, (Latin American Bureau, 1994).
Duncan Green, *The Silent Revolution: Rise of Market Economics in Latin America,* (Cassell, 1995).
J.J. Thomas, *Surviving in the City: The Urban Informal Sector in Latin America*, (Pluto, 1995).

Asia
K.C. Abraham, "Globalisation: A gospel and culture perspective", in *International Review of Mission,* (1996).
John Clammer, *Contemporary Urban Japan,* (Blackwell, 1997).
Jeremy Seabrook, *In the Cities of the South - Scenes from a developing world*, (Verso, 1996).
Dorothy Solinger, *Contesting Citizenship in Urban China*, (UP California, 1999).
Smriti Srinivas, *Landscapes of Urban memory: The Scared and the Civic in India's High Tech City*, (University of Minnestoa, 2001).

Australia
Katherine Gibson & Sophie Watson, *Metropolis Now: Planning and the Urban in Contemporary Australia*, (Polity / Pluto, 1998).

Europe
Martien Brintsmen and Hugo Vlug, *Faith in the City - Fifty years of the WCC in a secularised western context*, (Meinema-Zoetermeer/WCC, 1998).
Seppo Kjellberg, *Urban Ecotheology*, (International Books, 2000).

North American -Theology & Mission
Robert D. Carle & Louis DeCaro, *Signs of Hope in the City. Ministries of Community Renewal*, (Judson Press, 1997).

Tony Campolo, *Revolution and Renewal: How Churches are Saving our Cities* (WJKP, 2000).

Tony Carnes & Anna Kappathakis, *New York Glory,* (NYUP, 2000).

Harvie M. Conn & Manuel Ortiz, *Urban Ministry: The Kingdom, the City and the People of God*, (IVP, 2001).

Theodore Eastman, 'Mission of Christ in Urban America', in Philip Turner and Frank Sugeno, *Crossroads are for Meeting,* (SPCK USA, 1986).

Mark R Gornik, *To Live in Peace: Biblical faith and the changing inner city,* (Eerdmanns, 2002).

Clifford J. Green, ed., *Churches, Cities and Human Community - Urban Ministry 1945-85*, (Eerdmanns).

Nile Harper, *Urban Churches: Beyond Charity Towards Justice*, (Eerdmans, 1998).

Lovell Livesey, *Public Religion and Urban Transformation,* (NYU, 2000).

Robert Orsi, *Gods of the City,* (Indiana University Press, 2000).

Eleanor Scott Meyers, ed., *Envisioning the New City - A Reader in Urban Ministry,* (WJKP, 1992).

Eldin Villafañe, *Seek the Peace of the City,* (Eerdmanns: Grand Rapids, 1995).

Jim Wallis, *Faithworks,* (SPCK, 2002).

Mark Warren, *Dry Bones Rattling,* (Princeton, 2001).

North American – Cities

Mike Davis, *City of Quartz,* (Picador, 1996); *Magical Urbanism: Latinos Reinvent the American City,* (Verso, 1999).

Andres Duany, Elizabeth Plater-Zyberk & Jeff Speck, *Suburban Nation: The Rise of Sprawl and the Decline of the American Dream,* (North Point, 2001).

Eben Fodor, *Better not Bigger,* (NSP, 1999).

Roberta Brandes Gratz, Norman Mintz, *Cities Back from the Edge: New Life for Downtown,* (John Wiley, 1998).

Paul S. Grogan, Tony Proscio, *Comeback Cities: A Blueprint for Urban Revival,* (Westview, 2000).

Dolores Hayden, *The Power of Place,* (MIT Press, 1996).

Rem Koolhas et al., *Guide to Shopping,* (Taschen, 2001).

John Norquist, *The Wealth of Cities: Revitalising the Centres of American Life,* (Addison Wesley, 1998).
Robert Putnam, *Bowling Alone: The Collapse and Revival of American Community*, (Simon & Schuster, 2000).
Dimitrious Roussopoulos, *Public Place: Citizen Participation in Neighbourhood and Cities,* (Black Rose, 2000).
Victor Valle & Rodlfo Torres, *Latino Metropolis,* (University of Minnesota, 2000).

New Political, Economic & Social Analysis

Thomas Frank, *One Market Under God,* (Secker and Warburg, 2000).
Anthony Giddens, *Beyond Right and Left*, (Polity Press, 1994); *Third Way*, (Polity Press, 1998).
Noreena Hertz, *Silent Takeover*, (Heinnemann, 2001).
Will Hutton, *The State we're in*, (Vintage, 1996); *The World we're in*, (Little Brown, 2002).
Will Hutton and Anthony Giddens, *On the Edge*, (Jonathan Cape, 2000).
Michael Jacobs, *Politics of the Real World,* (Earthscan, 1996).
Naoim Klein, *No Logo*, (Harper, 1999), *Fences and Windows*, (Harper, 2002).
George Monbiot, *Captive State: The Corporate Take-over of Britain,* (Methuen, 2000).
Geoff Mulgan, *Life after Politics: New Thinking for the Twenty-First Century*, (Collins, 1997).
Real World Coalition, *From Here to Sustainability,* (Earthscan, 2001).

British Reports

Church of England reports
Archbishop of Canterbury's Commission on Urban Priority Areas, *Faith in the City: A Call to Church and Nation*, (CHP, 1985).
Archbishop's Advisory Group on UPAs, *Living Faith in the City*, (General Synod, 1990).
Bishops' Advisory Group on UPAs, *Staying in the City*, (CHP, 1995).

Other church reports
The Cities - A Methodist Report, (NCH: Action for Children, 1997).
Unemployment and the Future of Work, (CCBI, 1997).

British Analysis & Theology

Analysis
Ash Amin, Doreen Massey and Nigel Thrift, *Cities for the many, not the few*, (Policy Press, 2000).
Tim Blackman, *Urban Policy in Practice*, (Routledge, 1994).
David Boyle, *Building Futures*, (W.H. Allen, 1989).
David Byrne, *Social Exclusion*, (Open University, 1999).
Tim Butler and Michael Rustin, *Rising in the East: The Regeneration of East London*, (Lawrence and Wishart, 1996).
Nick Davies, *Dark Heart - The Shocking Truth about Hidden Britain*, (Chatto & Windus, 1997).
Janet Foster, *Docklands: Cultures in Conflict, Worlds in Collision*, (UCL, 1999).
Stephen Graham and Simon Marvin, *Telecommunications and the City: Electronic spaces, urban places,* (Routledge, 1996).
Paul Harrison, *Inside the Inner City*, (Penguin, 1983).
Michael Pacione, *Britain's Cities: Geographies of Division in Urban Britain*, (Routledge, 1997); *Urban Geography,* (Routledge, 2001).
Anne Power and Katharine Mumford, *The Slow Death of Great Cities? - Urban abandonment or urban renaissance*, (JRF York, 1999).
Anne Power and Richard Rogers, *Cities for a Small Country,* (Faber, 2000).
Towards an Urban Renaissance - Final report of the Urban Task Force, chaired by Lord Rogers of Riverside, (E&FN Spon, 1999).

Urban Theology & Practice
Michael Northcott, ed., *Urban Theology: A Reader*, (Cassell, 1998).
Mary Beasley, *Mission on the Margins*, (Lutterworth, 1997).
Nicholas Bradbury, *City of God*?,(SPCK, 1990).

Liz Carnelly, "Prophecy, Race and Eastenders" in *Modern Believing,* 36, (1995).

Andrew Davey, "London as theological problem", in *Theology, May* (1998).

Ian Duffield, ed., *Urban Christ: Responses to John J. Vincent,* (UTU, 1997).

David Ford, "Faith in the Cities: Corinth and the Modern City" in Colin Gunton and Daniel Hardy, eds., *On Being the Church,* (T&T Clark, 1989).

Timothy Gorringe, *A Theology of the Built Environment: Justice, Empowerment, Redemption,* (CUP, 2002).

Laurie Green, *Power to the Powerless,* (Marshalls, 1989); *Urban Ministry and the Kingdom of God,* (SPCK, 2003).

Anthony Harvey, ed., *Theology in the City - A Theological Response to Faith in the City,* (SPCK, 1989).

Kenneth Leech, *Through our long exile,* (DLT, 2001).

Ann Morisy, *Beyond the Good Samaritan: Community Ministry & Mission,* (Mowbrays, 1997).

John Proctor, *Urban God,* (BRF, 2002).

Chris Rowland and John Vincent, eds., *Liberation Theology UK,* (UTU, 1995); *Gospel from the City,* (UTU, 1998); *Liberation Spirituality,* (UTU, 1999); *The Bible and Practice,* (UTU, 2001).

Hilary Russell, *Poverty close to home -A Christian Understanding,* (Mowbrays, 1995).

Peter Sedgwick, ed., *God in the City,* (Mowbrays, 1995).

Peter Selby, *Grace and Mortgage,* (DLT, 1997).

Philip Shedrake, *Spaces for the Sacred,* (SCM Press, 2001).

Norman Shanks, 'Mission and Urbanisation' in *Theology in Scotland,* March, (1996).

Michael Simmons, ed., *Street Credo: Churches in the Community,* (Lemos & Crane, 2000).

John Vincent, *Hope from the City,* (Epworth, 2000).

Graham Ward, *Cities of God,* (Routledge, 2000).

Racism and ethnicity in Britain (including black theology)
Les Back, *New Ethnicities and Urban Cultures,* (UCL Press, 1996).

Robert Beckford, *Jesus is Dread - Black Theology and Culture in Britain*, (DLT, 1998); *Dread and Pentecostal – A political theology for the black church in Britain*, (SPCK, 2000); *God of the Rahtid: redeeming rage*, (DLT 2001).
Roswith Gerloff, *A Plea for Black British Theologies*, (Peter Lang, 1992).
David Haslam, *Race for the Millennium*, (CHP, 1996).
Ken Leech, *Struggle in Babylon*, (Sheldon, 1989).
Tariq Modood, Richard Berthoud et al., *Ethnic Minorities in Britain: Diversity and Disadvantage: The Fourth National Survey of Ethnic Minorities*, (London: Policy Studies Institute, 1997).
Lord Parekh, *The Future of Multi-Ethnic Britain*, (Profile, 2000).
Kwesi Owusu, *Black British Culture and Society - A Text Reader*, (Routledge, 2000).
John Wilkinson, *The Church in Black and White*, (St Andrews, 1994).

Journals

CITY- analysis of urban trends, culture theory, policy, action, (Carfax Publishing Ltd, Taylor and Francis Ltd, Rankine Road, Basingstoke, Hants, RG24 8PR).
Environment & Urbanization, (IIED, 3 Endsleigh St. London, WC1H 0DD).
Urban Age:
http://www.worldbank.org/html/fpd/urban/urb_age/urb_age.htm

Miscellaneous

Church in the city, historical context

Jeffrey Cox, *The Churches in a Secular Society: Lambeth 1870-1930*, (OUP, 1982).
Hugh Mcleod, *Class and Religion in the late Victorian City*, (RKP, 1974); *Piety and Poverty: Working Class Religion in Berlin, London and New York, 1870-1914*, (Holmes & Meier, 1995).
Jeremy Morris, *Religion and Urban Change: Croydon 1840-1914*, (RHS, 1992).
E.R. Wickham, *Church and People in an Industrial City*, (Lutterworth, 1957).

New Testament background

Richard Batey, *Jesus & the Forgotten City*, (Baker, 1991).
John Dominic Crossan, *The Birth of Christianity*, (Harper, 1998).
John Dominic Crossan & Jonathan Reed, *Excavating Jesus*, (Harper, 2001).
William R. Herzog, *Jesus, Justice & the Reign of God. A Ministry of Liberation,* (WKJP, 2000).
Robert Jewett, *Paul: Apostle to America,* (WKJP, 1994).
Wayne Meeks, *The First Urban Christians*, (Yale, 1983).
Justin Meggitt, *Paul, Poverty and Survival*, (T&T Clark, 1998).
Marianne Sawicki, *Crossing Galilee*: *The architecture of contact in the occupied land of Jesus*, (TPI, 2000).
Gerd Theissen, *The Historical Jesus*, (SCM, 1998).

Older Texts (mostly out of print)

Classics

Ray Bakke, *The Urban Christian*, (MARC/ECUM, 1987).
Harvey Cox, *Secular City*, (SCM, 1965).
Jaques Ellul, *The Meaning of the City*, (Paternoster, reprint 1997).
Bruce Kendrick, *Come out the Wilderness*, (Collins, 1965).
Colin Marchant, *Signs in the City*, (Hodder, 1985)
Paul Moore, *The Church Reclaims the City*, (SCM, 1965).
David Sheppard, *Built as a City*, (Hodder, 1974); *Bias to the Poor*, (Hodder, 1983).
Austin Smith, *Passion for the Inner City*, (Sheed, 1983).
Stephen Verney, *People and Cities*, (Fontana, 1968).
John Vincent, *Starting All Over Again*, (WCC, 1981); *Into the City*, (Epworth, 1982).
Jim Wallis, *Call to Conversion*, (Lion, 1982).

Videos

Peace to the City, (WCC, 1997).
*Agents of Change, (*World Vision, 1995).
Renewal and Regeneration, (Diocese of Liverpool, 2001).
Understanding Cities, (Open University, 1999).

Appendix II: Useful Addresses

Board of Social Responsibility, Urban Community Affairs:
Revd Dr Andrew Davey
Church House
Great Smith Street
London
SW1P 3NZ

Church Urban Fund
Ms Fran Beckett
1 Millbank
London
SW1P 3JZ

Institute for Urban Theology
Revd Dr Ian Duffield, Revd Dr John Vincent
Urban Theology Unit
210 Abbeyfield Road
Sheffield
S4 7AW

Regenerating Communities
Revd Dr Christopher Baker
William Temple Foundation
Luther King House
Brighton Grove
Manchester
M14 5JP

Touchstone
Revd Geoff Reid
30 Merton Road
Bradford
BD7 1RE

Unlock (formally Evangelical Urban Training Project)
336A City Road
Sheffield
S2 1GA

Urban Bulletin (Bi-Annual)
Ms Ann Weatherly
Bethnal Green Mission Church
305 Cambridge Heath Road
London
E2 9LH

Urban Presence
Mr Derek Purnell
Nazarene Theological College
Dene Road
Manchester
M20 2GU

Urban Theology Collective
Revd Peter Francis
St Deiniol's Library
Hawarden
Flintshire
CH5 3DF

Urban Theology Unit
Revd Dr John Vincent
210 Abbeyfield Road
Sheffield
S4 7AW

John Vincent
john@utusheffield.fsnet.co.uk

Appendix III:
The Contributors

Elaine Appelbee has worked in Bradford since 1977, predominantly in community development work. From 1991- 2000 she was Bishop's Officer for Church in Society for the Diocese of Bradford, encouraging the church to play a strategic role in regeneration. In 2000 Elaine took up the post of Director of the Bradford Health Action Zone and in November 2001 she was seconded to be Neighbourhood Renewal Director for the Local Strategic Partnership in Bradford, Bradford Vision.

Peter Atkinson is Vicar of Aylesbury, Bucks. He is also Faith in the City Co-ordinator for the Diocese of Oxford, and Advisor to Urban Priority Area parishes.

Christopher Baker worked in parish life and adult education in Milton Keynes 1994 –1998, where he was also a co-founder of The Well Community in Milton Keynes – an ecumenical Christian community committed to exploring issues of hospitality and justice. He is currently Development Officer with the William Temple Foundation.

Geoff Curtiss has been Rector of All Saints Episcopal Parish, Hoboken, New Jersey, since 1980. He leads ecumenical urban ministry courses with John Vincent and the Urban Theology Unit, and is opening a UTU study and resource house in Hoboken.

Andrew Davey was Archbishop's Officer for Urban Priority Areas at Church House, Westminster, and is now Assistant Secretary in the Anglican Board of Social Responsibility. His Sheffield Doctorate was on *Theology and Church in the Urban Context*. His book on *Urban Ministry* was published by SPCK in 2001.

Ian K Duffield is Vicar of St Leonard's Norwood, Sheffield, and a lecturer on the Core Staff of the Urban Theology Unit where he is supervisor for postgraduate in-service degrees. He edited the volume, *Urban Christ,* (UTU, 1997) and co-authored *Crucibles,* (UTU, 2000).

Peter Francis is Warden and Chief Librarian at St Deiniol's Library, Hawarden, Flintshire. As an Anglican Priest he has lived and worked in the West Midlands, the East End of London and Scotland, where he was Provost of St Mary's Cathedral, Glasgow. He is editor of *The Grand Old Man,* (Monad Press 2000); *The Gladstone Umbrella,* (Monad Press 2001) and co-editor of two forthcoming books: *Cinema Divinite* exploring the dialogue between film and theology, and *God and Country,* theological reflection on rural issues in Britain.

Peter Howard was brought up in Newham, East London. He trained for the Ministry at St John's, Nottingham and has served and studied in Birmingham and West Yorkshire. Since 1992 he has been Vicar on the Heartsease Estate in Norwich.

Nerissa Jones was Vicar of St. Chad's Parish Church, Wood End, Coventry. She was previously Parish Deacon at St Botolph's, Aldgate. She was made a Canon of Coventry Cathedral in June 2001. Since 2001 she has moved from Urban Coventry to Rural Dorset.

Stuart Jordan is a Methodist Minister and Secretary to the Methodist London Committee. Previous appointments included university chaplaincies and inner city ministries in Manchester and London. His PhD research examined the reception of liberation theology in the United Kingdom. He is a contributor to P. Richter (ed.), *God's Here and Now: Social Contexts and the Ministry of the People of God,* (DLT, 1999).

Colin Marchant is a Baptist minister. After Birmingham housing estate and Luton central church ministries, he has lived and worked in Newham, East London since 1965. After pastoral work, social action and community work, he now teaches Urban Ministry and Church Planting at Spurgeon's College, London. He is author of *Signs in the City,* (Hodder, 1985) and a *History of Urban Mission in Britain*.

Ian S McCollough has been a Methodist and a Local Preacher for 30 years. He worked as a Research metallurgist and also trained as a psychotherapist. General manager of a church sponsored Community Programme, 1981-86. Since 1987 he has been the Faith in the City Development Worker in the Diocese of Sheffield. Joint Manager, Churches' Regeneration Initiative in South Yorkshire. Member of the Churches Regional Commission for Yorkshire and the Humber. Member of Sheffield First Partnership. Churches' Together in South Yorkshire representative on the Churches' Regional Commission for Yorkshire and the Humber. Recent member of Sheffield First Partnership. Co-founder and Director of IMPACT, (Communities in Partnership for Action). Currently working to develop a city-wide strategy to tackle debt.

Ann Morisy is Community Ministry Adviser in the Diocese of London, working particuarly in Urban Priority Areas in London. She wrote *Beyond the Good Samaritan* (Mowbray, 1997), and her next book will be published in February 2004.

Michael Northcott teaches Christian Ethics in the University of Edinburgh and is a priest at St James' Church, Leith, in the Scottish Episcopal Church. He is editor of *Urban Theology: A Reader* (Cassell, 1998), and his most recent book is *Life after Debt: Christianity and Global Justice,* (SPCK, 1999).

Derek Purnell is from a working class housing estate background and was a telephone technician. He attended a Missionary Training College and pastored an inner city Independent Evangelical Church. He is now co-director and Consultant with Urban Presence, which he jointly founded. This includes developing an Urban Ministry course at the Nazarene Theological College where he also studied.

Helen Reid has a PhD in Sociology from Leeds University, and was a member of the staff team of Touchstone in inner city Bradford, with special responsibility for the development of Inter-Faith work. She is now Director of Faith to Faith.

Greg Smith is employed part time as Senior Research Fellow at the Centre for Institutional Studies in the University of East London and also does freelance and voluntary consultancy and capacity building. At the time of writing he had lived and worked for over 25 years in the church, community and voluntary sectors in the London borough of Newham. He was employed as research officer /consultant for Aston Mansfield Community Involvement Unit from 1991 to 2001. During that period he has helped community groups carry out major surveys on disability, poverty and health, interfaith attitudes, caste discrimination personal support networks, church and voluntary sector networking. In a previous job he worked for the Evangelical Coalition for Urban Mission and wrote extensively about the church in Urban Priority Areas. In 2002 he and his family moved into exile in Preston, Lancashire.

John Summers became vicar of St Barnabas, Plymouth, in 1981 and also St Michaels, Devonport, in 1998. After Fulham and naval chaplaincy, he retired in 2000. From 1994 he has been influenced by Latin American Liberation theology and in his two parishes has been developing a *New Way of Being Church*, with "neighbourhood groups" as the basic working unit of being church.

John Vincent is part-time lecturer at the Urban Theology Unit, which he founded in 1969, and supervisor of the Contextual, Urban and Liberation Theologies MPhil/PhD of the Biblical Studies Department of Sheffield University, of which he is an honorary lecturer. He was Joint Chair of The Methodist Report on *The Cities*. His latest book is *Hope from the City*, (Epworth, 2000).

Notes

1 Mary Drew, "Mr Gladstone's Library at St Deiniol's Hawarden", in *Nineteenth Century and After*, (June, 1906).
2 Uncatalogued St. Deiniol's MSS 1893 undated in Gladstone's hand.
3 Uncatalogued St Deiniol's MSS 1895.
4 *Faith In The City*, (Church House Publishing, 1985).
5 Joe Hasler, *Mind, Body and Estates*, National Estate Churches Network, c/o Urban Bishops' Panel, Church House, London SW1P 3NZ.
6 Don Rudalevige, *Urban Mission Training: The UTU in the US*, Urban Program Consultants, 15 Pleasant Avenue, Portland, Maine 04103.
7 Nick Davies, *Dark Heart: The Shocking Truth about Hidden Britain*, (London: Chatto, 1997).
8 See especially the annual Report on *Child Poverty*, produced by NCH Action for Children. In December 2000, we had two good surveys: the Report, *What Works in Reducing Inequalities in Childcare*, from Barnardo's, highlighting again the effects of poverty on child health; and the Report on *Poverty 2000*, from the Joseph Rowntree Foundation, indicating that 9 of 50 poverty indicators had worsened during the year.
9 Bob Holman, *Faith in the Poor*, (Lion Publishing, 1998); Nick Danziger, *Danziger's Britain: A Journey to the Edge*, (Flamingo, 1996). See also *Poverty First Hand: Poor People Speak for Themselves*, eds., Peter Beresford, David Green, Ruth Lister and Kirsty Woodard, (Child Poverty Action Group, 1999).
10 See John Vincent, *Hope from the City*, (Epworth Press, 2000), Chapter 17: "Incomers – and Jesus' Ministry of Incarnation", pp. 126-134.
11 Cf. John Vincent, "Regeneration and Capacity Building", in *Crucible*, October-December 2000, pp. 14-24.
12 *Faith in the City*, Archbishop's Commission on Urban Priority Areas, (London: Church House Publishing, 1985).
13 *The Cities*, Methodist Church Report, (London: NCH Action for Children, 1997).
14 *Indices of Deprivation 2000*, (London: Department of Environment, Transport and the Regions, 2000). See DETR *Update*, November 2000.
15 *Poverty Audit*, (London: New Policy Institute, December 2002).
16 *Faith in the City*, pp. 3-26.
17 *Faith in the City*, pp. 27-46.
18 Department of the Environment, Transport and the Regions, *Our Towns and Cities in the Future*, Issued 30 November 2000.

[19] *Highway Story 1989....*;West Doncaster Christian Unemployment Group (adapted).

[20] Red House was one of 5 centres in the UK built as a Community Education and Resource Centre following the Plowden Report. Its recent closure has been followed by that of the library in Denaby, both at a time when regeneration incentives are coming on a stream.

[21] Manchester scores number 3 (after Liverpool and Newham) on the government's new Index of Local Deprivation (DETR 1998).

[22] 1991 Census, The actual figure is 37% - national average is 24%.

[23] Joseph Rowntree Foundation report: *The Slow Death of Great Cities?* (1999).

[24] *A profile of poverty and health in Manchester* - Steve Griffiths, Manchester City Council, (November 1998).

[25] Charles Murray, "The Emerging British Underclass", in *Charles Murray and the Underclass: The Developing Debate,* ed. Ruth Lister, (London: IEA in association with the Sunday Times, 1996), 26.

[26] Ruth Lister, "Introduction in search of the Underclass" in *Charles Murray and the Underclass...,*10.

[27] Charles Murray, "Rejoiner" in *Charles Murray and the Underclass...,*p83

[28] Rosino Gibellini, *The Liberation Theology Debate,* (London: SCM Press Ltd., 1987), 14. This description, coming out of Latin America, sees the challenge to the church not to respond principally to the non-believer, but to the non-person. There are obvious dissimilarities here except for a group that is developing outside of recognised society.

[29] William Booth, *In Darkest England,* (London: Charles Knight & Co Ltd, 1970), 71. Casual Wards were night refuges for unemployed casual labourers. They had to work for their board and lodgings, this often meant they were released too late each day to get work.

[30] Joan C Brown, "Focus on Single Mothers" in *Charles Murray and the Underclass...,* p64.

[31] Rt. Rev. James Jones speaking at Manchester Diocesan Evangelical Union meeting, Manchester Cathedral, 24/1/00.

[32] A social process that often takes place following conversion whereby the social conditions are improved due to change in life style and personal aspirations and horizons are extended. A.D Gilbert states "Lift is to be distinguished from upward social mobility, although the two are closely connected. It describes the social and cultural estrangement of members of a religious group from the social environment in which they were recruited." Gilbert, *Religion and Society in Industrial England: Church, Chapel and Social*

Change 1740-1914, (London: Longman, 1976), 158-159. See also Roy Joslin, *Urban Harvest,* (Welwyn: Evangelical Press, 1982), 28-29.

[33] Manchester and Salford inner-city Partnership Group, *Manchester And Salford Inner Area Study,* (Manchester: Dept of the Environment, 1978), 1.

[34] North Manchester Health Promotion Unit, *Time For A Change,* (Manchester: North Manchester Health Authority, 1991), 1.

[35] "Redemption and *lift*", while a positive experience for the individual often has negative implications as C. Peter Wagner suggests "But as this process develops, a gap between the Christian and his unsaved friends opens wider and wider, until in some cases very little can be shared with them on a deeper personal level." C. Peter Wagner, *Your Church can Grow,* (Glendale: G/L Regal Books, 1977), 82.

[36] Greek: koinonia. This word is used to describe shared lives and partnership serving God.

[37] MCM was founded in 1837 and like many other City Missions was greatly influenced by David Nasmith.

[38] Dr Thomas Wolf, *Oikos Evangelism - the Biblical Pattern.* Hand out from Trinity Evangelical Divinity School, 1991), p.2. (Greek: oikov oikos, meaning household).

[39] Dr Thomas Wolf, *Oikos Evangelism...,* p.2.

[40] The Nature of the MCM was a Sodality or task orientated *Agency.* Eddie Gibbs in his book refers to Dr Ralph Winter's article 'The Two Structures of God's Redemptive Mission' who he states; "...argues the case for the Church to maintain what he terms 'modality' and 'sodality' structures. He draws a distinction between two kinds of community. The modality represents the settled community, and the sodality the apostolic band. The former places emphasis on being called and the latter on being sent. The modality is people orientated and diverse in its concerns, while the sodality is task-orientated and single-minded." Gibbs, E., *I Believe in Church Growth,* (London: Hodder and Stoughton, 1981), pp.344-345. Sodality is being used in the context of technical 'Church Growth' terminology not with reference to a charitable society within the Roman Catholic Church.

[41] *Manchester Guardian* 3rd May 1837. The Manchester City Mission was founded in 1837 under the influence of David Nasmith and continues today.

[42] Robert Lee, *Ten Fruitful Decades* (London: Pickering and Inglis, 1937.), pp.115 - 118.

[43] *Sixty-Second Annual Report of the Manchester and Salford Town Mission,* (Manchester, 1899), [chart between] pp.14 & 15.

[44] National S.A.T.S. tests 1998. (43% of pupils achieved level 4 in English and 20% in Mathematics compared with 64%/58% National figures and 61%/60% for Norfolk.) D.E.S. H.M.S.O. 1998.

[45] C.f. Isaiah 25:6 Matt. 22:3ff , 26:29ff, Rev. 19:7ff.

[46] 1Kings 17:13.

[47] Dave Rimmer, *Harpers and Queen*, February 1986, p. 78m quoted Ruth Finnegan, *Tales of the City*, Cambridge University Press, 1998. p. 42.

[48] Christopher Baker, *Towards a Theology of New Towns – the implications of the New Town experience for Urban Theology*, Ph.D thesis, (University of Manchester, 2002). See also DHR Jones, *Planning for Mission: A Study in Church Decision-Making in New Towns*, (NTMA, 1971); Christopher Nankivell, *Religion and New Towns*, MSc Thesis, (University of Birmingham, 1979); and Barbara Wollaston, *Report on the Church Situation in the Eight New Towns of the London Ring*, Diocese of Southwark Report, (unpublished), 1961.

[49] See DHR Jones (op cit) p.89.

[50] *Family and Kinship in East London*, (London: Routledge, 1957).

[51] Maurice Creasey, *New Town Ministers Association Conference* (NTMA) Report 1971, p.52.

[52] For example, Vatican II, the Anglican-Methodist Accord and the British Council of Churches conference in Nottingham in 1964 which pledged full covenanted union between the churches by Easter 1980.

[53] For example, the Skelmersdale Ecumenical Centre, the Danesholme Communicare centre in Corby, the Church of Christ the Cornerstone in Milton Keynes.

[54] Estimates of the number of new homes to be built range from 3.3 to 4.4 million with 50-60% to be built on brownfield sites with the rest needing to be built on greenfield sites.

[55] Lewis Mumford, *The City in History*, (New York: Harcourt Brace, 1961).

[56] Lord Reith, *Reith Committee Report,* (London, HMSO, 1946), para 230.

[57] Cf. John D Davies and John J Vincent, *Mark at Work*, (London: Bible Reading Fellowship, 1986). Also John Vincent, *Hope from the City*, (Epworth Press, 2000), pp. 19-25, 36-41.

[58] Duncan Wilson, "Gospel Values in Inner City Churches", in Chris Roland and John Vincent, eds., *Gospel from the City*, (Sheffield: Urban Theology Unit, 1997), pp. 86-106, pp. 92-95.

[59] William R Herzog III, *Jesus, Justice and the Reign of God: A Ministry of Liberation*, (Louisville: Westminster John Knox Press, 1999).

[60] Moby Farrands, "Gospel Stories in Radford", in *Gospel from the City,* (footnote 2 above), pp. 57-63.

[61] John Howard Yoder, *The Politics of Jesus*, (Grand Rapids: Wm B Eerdmanns, 1972).

[62] Leonie Sandercock, *Towards Cosmopolis: Planning for Multi-Cultural Cities*, (London: John Wiley & Sons, 1998).

[63] David Harvey, *Justice, Nature and the Geography of Difference*, (London: 1999).

[64] Juliet Kilpin, *Urban Expression in London*, Brochure, (1999).

[65] Isaiah, Chapter 58:1-12, *The Good News Bible*.

[66] Kissane, E.J., *The Book of Isaiah*, Volume 2, (Browne and Nolan Ltd, 1943), p232.

[67] Kissane, *ibid*, p236.

[68] Lambourne, R.A. *Community, Church and Healing*, (Darton, Longman and Todd, 1963), p25.

[69] Newbiggin, L., "The Welfare State: A Christian Perspective" in *Theology*, May 1985.

[70] Verney, S., "Metanoia", *Christian Magazine*, 1992.

[71] *Powerful Whispers*, eds., Elaine Appelbee and Geoff Reid, (Bradford Metropolitan Faith in the City Forum, 1996).

[72] Local Anglican and Methodist churches funded the Faith to Faith Project from 1998-2001. A key aim of the project was to encourage Christians to think theologically about living in a multi-faith city. Further, to build on this by encouraging the development of positive relationships between people of different faiths.

[73] References: Patrick, Gail and Helen Reid, 1999; *A Faithful Future: Churches in Great Horton and Lidget Green, Bradford and the potential for involvement in multi-faith initiatives*, Bradford: The Touchstone Centre; and Burlet, Stacey and Helen Reid, 1997; *Faith in our Future: People of faith, social action and the city of Leeds*, Leeds: Community Religions Project, University of Leeds.

[74] The interviews drew on the methodology of the Community Religions Project at the University of Leeds and in particular on the Inter-Religious Social Action Research Project, (Burlet and Reid, 1997).

[75] Frederick Buechner, *The Longing for Home*, (San Francisco: HarperSanFrancisco), p. 110.

[76] Walter Brueggemann, *Theology of the Old Testament*, (Minneapolis: Fortress Press, 1997), p.718.

[77] Norman K Gottwald, *A Light to the Nations*, (New York: Harper & Row), pp. 372ff.

[78] Brueggemann, *Theology of the Old Testament*, p. 149.

329

[79] Brueggemann, *Cadences of Home: Preaching among Exiles*, (Louisville: Westminster John Knox Press, 1997), pp.4-11.

[80] Brueggemann, *Cadences of Home: Preaching among Exiles*, p.8.

[81] Viktor Frankl, *Man's Search for Meaning*, (London: Hodder & Stoughton, 1964).

[82] Ann Morisy, *Beyond the Good Samaritan: Community Ministry and Mission*, (Mowbray, 1997).

[83] Michael Ignatieff, *The Needs of Strangers*, (London: Hogarth Press 1984).

[84] Ignatieff, p. 10.

[85] Daniel Taylor, *The Healing Power of Stories*, (Dublin, Gill and Macmillan, 1996), p.99.

[86] Ibid p. 12.

[87] Ibid p. 55.

[88] Paulo Freire, *Pedagogy of the Oppressed*, (London: Penguin Books, 1972).

[89] Newham Directory of Religious Groups, (3rd Edition 1999). Aston Community Involvement Unit, Durning Hall, Earlham Grove, London R7 9AB.

[90] Religious Trends - linked with [2].

[91] Harvey Cox, *The Secular City*, (S.C.M. Press, 1965).

[92] Harvey Cox, *Fire from Heaven*, (Cassell, 1996).

[93] Deborah Padfield, *Hidden Lives - Stories from the East End*, (London, 1999).

[94] The Archbishop of Canterbury's Commission on Urban Priority Areas, *Faith in the City*, London: Church House Publishing, 1985, p67.

[95] For Iona Community 'Colomban Houses', see Ronald Ferguson, Chasing the Wild Goose, (London: Collins, 1988).
For Ashram Community Houses and Projects, see John Vincent, *The Jesus Thing*, (London: Epworth Press, 1973); *Alternative Church*, (Belfast: Christian Journals, 1976).

[96] On The Furnival and its Cellar Project see John Vincent, *Hope from the City*, (Peterborough: Epworth Press, 2000), pp.75-78.

[97] Information on Broad-Based Organising may be obtained from Citizen Organising, Bristol.

[98] See "New Strategies for Mission", *Epworth Review*, 26. 2, April 1999, pp. 26-32.

[99] Karl Marx, *Collected Works*. Volume 5. (Moscow: Progress Publishers, 1976), p.5.

[100] John De Gruchy, *Theology and Ministry in Context and Crisis: A South African Approach*, (London: Collins Flame 1987), p.31.

[101] Leonie Sandercock, *Towards Cosmopolis-Planning for Multicultural Cities*,

(John Wiley and Sons, 1998).
[102] p.164.
[103] p.205
[104] p.163
[105] Enrique Dussel, *Ethics and Community*, (Tunbridge Wells: Burns and Oates, 1988), p.9.
[106] Sandercock, p.218.
[107] p.218-9
[108] Robert Schreiter, *The New Catholicity: Theology between the Global and the Local*, (Maryknoll: Orbis, 1997), p.94-5.
[109] p.97
[110] p.97
[111] See *Participation Works! 21 Techniques of Community Participation for the 21st Century*, (London: New Economics Foundation, 1999).
[112] *Towards an Urban Renaissance* - Final report of the Urban Task Force, chaired by Lord Rogers of Riverside, (London: E&FN Spon, 1999).
[113] *Urban Renaissance-Sharing the Vision*, (DETR, 1999), p.22.
[114] Compiled by URBED, MORI and Bristol University, (DETR, 1999).
[115] Jonathan Gancey, *The Guardian*, Monday 15th March, 1999.
[116] David Harvey, *Justice, Nature and the Geographies of Difference*, (Blackwell, 1996), p.419.
[117] Harvey, p.419.
[118] See Decca Aitkenhead, 'Urban meltdown', *The Guardian*, 23rd August 1999.
[119] Rob Furbey, 'Urban Regeneration: Reflections on a Metaphor', (CRESR, Sheffield Hallam University, 1999).
[120] Daily Telegraph, 15th Oct 1988, quoted by Furbey.
[121] see Walter Brueggemann, *The Land - Place as Gift, Promise and Challenge in Biblical Faith*, (SPCK 1977), p187.
[122] Murray Bookchin, *The Limits of the City*, (Montreal: Black Rose Books, 1986).
[123] Jane Jacobs, *The Death and Life of Great American Cities*, (New York: Random House, 1961).
[124] Philip Bond, 'Perception: From Modern Painting to the Vision in Christ' pp. 220-242, in John Milbank, Catherine Pickstock and Graham Ward, eds., *Radical Orthodoxy: A New Theology*, p. 220.
[125] Ibid, p. 221. And see also Timothy Gorringe, *A Theology of the Built Environment*, (Cambridge: Cambridge University Press, 2002).

126 I have explored this issue in some depth in Michael Northcott, *The Environment and Christian Ethics,* (Cambridge: Cambridge University Press, 1996). See in particular the critical discussion of the fact-value distinction in modern philosophy and culture in chapter 6.

127 Bond, 'Perception', p. 221.

128 Richard Sennett, *The Conscience of the Eye: The Design and Social Life of Cities,* (New York: W. W. Norton, 1990), p. 6.

129 Ibid, p. 10.

130 Ibid, p. 12.

131 Walter Benjamin, *The Arcades Project,* trans. Howard Eiland and Kevin McLaughlin, (Cambridge, MA: Belknap Press, 1999).

132 For an account of Morris's workshops see Fiona MacCarthy's superb biography *William Morris: A Life for Our Times,* (London: Faber and Faber, 1994).

133 John Ruskin, *Sesame and Lilies,* cited Sennett, *Conscience of the Eye,* p. 20.

134 John K. Galbraith, *The Affluent Society,* Fourth British Edition, (London: Penguin, 1987).

135 Sennett, *Conscience of the Eye,* p. 29.

136 For an example of this approach in English urban theology see the essay by David Ford and Al McFadyen on 'Praise', pp. 95-104, in Peter Sedgwick, ed., *God in the City,* (London: Mowbray, 1995). See also Jacques Ellul, *The Meaning of the City,* (Grand Rapids, MI: Eerdmans, 1970).

137 Benjamin, *Arcades Project,* p. 11.

138 John Milbank, 'On Complex Space', pp. 268-292 in John Milbank, *The World Made Strange: Theology, Language and Culture,* (Oxford: Blackwell, 1997), p. 277.

139 Ibid, p. 279.

140 Ibid, p. 282.

141 Sasskia Sassen, *Cities in a World Economy,* (Thousand Oaks, CA: Pine Forge Press, 1994), p. 4.

142 Ibid, p. 213.

143 Ibid, p. 216.

144 Seyla Benhabib, *Situating the Self: Gender, Community and Postmodernism in Contemporary Ethics,* (London: Routledge, 1992).

145 Charles Leadbetter, *Living On Thin Air: The New Economy,* (Harmondsworth: Penguin, 2000).

146 See further Northcott, *Environment and Christian Ethics,* Ch. 5.

147 Miroslav Volf, *Exclusion and Embrace: A Theological Exploration of Identity, Otherness and Reconciliation,* (Nashville: Abingdon, 1996), p. 78.

[148] Ibid, p. 67.
[149] Ibid, p. 72.
[150] Ibid, pp. 73-74.
[151] William Cavanaugh, *Torture and Eucharist: Theology, Politics and the Body of Christ*, (Oxford: Blackwell, 1998), p. 214.
[152] Ibid.
[153] Ibid, p. 218.
[154] Ibid. p. 233.
[155] Ibid, p. 271.
[156] Ibid, p. 269.
[157] Ibid, p. 272.
[158] Michael Northcott, 'A Place of Our Own', pp. 119-138 in Sedgwick, ed., *God in the City*.
[159] Volf, *Exclusion and Embrace*, p. 225.
[160] Ibid, p. 230.
[161] Cavanaugh, *Torture and Eucharist*, p. 246.
[162] Forty years ago, the captivity of the churches to the agenda of the suburbs was identified by Gibson Winter in his book *The Suburban Captivity of the Churches: An Analysis of Protestant Responsibility in the Expanding Metropolis*, (New York: Doubleday & Co., 1961).
[163] At UTU, for more than twenty years, this starting point for theology has been registered by inviting students at the beginning of various courses to engage in a *Situation Analysis*. Before Bible and theology are considered, the reality of a person's location is held up for investigation and exploration.
[164] Cf. Paul Tillich's autobiographical sketch, "On the Boundary", originally published as Part I of *The Interpretation of History* (1936), revised and newly translated in *The Boundaries of Our Being*, (London: Fontana, 1973), pp.285-350.
[165] Visitors and students at UTU arc encouraged to consider their vocation and discipleship, with an emphasis on the vocation to live, work, and minister within the inner city or deprived urban areas. Cf. Elisabeth Mitchell's article in Urban Christ, (UTU, 1997), pp.10-13.
[166] Mark 4:6.
[167] In addition to the Situation Analysis (see above) there is a need for Social and Structural Analysis which seeks to understand the deeper forces at work. See, for example, Joe Holland & Peter Henriot, *Social Analysis. Linking Faith and Justice*, (Revd and enlarged edn. Maryknoll, NY: Dove Communications & Orbis Books, 1983).

333

[168] At UTU, doing theology always includes the consideration of Biblical Antecedents, i.e. identifying where in the Scriptures there are parallels or resonances between the people of God then and now.

[169] At UTU, Situation and Structural Analysis interact with theological reflection, utilising Biblical Antecedents, leading towards action, often expressed in terms of a practical planned project in ministry to effect change or transformation.

[170] See Paul Tillich, *Systematic Theology*, Vol.1, (Combined Volume, Welwyn, Herts: James Nisbet & Co., 1968), pp.67-73.

[171] Ian K Duffield, ed., *Urban Christ*, (UTU, 1997), p.20.

[172] At UTU we sometimes find ourselves using these terms interchangeably. For us they are related terms.

[173] This is related to, but not to be confused with Karl Barth's 'dialectical theology'.

[174] This is related to, but not to be identified exhaustively with, Paul Tillich's 'method of correlation' (see above).

[175] This designation was used by national government and adopted by *Faith in the City* (1985), and applied at ecclesiastical parish level.

[176] See the series of books, under the general title *British Liberation Theology*, published by UTU and edited by Chris Rowland & John Vincent.

[177] UTU as a place of study seeks to provide a forum for such engagement and learning.

[178] The differences in context are discussed for example in V. Jones, *What is Our Theology of Liberation?*, Christian Socialist Movement Pamphlet No. 1, (London 1985); J.J. Vincent, *Liberation Theology from the Inner City*, (Sheffield: UTU, 1989), p.11.

[179] eg. C. Marchant, *Signs in the City*, (London: Hodder & Stoughton, 1985); A. Smith, *Passion for the Inner City*, (London: Sheed & Ward, 1983).

[180] The process began with the report - Archbishop of Canterbury's Commission on Urban Priority Areas, *Faith in the City*, (London: Church House Publishing, 1985), and subsequently continued with two readers P. Sedgwick, ed., *God in the City*, (London: Mowbray, 1995) and M. Northcott, ed., *Urban Theology: a Reader*, (London: Cassell, 1997).

[181] *The Cities: A Methodist Report*, (London: The Methodist Church and NCH Action for Children, 1997).

[182] Eg R.S. Greenway, ed., *Discipling the City*, (Grand Rapids: Baker, 1992); R.S. Greenway & T.M.Monsma, eds, *Cities: Missions' New Frontier*, (Grand Rapids: Baker, 1994).

[183] Moltmann's characterisation of Political theology might also apply to Urban theology in *its* relationship to Liberation theology: 'Political theology is *internal critique* of the modern world. Liberation theology is *external critique* of the modern world': J.Moltmann "Political Theology and the Theology of Liberation" in J. Rieger, ed., *Liberating the Future*, (Minneapolis: Fortress Press, 1998), p.73.

[184] *A Theology of Liberation*, (London: SCM Press, 1971), p. 36.

[185] G. Gutiérrez, "Liberation Theology and Proclamation" in *Concilium* 6.10 (1974) p.69.

[186] Vatican opposition to liberation theology focused especially on Leonardo Boff's book, *Church: Charism and Power*, (London: SCM Press, 1985). See also H. Cox, *The Silencing of Leonardo Boff*, (London: Collins, 1988).

[187] See, for example, P. Sedgwick, who suggests three central theological categories of 'sin, redemption and salvation' and then calls for them to be related to a Trinitarian framework, 'Mapping an Urban Theology' in *God in the City*, p.xvi.

[188] J. Sobrino, *The True Church and the Poor*, (London: SCM Press, 1985), p.11.

[189] Cf. Schreiter's insistence that 'both prophets and poets are essential to the theological process, but the process cannot be reduced to either one of them, cited in *Urban Theology*, p.26.

[190] J. Comblin, *Called for Freedom: The Changing Context of Liberation Theology*, (Maryknoll: Orbis, 1998), p.97.

[191] Andrew Davey's contribution above is one such attempt at a broadened perspective.

[192] Greg Smith, *Newham Directory of Religious Groups*, 3rd edition, (1998).

[193] G. Gutiérrez, "Liberation Theology and the Future of the Poor" in J. Rieger, *Liberating the Future*; pp.96-123; C. Villa Vicencio 'Liberation and reconstruction: the unfinished agenda' in C. Rowland, ed. *The Cambridge Companion to Liberation Theology*, (Cambridge: Cambridge University Press, 1999), pp.153-176.

[194] *Liberating the Future*, p. 104.

[195] ibid. p.123.

[196] The Archbishop of Canterbury's Commission on Urban Priority Areas, *Faith in the City*, (London: Church House Publishing, 1985), p.67.

[197] Ibid p.66.

[198] Ibid p.70.

[199] Cf. my definitions in 'A New Theology and Spirituality' in *Liberation Spirituality*, ed., Chris Rowland & John Vincent, (Sheffield: UTU, 1999), p.95-106, p.104.

[200] Each of the contributors to *Liberation Spirituality* works in an urban context.

[201] John Vincent, *Hope from the City*, (London: Epworth Press, 2000), p.36.

[202] Cf. Frederick Herzog, *God-Walk: Liberation Shaping Dogmatics*, (Maryknoll: Orbis Books, 1988).

[203] David Ford and Laurie Green, 'Distilling the Wisdom', in *God in the City, Essays and Reflections from the Archbishop's Urban Theology Group*, ed., Peter Sedgewick, (Mowbray, 1995), pp.16-24, p.17. A good example is T.J. Gorringe, *A Theology of the Built Environment*, (Cambridge: University Press, 2002).

[204] See my article, "An Urban Hearing of the Gospel" in *Gospel from the City*, ed. Chris Rowland and John Vincent, (Sheffield: UTU, 1997), pp. 105-116; and Laurie Green, "Gospel from the Underclass", *ibid*, pp.117-125. I have pursued this line in two recent articles in *Expository Times*: "Outworkings: A Gospel Practice Criticism", October 2001, pp.16-18, and "Outworkings: Gospel Practice Today", August 2002, pp.367-371. See further my article "Theological Practice", *Theology*, forthcoming.

[205] For the importance of Incarnation in urban theologising in various traditions, the following may be compared: Roman Catholic: Austin Smith, *Passion for the Inner City*, (Sheed & Ward, 1983); Evangelical: Dorothy Harris, "Incarnation as a Journey in Relocation", in B.J. Nicholls & B.R. Wood, eds., *Sharing the Good News with The Poor*, (Paternoster/Baker House, 1996), pp.175-188; Methodist: *The Cities: A Methodist Report*, pp. 209-10. Cf. also my *Hope from the City*, pp. 126-134. Sally Nash, "Supporting Urban Youth Workers", studies the "International Youth Ministry" of Youth For Christ workers on housing estates (DMin Dissertation, UTU/Sheffield University, 2003).

[206] Cf. my comments in "Developing Contextual Theologies", *Epworth Review*, July, 2000, pp. 62-71. Reprinted in Duffield, Jones, Vincent, *Crucibles: Creating Theology at UTU*, (Sheffield: Urban Theology Unit, 2000), pp. 23-32.

[207] Alistair McFadyen, "The UPA as the place of demons?" in *God in the City*, pp.178-190, p.183.

[208] I develop this in *Theology from the City*, (Epworth Press), forthcoming.

[209] *Our Towns and Cities: The Future*, (London: Office of the Deputy Prime Minister, 2000). See now *Towns and Cities: Partners in Urban Renaissance*, (London: Office of the Deputy Prime Minister, 5 vols., 2002).

[210] Cf. my "Thoughts form the Urban Summit: Dystopic Utopia" in *Urban Bulletin*, Spring 2003.

[211] Cf. comments and references in *Hope from the City*, pp. 154-157.